SOCIAL POLICY

POLITICS EDITOR
William Robson
B.Sc.(Econ.), Ph.D., Ll.M.
*Professor Emeritus of Public Administration
in the University of London*

Social Policy

in the Twentieth Century

T. H. MARSHALL
Professor Emeritus of Sociology
in the University of London

Hutchinson of London

Hutchinson & Co. (Publishers) Ltd
3 Fitzroy Square London W1

London Melbourne Sydney Auckland
Wellington Johannesburg and agencies
throughout the world

First published 1965
Second edition 1967
Reprinted 1968
Third (revised) edition 1970
Reprinted 1972
Fourth (revised) edition 1975
Reprinted 1977, 1979

Set in Monotype Times
Printed in Great Britain by The Anchor Press Ltd
and bound by Wm Brendon & Son Ltd
both of Tiptree, Essex

ISBN 0 09 122621 x (paper)

Contents

Preface to the Fourth Edition

In the third edition of this book, published in 1970, Part Two was extensively revised. In this edition it has been even more thoroughly rewritten. There were two reasons for this. In the first place I felt sure that this was the last revision I should make, and there were some thoughts that I wanted to include in it. Secondly, the change of government in June 1970 had made some parts of my book look very ill-balanced. I had given much space to plans of the Labour government which had never materialized, and there was, of course, nothing about the important legislation carried through by the Conservative government which followed. It was clear that, owing to the sharp disagreement on some central issues, the situation was unstable, and further changes of policy might be expected in the not too distant future. So I decided to focus attention as much as possible on basic issues and current ideas about alternative ways of dealing with them, in the hope that this would enable the book, in its final shape, to retain its value for some time in spite of the swings of political fortune. The wisdom of this decision was demonstrated when, in March 1974, a month or two before the work was due to go to the printer, the Labour Party returned to power under conditions which made it certain that there would be another general election in the autumn. The situation was very unstable, but it was not too difficult to identify the dominant social problems of the day and to explain the areas of agreement and disagreement between the various policies current at the time, even though one could not be sure which policies would ultimately prevail. I was enabled to throw a little light on the latter point when space was found to accommodate a short Postscript, written in November 1974, after the new Labour government had announced the main lines of its programme.

Part Two of the book was originally entitled 'Social Policy at

Mid-Century', but this is no longer appropriate for an account of things as they appeared in 1974. So I have borrowed a title used by Gunnar Myrdal, 'Beyond the Welfare State', to indicate that social policy has entered a new phase differing from that through which it passed in the years immediately following the Second World War. My feelings about this development are most fully expressed in the last two chapters of the book, on 'Poverty' and on 'Problems and Prospects of the 1970s', both of which are almost completely new. I have also added an Introduction to explain my latest views on the nature of social policy and the scope of a book of this kind.

The five years since the third edition appeared have also seen great progress in the subject of social administration, both in range and in depth. More research is being done than before on such matters as the impact of social casework and the relations between social insurance and taxation, while the study of poverty has been extended. Three important new periodicals have appeared. Two of these are annuals – namely the volume on *Social Trends* produced by the Central Statistical Office, and the *Year Book of Social Policy in Britain*, edited by Kathleen Jones; the third is the *Journal of Social Policy*, founded with the aim of exploring the basic issues, principles and values which underlie and inspire social administration. I have found it invaluable, and am particularly grateful to Kathleen Slack for her excellent 'Social Administration Digest' which appears in every issue, and for her readiness to answer my supplementary questions. I am grateful also to other colleagues who have shown a similar readiness, among whom I would mention Brian Abel-Smith, David Donnison, Tony Atkinson, Kit Russell, Sally Sainsbury and Chris Lewis of the Central Statistical Office.

20 November 1974

Preface to the First Edition

As this book is based not on original research but on secondary authorities and official publications, my debt to those who have worked in this field is enormous and obvious. I am particularly grateful to my former colleagues at the London School of Economics, most of whom are now members of the remarkable team headed by Professor Titmuss, for what I learned from working with them and for the response I received from the inquiries I addressed to some of them—from Dame Eileen Younghusband on social workers, Mrs Cockburn on housing, Mrs McDougall on mental health, Mr Carrier on demographic problems, and Mr Bird on some intricacies of our tax system.

Conscious as I was of my lack of first-hand knowledge of the major social services, I decided to seek interviews with some of those actually engaged in the work and I chose for this purpose three very different areas—London (the LCC), Leicester, and the County of Cambridgeshire. I was fortunate in obtaining introductions in the first case from Mrs Peggy Jay, in the second from Professor Neustadt, and in the third from Lady Adrian and Mr Michael Pease. All those I approached were generous in giving me their time and took great trouble in telling me the things I wanted to know, for all of which I here express my gratitude. They are in *London*, in addition to Mrs Jay herself (Vice-Chairman of the Welfare Committee and member of the Children's Committee), Mrs Durbin (member of the Housing Committee, a Rent Tribunal, and other bodies), Mr Lloyd Jacob (Head of the General Division of the Welfare Department), Miss Taylor (Chief Inspector of Child Care), and Mr Balchin (Assistant Director of Housing); in *Leicester* Dr Moss (Medical Officer of Health), Mr Powell (Director of Welfare Services), Mr Evans (Children's Officer), and Mr Hadfield (City Housing Manager); in *Cambridge* Dr Tyser (Medical Officer of Health), Miss Valentine (Children's Officer), and Mr Hitch (County Welfare Officer).

Last, but by no means least, I am indebted to Professor W. A. Robson who first proposed that I should write this book and without whose initiative and encouragement it would never have been written.

Introduction:
What is social policy?

'Social policy' is a term which is widely used but does not lend itself to precise definition. The meaning given to it in any particular context is largely a matter of convenience or of convention. The conventional approach will tell us which areas of government action are generally accepted as belonging to the 'social' sphere. Convenience, in this case, will determine what it is possible to deal with adequately in this book. Neither will explain what the subject is really about. For that we must look, not simply at the measures adopted, since these are but means to an end, but at the nature of the end itself—at the objectives which 'social' policy pursues in a way in which other policies do not. Let us begin with convention, then plunge into the deep waters of objectives and leave convenience to the end.

Convention in this matter is international, at least in part. It is most decisive in its inclusion, and definition, of social security. A Convention adopted by the International Labour Organization in 1952 specified, under 'Social Security', measures for maintaining income during sickness, unemployment and old age, family allowances and the provision of medical care. The last item was, presumably, included because in most countries this requirement is met, not by a national health service, but by social insurance to cover the greater part of medical costs. The British custom is to treat what we now call *health care* as a separate item outside of *social security* which thus becomes synonymous with the system of cash benefits. This makes good sense, because it allows health to move over to the place where it properly belongs, next to *welfare*. A fourth item, which has a prominent place in, for instance, the social reports of the European Economic Community, is *housing*. Here definition becomes more difficult, partly because of the intricate involvement of public action with private enterprise in the housing market, and partly because housing policy merges into town and country planning which, if studied in depth, would lead us beyond the frontiers of social policy, as conventionally understood. As a fifth item we can add *community services*. In these, although they exist for the benefit of individuals, the services themselves are not personal. Their aim is to contribute to the creation or maintenance of a neighbourhood, both physical and social, fit to satisfy the needs of its inhabitants. This category of social policy has gained in prominence in recent years and there is much talk today of 'community health' and 'community development'. Finally there is one other major service which has every right to be classed as 'social', namely *education*, but convention does not usually admit it into the fold, perhaps because it is too large a subject, or because it raises too many issues peculiar to itself.

The objectives of these policies are indicated by the words used to designate them—security, health and welfare. Of these welfare, in its most general sense, is the only true end product, one to which an assured cash income, a healthy body and, one could add, a house to live in are among the most important contributors. This was recognized when we coined the phrase 'the Welfare State' to describe the post-war social and political order. The term was meant to refer to the end achieved, not to the means employed, and when critics speak of it as 'the Social Service State' they rather suggest that the means employed have become more important than the ends at which they aim. Be that as it may, the avowed objective of twentieth-century social policy is welfare. So what can we say about it? We are concerned here, not with etymology or historical usage, but simply with the meaning given to the word today in the context of social policy. This meaning is undoubtedly more personal, more subjective than that of its sister-word 'wealth'. It has a mixed reference which embraces both the experience of well-being and the conditions which produce it. To say that a man 'fares well' implies that he is both doing well and feeling well. A programme which takes welfare as its objective must be planned on the assumption that there is normally some correlation between these two aspects—the external conditions and the internal experience. It can then operate on the external conditions. But when action reaches the level of personal contact with the intended beneficiary, as it does at some point almost everywhere in the social policy world, then it becomes possible to modify the initial assumption so as to take account of individual differences in respect both of the needs to be met and of the response to the kinds of help offered. The parts played by these two approaches, the assumed correlation and the assessment of the individual case, vary from service to service.

Ever since the invention of social insurance standard cash benefits have been assessed according to a *presumption* as to the amount of income needed to enable the *average* beneficiary to achieve the level of welfare to which he is held to be entitled. Hence the attempts to draw a poverty line, to define the subsistence level, to estimate what is needed to sustain family welfare as the children arrive and grow up, or to decide what the relationship should be between a man's retirement pension and his previous earnings. Only those cases which are overlooked or inadequately provided for by the general system are treated individually and, since they are marked out as exceptions, this individual treatment is felt to be invidious. So twentieth-century social policy in the matter of cash benefits has been under constant pressure to reduce to a minimum the number of cases requiring individual investigation of an invidious kind while seeking ways of bringing the approximations closer to the realities. But this problem has proved to be very intractable, and policy-makers in the 1970s are still looking for the answer.

The pressure in the health and welfare services has been, on the whole, in the opposite direction, towards personalizing the service as much as possible and protecting the individual from the harsh impact of those institutions, organizations, rules and regulations without which no personal service could be provided on a national, or even on a local, scale. Success in this endeavour depends greatly on the intervention of the professional, or the expert, between the bureaucratic machine and the individual client, or patient. The bureaucrat tends to assign cases to appropriate categories and order the prescribed treatment; this has a depersonalizing effect on the relationship. The professional by contrast, claims the right to judge each case on its merits and then to prescribe, or to recommend, what is in his opinion the best treatment for it, within the limits of the service of which he (or she) is the agent. The distinction between these roles is important, both in theory and in practice. But any authority, whether bureaucratic or professional, which touches on such intimate personal matters as health and welfare should be exercised with great circumspection and restraint. The relationship is in some ways easier to handle in medicine than in welfare. The concept of health is sufficiently precise and the standing of the medical profession is sufficiently high to win general agreement that the doctor knows best, nor need there be anything humiliating about his intervention. Welfare, by comparison, is a vaguer concept, the professional standing of the social worker is less eminent, the element of uncertainty when decisions must be taken is likely to be greater, and the intervention of the social worker can be felt to be humiliating. But decisions must be made, and made by the 'outsider' on behalf of the patient or client, though the decision may often consist in accepting and endorsing the client's own expressed preferences.

The purpose of this brief analysis is to identify the two most fundamental problems which confront a social policy which chooses welfare as its objective. The first, briefly and crudely expressed, is how to enable a mass-produced service to distribute a highly individualized product by means which are neither invidious, humiliating nor presumptuous. The second is how to manage its dual role of being both the servant and the master of its intended beneficiaries. A social service exists for the benefit of those it serves, but in the course of its operation a host of decisions must be taken, not by them, but on their behalf by 'outsiders' from policy-makers at the top to physicians and social workers at the point of impact. This discharge of a vicarious responsibility is often described—with derogatory intent—as 'paternalism'. But a social service cannot function without it, since it must be guided by a consistent system of values and it must take its own decisions about priorities. There is inevitably in social services a danger of excessive vicarious paternalism, which is enhanced by the imbalance of authority between the providers and the recipients of the service. In other spheres the antidote to a lopsided power situation has been found (or sought) in the organization of the weaker party, as in the case of trade unions. There has been relatively little of this in the social service world, where, until recently, the only effective pressure-groups were themselves run by 'outsiders', not by, but on behalf of, those immediately concerned. But recent years have seen a rapid expansion of activities of this kind, both defensive and aggressive, among those at the receiving end of social policy, of which the 'claimants unions' are a good example. It is very much on the progress of this movement that many people build their faith in 'community development'.

To return to welfare as an objective of social policy, it might be argued that it is in fact the ultimate objective of all policy, and also of the economic system as a whole. This is true in a sense, but in the case of social policy the relation between programme and objective is a more immediate one. The general pattern is one of action carried through until, so to speak, the product has been delivered into the hands of the person for whom it is intended; till then the job has not been finished. That is why we can speak of *individual* rights (or in some cases more accurately claims) to welfare. Economic policy, on the other hand, is concerned more with the 'common weal' than with individual welfare. Secondly, it has been represented by the present author and others that social policy uses political power to supersede, supplement or modify operations of the economic system in order to achieve results which the economic system would not achieve on its own, and that in doing so it is guided by values other than those determined by open market forces.

Finally we come to the question of convenience—the limitations this book imposes on this extensive subject. We shall try to cover: first, social security, in the sense of income maintenance, whether through social insurance or other methods of providing cash benefits; secondly, health care, whether it takes the form of a health service or of health insurance or a combination of the two; thirdly, social welfare, or personal social services; and fourthly, housing policy, particularly in so far as it aims at enabling less well-off families to obtain a home on terms that they can afford. Policies directed towards the health and welfare of communities rather than immediately of individuals will be considered in the context of those policy areas, as will also the roles of the agents through whom the policies are carried out. A novelty in this edition is a chapter on poverty in Part II. This has been introduced because of the key position the subject has come to occupy in the preoccupations of the 1970s, and also because it is a problem area on which all the other subjects converge—income, health, welfare and housing. The question of delinquency and its treatment will be dealt with only as it concerns juveniles and merges with the welfare services for children. Education, unfortunately, must be omitted. Finally, although the bias in both parts of the book is towards British history and policy, as much consideration as possible has been given to the affairs of other countries at a similar stage of development, and every effort has been made to examine problems and policies in general, and not in purely national, terms.

One | The first fifty years

1 | The legacy of the Victorian era

In the first volume of his autobiography Leonard Woolf writes: 'our youth, the years of my generation at Cambridge, coincided with the end and the beginning of a century which was also the end of one era and the beginning of another. . . . We found ourselves living in the springtime of a conscious revolt against the social, political, religious, moral, intellectual and artistic institutions, beliefs and standards of our fathers and grandfathers. . . . The battle, which was against what for short one may call Victorianism, had not yet been won, and what was so exciting was our feeling that we ourselves were part of the revolution.'[1] This is a personal recollection of the authenticity of which there can be no doubt, and it is supported by many historians who have maintained that the death of Queen Victoria marked the close not only of a reign but of an epoch.[2] But when we pause to consider these sweeping generalizations we remember how often young men of one generation have believed that they were waging a revolutionary war against the generation of their elders, and how many 'epochs' with profoundly significant opening and closing dates historians have discovered, and subsequently discarded. So it behoves us to be cautious; and it is the purpose of this chapter and the next to look at the situation in or around the year 1900 in order to see in what respects if any it really did mark the birth of a new era, especially in the field of social policy.

That year falls midway between what Trevelyan has called 'the two mid-Victorian decades of quiet politics and roaring prosperity'[3] and the appearance of what we have become accustomed to call the Welfare State. For Leonard Woolf it was the

[1] Superior figures refer to References p. 222.

time of *Sowing* (the title of his book). Can we transfer the metaphor from his personal life to our social and political history?
This would imply that the seed was sown, around the turn of the
century, in land that had been ploughed by an earlier generation,
and that the harvest was gathered by a later one. We shall see,
as we follow the passage of events from the first period to the last,
that the metaphor is, in many ways, a very appropriate one
indeed.

The industrial revolution, whatever may be the truth about its
beginning, most certainly had no end. For it is the essence of
industrialization that, once you are well 'over the hump', and
fully committed to the industrial way of life, the movement
never stops and (in all probability) the pace will get continually
hotter. It takes a society a little time to get accustomed to the
motion and to tidy up the bits and pieces which were thrown
out of place when the acceleration started. The thesis, just
quoted, about the mid-Victorian decades signifies that by then
Britain had achieved this adaptation and found its balance, or
at least that most of the people who mattered believed that this
was so. In a sense they were right, but in another sense they
were wrong. It was true that by the 1850s the old order had
vanished and a new order had taken its place. It was true, also,
that the more violent disturbances which had accompanied its
birth were over and that relative harmony prevailed. But much
still remained to be done to enable the immanent principles of
the new order to reach fulfilment. And when Victorian society,
in its age of confidence, embarked upon this task of fulfilment,
it set in motion forces within the system itself which led, by
natural and logical processes, to its transformation into something totally unforeseen and unfamiliar. In fact the transformation,
when it came, was shaped by a conscious effort on the part of
twentieth-century policy to create a social order essentially
different from that of the Victorians.

So far as industry was concerned, the triumph of the Victorian society was beyond dispute. 'The country regarded itself,'
says Ensor, 'as "the workshop of the world"—a phrase then
universal which expressed not an aspiration but a fact.'[4] The
boast was justified, but there were, nevertheless, two vital matters
to be settled within the industrial system itself, namely the
structure of the large business unit and the status of the organiza-

tions of the workers that these business units employed. A decisive step towards the settlement of the former was taken when Parliament, in 1855–6, established the legal basis for the operation of joint-stock companies with limited liability. There were some exclamations of horror from *The Times*, but the new shape of things was soon generally accepted. Some years later legislation, culminating in the Act of 1875, legalized collective bargaining by trade unions including (so it seemed) the right to strike. This too, appeared to be in tune with the spirit of the age. For did not the Royal Commission on Labour, of 1894, express the view that the 'occasional great trade conflict' to settle a major issue represented 'a higher stage of civilization' than continued local bickerings?[5] But when the trade unions began to make powerful use of their new liberties, these were challenged by the courts, and had to be reaffirmed, and strengthened, by Parliament in 1906. The truth, not fully realized at the time, was that an industrial system characterized by the consolidation of business into vast impersonal units and the combination of workers into national trade unions was a very different thing from the paradise of individual enterprise, free competition, and self-help which the Victorians imagined they had established. The logical elaboration of the principles of the Victorians, and the natural growth of the institutions they had founded, were leading to something which, though it might at first look like a fulfilment, was in fact a transformation; the seed sown in the ground which the Victorians had ploughed produced a crop unlike anything they had known or could easily imagine.

If capitalist industry was one of the pillars upholding the Victorian system, the other was responsible government, both central and local. After 1832 the cabinet was responsible to a House of Commons which in turn was aware of its responsibilities to the electorate, but it did not represent the people. The franchise was far too restricted for that. Only about 19 per cent of the adult males in the population had the vote, but the principle that men were sent to Parliament by the votes of their fellow-citizens had been accepted, and it was logically inevitable that, by a process of natural growth, parliamentary government should become representative as well as responsible. The mid-Victorians themselves took the crucial step in 1867 when they passed the Reform Act which just about doubled the proportion of the enfranchised. By the end of the century the system fell little short of manhood suffrage, but it was still based ostensibly on the idea that a man was qualified for the franchise by virtue of his substance as reflected in the annual value of his home. It was not until after the First World War that the right to vote was recognized as being a right of citizenship as such, to be enjoyed by men and women alike. However, in 1900 there was a legislative organ in sensitive touch with the public conscience and with the new streams of political thought flowing through the minds and from the pens of the Radicals and Socialists. And in the year 1906 the Labour Party first entered the political arena as a fully qualified competitor in the party game. Even contemporaries, without the help that historical perspective gives, saw, and said, that a new era of party politics had begun. Here, too, natural growth and logical processes were on the way to produce a transformation.

In local government, a matter of great importance in the history of social policy, the picture is not so clear nor the story so simple. The reformed Parliament had cleaned up what *The Times* once referred to as the 'chartered hogsties' of municipal government as early as 1835,[6] but no comparable reform had been under-taken in rural areas when the mid-Victorian age of prosperity and confidence began. Nor did the mid-Victorians make good this defect. When a new task emerged which required a firm hand and an honest mind to guide it they created new machinery for the purpose, first the Poor Law Guardians (with their special administrative areas) and then in 1870 the School Boards, while the urban Sanitary Authorities, under the permissive Act of 1848, largely created themselves by Private Bill very much as the fancy moved them. It is tempting to imagine that the 'sowing' could not have taken place had the ground not been prepared by the legislation which, between the years 1882 and 1894, brought the municipal corporations up to date and established a uniform and effective system of rural administration in the hands of the county, urban district, and rural district councils. But this interpretation cannot really be sustained. For, although a fair measure of concentration of functions in the hands of these bodies did eventually take place, the old tangle remained in being at least till 1929, by which time a new tangle was growing up to take its place, and heated debates about the reform of local government continued to the present day.* In fact, in the years around 1900 the only local government that could be counted as a power in the land was municipal government in the cities together with the specialized bodies just mentioned.

Turning now to the social policy which was enacted and executed by these political organs, it is convenient—since space does not allow a comprehensive survey—to group the salient features of the picture under four headings: education, industry, poverty, and health. Education falls outside the scope of this book, but a word must be said about it here, if only because it illustrates so well the thesis that natural growth in the second half of the nineteenth century prepared the way for transformation in the twentieth. For the Victorians, democracy and education were partners. A free society could not be orderly unless it was literate, and a self-governing society could not progress in peace unless it was educated. Since, therefore, education was required as much for the benefit of the society as for that of the individual, it was not too difficult to establish the case for holding the State responsible for seeing that it was both offered and accepted. Universal, compulsory, and therefore free elementary education was the corollary; it was implicit in the Act of 1870 and was made explicit in subsequent legislation. Thereupon some people concluded that, with democracy and education securely established, there was little more to be done in the way of social policy. But they were wrong even as regards education itself. Attention was next turned, naturally and logically, to technical and secondary education. And then the story of trade unionism repeated itself. The authorities which tried tentatively to invade the field of secondary education were told by the courts that they had no legal power to use public money in this way. In the counter-attack of the Act of 1902 they not only won back the ground they had lost but established a base for further advances in great depth. The eventual result was, once more, a transformation. The public elementary education of the nineteenth century was an inferior commodity provided for an inferior class, and it led straight into the lower reaches of the labour market. The twentieth century created an educational ladder from the primary

*Proposals for a drastic reorganization of local authorities were made in the Maud Report (*The Royal Commission on Local Government in England, 1966–9*, Cmnd. 4040, June 1969). Legislation followed in 1972.

school to the university, and adopted, in principle, the ideal of equal opportunity. It is true that it remained a good deal easier to mount the ladder from half-way up than to start from the bottom rung, but education in 1970 was profoundly different, both in structure and in quality, from what it had been when Queen Victoria died, and also from what the reformers of those days had had in mind.

When we look at industry, we see that the mid-Victorian State had already accepted its duty and asserted its right to intervene directly for the protection of workers in factories. It is true that, in accordance with the pure doctrine of individualism as understood at the time, it did not 'interfere' with the liberty of adult male workers but confined its attention (in theory) to women and children. In effect, as was quite clearly appreciated, the men benefited indirectly from some of the measures designed for the protection of the others. As the need to guard the workers not only against moving machinery but also against such insidious menaces to health as lead poisoning and noxious dust became more and more apparent, this principle was quietly dropped in the legislation of the 1890s dealing with matters of this kind. The significance of this departure from doctrinaire individualism is considerable, but it should not be misinterpreted. It did not mean that in future individualism was to be replaced by paternalism everywhere. Far from it. It meant only that paternalism was deemed acceptable in cases where the individual was powerless to protect himself, even if he wanted to, and where the ill-judged acts of the few might cause grave injury to the many. Each case must be judged on its merits, and many important instances could be cited, from that time to the present, in which the choice between individualism and paternalism proved difficult and the judgement was not unanimous. We shall meet such instances shortly in the field of public health.

But two other aspects of factory legislation are still more important. The first is the creation of the inspectorate, acting under the orders of the central government. We shall return later to the role of inspectors in nineteenth-century social administration. The point about the factory inspectors is that there was no local authority for them to work through; all power was concentrated at the centre, and this was done because it was clearly realized that 'conflicting interests, local influences, indisposition to carrying the law into effect, and other circumstances' might well make administration by local authorities ineffective, as indeed it proved to be when it was tried briefly in the case of workshops as distinct from factories.[7] Secondly, under this legislation first the factories, then the workshops, and eventually even the domestic premises of the manufacturers—that is to say their private property, their real estate, and, in certain circumstances, their homes—were treated as things for the use of which they could be publicly answerable and into which public officials had the right of entry in the ordinary course of their duty. In this way the second great principle of Victorian individualism, the principle of the inviolability of private property, was put on trial and found wanting. Certainly it was not overthrown, but it was dislodged from its position as a sacred dogma and made to submit like other humbler principles, to the modifications required by the circumstances in which it was applied.

Poverty is a subject that will figure so extensively in the later parts of this book that little need be said about it here. We can confine ourselves to identifying the concepts of poverty and of the Poor Law which prevailed during the period of Victorian confidence, within the framework of the concept of competitive capitalism. Poverty, one might venture to say, was regarded more as a social fact than a social problem. The problem was how to reduce the mass of apparent or self-declared poverty to the hard core of the genuine article. This was done by means of the deterrent effect of the workhouse test and the principle of 'less eligibility' (the condition of the pauper must be less attractive than that of the poorest person outside this category). This remained the accepted doctrine in official circles right through the period of confidence and for some time afterwards. But on the question what to do with the hard core of the genuine poor there were some doubts and some disagreement. Should they be treated harshly or generously, in the workhouse or outside it, as unfortunate citizens or as social outcasts? The answers were not clear, and in the soil of this perturbation of mind lay the seeds of the first great social reforms of the twentieth century.

There are two points of general significance which must be grasped if the events that followed are to be understood. The Victorians, we have just suggested, regarded poverty as a social fact. The poor, they reflected, are always with us, always have been and always will be. In the prosperous nineteenth century there should be fewer, rather than more, of them than at previous times. Their ever-present need was traditionally relieved by their families, the Church, the religious orders, and the neighbours. It was only in a supplementary way, to co-ordinate or to provide special types of service, that the public authorities stepped in. This is what one sees very clearly when one looks at a country like France in which religious institutions operated at full strength, or at the United States, particularly in the early years of its independence, where the neighbourhood generally felt quite capable of looking after its own affairs. But in Britain the power of religious institutions had been greatly curtailed by the Reformation, and the strength of the neighbourhood had been extensively undermined by the industrial revolution. In addition, for centuries the neighbourhood had been personified, for major administrative purposes, in the Justice of the Peace, who, though a genuine neighbour, was at the same time a public official and the agent of the central government. Now the Justices had been replaced by the Poor Law Guardians who, although still local worthies, seemed to have even less of the neighbourly spirit in them. Thus the traditional philosophy of poverty still persisted, but the social and institutional structure through which the philosophy could be translated into action had passed away.

The second point to grasp is that we must think in terms not of the poor but of the paupers. Pauperism was a status, entry into which affected not merely a part of a man's life, but the whole of it. He became a pauper for all purposes, and he carried his family with him. Paupers formed a distinct group of second-class citizens, deprived of most of the important rights of citizenship. The principal officer of the Poor Law Division of the Local Government Board, giving evidence before the Royal Commission of 1905–9, said that the status of pauper implied 'firstly, the loss of personal reputation (what is understood as the stigma of pauperism); secondly, the loss of personal freedom, which is secured by detention in a workhouse; and thirdly the loss of political freedom by suffering disfranchisement'. The pauper, he added, has in practice a right of relief, but 'his right is not a complete right for the necessary sanctions are lacking . . . he cannot sue for his relief', and that is precisely why it is the duty of the State to see that he gets his rights.[8] The comprehensive character of the status meant that certain essential services, especially those of health and education, were split in two. Sick and infirm paupers were attended by the Poor Law Medical Officer or entered the Poor Law Infirmary, and their children were sent to the Poor Law Schools or other establishments certified as available to them, while the other needy members of the society were provided for by the local Sanitary Authority and its Medical Officer of Health and the local School Board. The anomalies that resulted, as well as the hardships induced by the workhouse test and the rigid conception of pauperism, caused growing uneasiness as the nineteenth century drew towards its close, and provoked a frontal attack on the system in the early years of the twentieth.

Our fourth category of social policy, health, will also figure extensively in this book, but in some respects it is the most critical of all to the understanding of the period under review, and must therefore receive careful attention here. It is critical for two reasons: first, because it was most conspicuously in the field of public health that the battle was fought over the relative roles of central and local government and, one might almost say, even over the role of government as such, in the pursuit of welfare. Secondly, whereas the developments in the machinery of democratic government, in education, in the structure of industry and the processes of collective bargaining, and in factory legislation, can properly be regarded as the natural growth and logical evolution of the mid-Victorian system, it is a debatable question whether the measures taken in the field of public health were a natural fulfilment of Victorian democratic capitalism or an attack launched against it. Aneurin Bevan took the latter view, but he qualified it by adding that the system was quick to claim the credit for what had been imposed upon it by its attackers. Public-health measures, he said, have become part of the system, 'but they do not flow from it. They have come in spite of it. . . . In claiming them, capitalism proudly displays medals won in the battles it has lost.'[9] The question having been posed, one must make haste to admit that it cannot be answered. There are no valid arguments by which one interpretation can be proved right and the other wrong. And yet even a cursory glance at British history leaves the impression that the public-health measures were much less of a natural growth from within the system than any of the items listed above. They sprang from the determined efforts of a small number of men—doctors and civil servants—of outstanding ability, courage, and energy who can easily be identified as the pioneers of this great advance. They had to instil into the circles that controlled affairs both in industry and in local government something of their own knowledge and understanding and of their own attitude to life; their understanding not only of the medical but also of the social factors involved, and their attitude towards man's environment, which refused to treat it as something given, as something to be accepted as an expression of the unalterable laws of nature. It was equally necessary in this conceptualization of the environment, both physical and social, to see in it something different from a mere aggregation of individual actions and circumstances to which the principles of individual rights and freedoms could be applied. The physical environment created by men and the social environment composed of men must be handled according to principles peculiar to themselves, and it was for the recognition and general application of these principles that men like Chadwick and Southwood Smith were fighting. One of the most notable examples of the utter failure to grasp this point is the leading article in *The Times* of 1 August 1854, celebrating the downfall of these two men and the suppression of the Board of Health. 'If there is such a thing as a political certainty among us, it is that nothing autocratic can exist in this country. The British nature abhors absolute power. . . . The Board of Health has fallen.' And it continues: 'We all of us claim the privilege of changing our doctors, throwing away their medicine when we are sick of it, or doing without them altogether whenever we feel tolerably well. . . . Esculapius and Chiron, in the form of Mr Chadwick and Dr Southwood Smith, have been deposed, and we prefer to take our chance of cholera and the rest than be bullied into health.'

This passage covers three distinct points. The first is concerned with the limits of bureaucratic power and in particular with the relations between the central bureaucracy and the allegedly democratic local authority; we shall return to this in a moment. The second refers to the right of the individual to choose for himself. But this is a right which, as we saw in the case of the Factory Acts, applies only where there is a real power to choose and when the choice made by one man cannot endanger the health and welfare of others. The third point concerns the environment and is a complete *non sequitur*. It would have been impossible to cope with 'cholera and the rest' without the help of bureaucracy guided by the best scientific knowledge of the age, and the man who decided to 'take his chance' was a menace to the health of his neighbours. Fortunately *The Times*'s song of victory was premature, and the public-health movement continued to advance.

Before we close this chapter there is one question to be considered which is relevant to all areas of social policy. It is the question of the means by which a central government (1) gathers information about the social problems with which the policy is to deal; (2) having decided on its policy, explains to its local executives, whether they are its own servants or autonomous local authorities, what they are to do; (3) keeps a watch to see if they are doing it, and (4) puts pressure on them, if they are not, to make them do it. Some provision to meet these needs is a prerequisite of any social policy, and it is therefore important to know whether the twentieth century inherited from the nineteenth a serviceable equipment for these purposes. The answer to (1) is the almost fabulous list of reports of Royal Commissions and Select Committees, admittedly somewhat unequal in quality, which were one of the outstanding contributions of the period to the apparatus of government. The answer to questions (2) and (3) is, apart from routine Ministry circulars, the inspectorate. There were inspectors for the Factory Acts, for education, for the Poor Law (Assistant Commissioners), and for public health. Their relations with the local executives of policy varied. The factory inspectors had no local agents to work through. For education and the Poor Law there were the *ad hoc* Boards created by government for the purpose, and therefore having something of the character of government agents. In public health the Sanitary Authorities were an integral part of general local government, and often showed the independence characteristic of its institutions. But, whoever it was that they were dealing with, the inspectors occupied a key position which they exploited as fully as contemporary ideas about the liberty of the subject and local dislike of bureaucratic interference permitted. The procedure laid down for them consisted of inspection, report and advice; it did not include dictation. So the answer to

question (4) above is that the pressure on local agents to implement central policy was exerted rather patchily, often indirectly
and not always effectively. But the result was better than one
might have expected.

In the mid-Victorian age of confidence there was a continuous
resistance to the encroachment of the central government in local
affairs, but the encroachment went on. The machinery at the
centre was steadily expanding, and we are told that the twenty
years ending in 1854 saw the addition of twenty permanent
central agencies to the apparatus. Also, even when no uniform
pattern could be imposed by authority on local administration,
the device was used with considerable effect of designing models
which most of the local authorities were only too glad to copy.
So, by the time the period of confidence ended and the nineteenth
century drew to a close, the ideas, the habits, and the machinery
of government had developed to a point at which the obstacles
to the new urge in social policy were not insuperable. Whatever
we may think about the exact interpretation of the phrase 'the
Welfare State', we can appreciate the force in David Roberts's
judgement that during the mid-Victorian epoch the ordinary
Englishman had become 'the beneficiary of a state that assumed a
responsibility for the well-being of its citizens. However limited
that responsibility, however meagre compared to the responsibilities assumed by Whitehall today, it did mark the beginning
of the Welfare State.'[10]

2 | Problems and policies at the turn of the century

It was argued in the last chapter that during the period of Victorian confidence in the social order the ground was being prepared for the new developments of the twentieth century in part by the natural and logical evolution of the social order itself. But in the last quarter of the nineteenth century the situation was changed by a series of events and discoveries which severely shook the confidence of the Victorians and seemed to betray unsuspected weaknesses in their society. One of the most important effects was to provide fresh ammunition and a more receptive audience for the various critics of the system whose utterances until then had not greatly disturbed the general calm, but who were now in a position to challenge the dominant orthodoxy. The distinction here made between events and discoveries may be a little arbitrary, but it is useful. It serves to distinguish between occurrences which struck society with a new impact, and the fruits of deliberate, planned inquiries which revealed conditions that had existed for some time, and thus convicted the public mind of having been lulled into a false complacency.

The principal event was the depression which attacked the economy of the Western world in the last quarter of the century. In Britain it came at a time when the competition of foreign industries had made manufacturers doubt whether the country was still entitled to call itself the 'workshop of the world', and it was accompanied by the new and alarming phenomenon of mass unemployment. In 1882, in spite of the gathering clouds, the *Spectator* could write: 'Britain as a whole never was more tranquil and happy. No class is at war with society or the government: there is no disaffection anywhere, the Treasury is fairly full, the

accumulations of capital are vast.'[1] Very soon, however, the unemployed were demonstrating in Hyde Park, and in 1886 Hynd-
man, leader of the Marxist wing of the Socialist forces, was
addressing packed crowds in Trafalgar Square, with John
Burns waving a red flag and shouting, 'When we give the word
for a rising will you join us?' There followed rioting, arrests,
prosecutions, and—most significantly—acquittals. The Mansion
House fund for the unemployed, 'which had long lingered, half
moribund, at about £3000, rose in the four days after the riot to
£20 000', and a fortnight later reached £60 000.[2] This was tan-
gible evidence of the extent of public sympathy. The corresponding
crisis in the United States came a little later, in the years 1894
to 1898, when the percentage of unemployed in manufacturing
industry and transport rose from a level of around 5 per cent
to a maximum of 16·7 per cent and the depression was described
as 'extreme', 'deep', 'severe', and 'intense'.[3] The comments of
historians on events in the two countries are very similar. In
England, says Ensor, 'the slump gave Victorian courage and
optimism the severest shock that it had yet received'.[4] In the
United States, we are told, 'it was clear that the country was
being profoundly shaken, that men everywhere were beginning
to envisage a turning-point in national development'.[5]

The shaking engendered a new attitude to social problems.
According to the old orthodoxy the prime cause of social distress
and destitution was to be found in the persons or individual
circumstances of the victims, and it was usually identifiable as
moral weakness. There was considerable resistance to admitting
the presence of impersonal social causes, because this implied
an inherent defect in the system itself. The shock administered
by the spectacle of mass unemployment did much to break this
resistance, because it was evident that the unemployed in Trafalgar
Square were not a collection of weaklings or idlers, but the product of an impersonal phenomenon called 'unemployment', a
word that had only recently been introduced into the vocabulary.
Close on the heels of these events came the famous strikes of the
match-girls and the dockers, in 1888–92, in which once more
public sympathy was on the side of those protesting against their
lot. And this time it was not a question of people who had been
ejected from an economic system which, for the moment at least,
had no use for them. The complaints were voiced by men and

women whose labour was in demand but who were not thereby enabled to rescue themselves from conditions of extreme poverty.

In this sense these strikes were not only events; they were also discoveries. They brought to light new facts about the standard of living of the unskilled workers. And they coincided in time with other discoveries of still wider import. The new enlightenment about the depth and extent of urban poverty erupted in the 1880s with the publication, first of *The Bitter Cry of Outcast London* (1883), and then of the more widely publicized studies by Charles Booth of the people of London (1889) and by Seebohm Rowntree of the people of York (1901).[6] These books created a sensation, and the facts reported in them passed immediately into general currency as established truths, and were quoted with telling effect in the highest circles. 'We know, thanks to the patience and accurate scientific investigations of Mr Rowntree and Mr Charles Booth, that there is about 30 per cent of our population underfed, on the verge of hunger.' So wrote Leo Chiozza Money in his widely read and very influential book *Riches and Poverty*.[7] The tone is typical; it is that of a man announcing a discovery, not quoting an opinion. And yet these two local studies provided only a slender basis for a general statement of this kind. A little later Lloyd George, at the outset of his campaign for social reform, was equally emphatic. Booth and Rowntree, he said, have 'revealed a state of things, especially in the towns, which it would be difficult even for the orators of discontent to exaggerate. There are ten millions in this country enduring year after year the torture of living while lacking a sufficiency of the bare necessities of life.'[8] This was in 1906, when the road to old-age pensions and national insurance still lay ahead of him, beset with hazards both known and unknown; he needed the popular support that these shocking truths might win for his social programme.

A second source of new information to which historians frequently refer is the Report of the Interdepartmental Committee on Physical Deterioration of 1904. It is indeed relevant to the story, but not so much because it administered a shock as because it was set up to investigate a shocking discovery which had already been announced. This was the report of the military authorities on the high rate of rejection, on medical and physical grounds, of recruits during the South African War. They concluded from this experience that the physical state of the population had deteriorated. The Interdepartmental Committee, on the contrary, decided that it had not. The statistics, they said, had been mishandled and misinterpreted, and they expressed the hope that their work might have some effect in 'allaying the apprehensions of those who, as it appears on insufficient grounds, have made up their minds that progressive deterioration is to be found among the people generally'.[9] But, on the basis of quite different evidence, they showed that some very shocking conditions existed in certain sections of the population, especially in the poorer parts of the big cities. They made a strong appeal for action to alleviate overcrowding, pollution of the atmosphere and underfeeding, and for the medical inspection of school children.

A third disclosure concerned the sweated industries. It was not so much the report of the House of Lords Committee of 1888 on sweating, though the mere fact of its appointment was full of significance, nor the brilliant study made by Beatrice Webb, that administered a sudden shock to the public mind, but rather the Sweated Industries Exhibition organized by the *Daily News* in 1906. Here could be seen particulars about the hours of work and the earnings of the sweated workers (mostly women and children), examples of the work they produced, demonstrations of the skill and labour they put into it, and models of the rooms in which they toiled. The effect was irresistible. Finally one might add the growing body of knowledge about the housing of the people, although here the story lacks the element of sudden discovery. However, for those who knew the facts, the situation was sufficiently alarming. As far back as 1885 a Royal Commission had reported that, although the improvement in the housing of the poor in the past thirty years had been enormous, 'yet the evils of overcrowding, especially in London, were still a public scandal, and were becoming in certain localities more serious than they ever were'.[10] In 1900 the Prime Minister was telling the Conservative Party that they should 'devote all the power they possess to getting rid of that which is really a scandal to our civilization . . . I would earnestly press upon all over whom my opinion may have any weight that the subject which should occupy their attention more than any other social subject is that of providing adequate and healthy accommodation for the working classes'.[11]

Thus the pride of Britain was assaulted from all directions. Her cities were breeding young men unfit to fight for her, there were workers in her industries reduced to conditions to which only a Dickens could do justice, a third of her inhabitants were living in absolute poverty or on the edge of it, and the slums of her towns were a public disgrace. The combined effect of these discoveries was great enough to change the political atmosphere and to create possibilities for new and more determined action. The previous generation had realized that these problems existed, but had not grasped their magnitude. Consequently their treatment of them remained, as it were, peripheral, as though concerned only with the fringes of society and not with large sections of its ordinary members. The new situation demanded a reappraisal of the rights of the citizen and of the obligations of the State towards him.

The recognition of the need for such a reappraisal and the attempts made to meet this need deeply disturbed the political thinking of the period and left their mark on the programmes of the political parties. It is remarkable how often in the speeches and writings of these years one meets the words 'Socialist' and 'Socialism'. It is obvious that the representatives of the old orthodoxy felt it necessary to take up some position with regard to this new doctrine—to belittle it, to appropriate it, or to fight it. And it is equally obvious that many of them had only the vaguest idea what it was; which was not surprising, since even those who called themselves Socialists were not in agreement on this point. Definitions of Socialism varied greatly. Dicey, in his book *Law and Public Opinion in England*, published in 1905, called the years from 1865 to 1900 'The Period of Collectivism', and he defined collectivism as 'the school of opinion often termed (and generally by more or less hostile critics) Socialism, which favours the intervention of the State, even at some sacrifice of individual freedom, for the purpose of conferring benefit upon the mass of the people'.[12] He elaborated the definition by specifying the types of State action he had in mind, and giving examples.

This definition is broad enough to cover practically all the policies of social reform that were taking shape at the turn of the century. For they all sprang from the belief that the State was responsible (in some measure) for the welfare of 'the mass of the people' and that it was endowed with the authority to interfere

(to some extent) with individual freedom and economic liberty
in order to promote it. The novelty of this idea lay in its divergence
from the former view that the State was concerned only with
the destitute and the helpless, and that its action on their behalf
must not impinge upon the ordinary life of the community.
And Dicey was quite right in saying that this was what most
people meant by 'Socialism'—except, of course, for the real
Socialists, who meant much more by it. But he was wrong in
suggesting that the term was used mostly by the hostile critics of
Socialism. It is true that 'Tory Socialist' was originally a term of
abuse applied to those Conservatives whose humanitarian feelings
had enticed them along paths which seemed to lead straight to
Radicalism.[13] But the Radicals themselves frankly admitted, or
one might almost say proudly proclaimed, that their programme
was compounded of Socialism. To Dicey the 1885 programme was
merely moving 'in the direction of socialism',[14] but Joseph
Chamberlain, its principal author, was more emphatic. The aim
of the Radicals was, he said, a government 'in which all shall
co-operate in order to secure to every man his natural rights,
his right to existence, and to a fair enjoyment of it. I shall be
told tomorrow that this is Socialism . . . of course it is Socialism.
The Poor Law is Socialism; the Education Act is Socialism; the
greater part of the municipal work is Socialism; and every
kindly act of legislation, by which the community has sought
to discharge its responsibilities and obligations to the poor, is
Socialism; but it is none the worse for that.'[15]

The thinking behind this statement is confused, but the senti-
ment and the intention are clear. It was becoming necessary to
assert a belief in the responsibility of government for the welfare
of the people and to deny to the official Socialists any monopoly
of good intentions by borrowing their name and rendering it
innocuous. Hubert Bland, the Fabian, put the point very clearly
in his comment on the famous utterance of a leading Liberal.
'Why does that extremely well oiled and accurately poised
weathercock, Sir William Harcourt, pointing to the dawn, crow
out that "we are all Socialists now"?' And his answer to his own
question was that no politician could address a political meeting
at that time without making some reference 'of a socialist sort
to the social problem'.[16] Naturally this kind of talk angered the
Socialists proper, because it obscured the real nature of the

conflict of opinion. They were not at war with Tory Socialists or Radical Socialists, and were even prepared to support them when they agreed on particular measures. But they were the implacable enemies of the traditional Liberalism of the nineteenth century, the Liberalism of Gladstone and *laissez faire*. And they thought, and hoped, that it was dying.

In 1889 the *Nineteenth Century* published a symposium of articles on the 'Liberal Collapse'. 'The Liberal Party,' wrote Sidney Low, 'is once more in trouble about its soul', and Keir Hardie and Ramsay MacDonald, speaking for the Independent Labour Party, explained what the trouble was. Liberalism had assumed that 'the man politically enfranchised would be economically free; but experience was proving that the hope was thoroughly false, and Liberalism had nothing else to put in its place'.[17] And three years later Sidney Webb returned to this theme in the same journal. Gladstonian Liberalism, he said, was extinct because it had an 'atomic conception of society'. 'Its worship of individual liberty evokes no enthusiasm. Its reliance on "freedom of contract" and "supply and demand" . . . now seems to work out disastrously for the masses', because they lack the means to make their demand effective even for the minimum conditions of well-being. The freedom which the ordinary man now wants 'is not individual but corporate freedom'.[18]

But, though Gladstonian Liberalism might be defunct, a new Liberalism was arising which, under the leadership of Asquith, Lloyd George, and Winston Churchill, was destined to carry social policy forward on the first stage of its journey towards the Welfare State. It accepted fully that common element in the new outlook which Chamberlain and others called 'Socialist'. Churchill, in 1906, declared that 'the fortunes and the interests of Liberalism and Labour are inseparably interwoven; they rise from the same forces'. And he urged his followers not to be discouraged if some old woman came along and told them their measures were 'socialistic'. He even admitted that 'the whole tendency of civilization is . . . towards the multiplication of the collective functions of society', but he insisted nevertheless that the Liberalism he championed was in essence the very antithesis of Socialism, because Liberalism wanted only to humanize the system of free enterprise, whereas Socialism would destroy it.[19] By 1906 the question was no longer whether the State was responsible for the welfare of the masses, instead of merely for the relief of the destitute. This was generally agreed, and after all the masses now had the vote. The problem was to decide on the extent of the responsibility and above all on the means by which it should be discharged. And here consensus ended and political conflict began. And when we look more closely at the clash of opinions we shall see that the issues raised were fundamentally the same then as they are now.

We can identify three main schools of thought. First there is the genuine Socialist school. This starts from the belief that the 'capitalist system' of private enterprise and a free market economy is inefficient and unjust. It is a kind of anarchy that should be replaced by a rational order of things planned and directed by the political power. In such an order, not only would the normal needs of everybody be met automatically by the operation of the system itself, but many of the needs that now clamour for satisfaction would no longer exist, since their cause—primarily poverty, squalor, and insanitary conditions of life—would be eliminated. Social progress, therefore, should be marked by a reduction, not an increase, in the special social services which are extraneous and supplementary to the working of the social and economic system itself.

This was the line of thought pursued at first by the Fabians. They had so much faith in the efficiency of a Socialist economy that they paid little attention to social policy as such. They thought that under Socialism, most of our social problems would disappear. Sidney Webb, looking back in 1920 at those early pioneering days of simple enthusiasm, admitted that he and his friends had behaved 'as if society were, or ought to be, composed entirely of healthy adults, free from accidents and exempt, if not from death, at any rate from senility'.[20] This is, no doubt, a piece of deliberate self-parody, but it is true that Graham Wallas, in his chapter in the original *Fabian Essays*, had dismissed very lightly the whole question of those who, in a Socialist society, would be unable to provide for themselves. 'There would always remain the sick, and infirm, and the school children, whose wants would be satisfied from the general stock without asking them to bear any part of the general burden.'[21] The essential thing was to socialize the system itself.

The second school of thought was the most strongly represented at the time. Its adherents admitted that the economic system left many needs unsatisfied and distributed its rewards inequitably, but held that in the purely economic tasks of production and distribution of goods it was superior to anything else that might be put in its place. They therefore did not wish to see any drastic change in the system. But, since they believed that the system could not cure its social defects itself, they recognized the responsiblilty and the right of the State to interfere and compulsorily to modify and supplement its operations. For the members of this school of thought, therefore, the first task of the twentieth century was to extend the social services and increase what Churchill called the 'collective functions' of society, until the ideal balance between private enterprise and public provision and control was attained. The outstanding examples of this approach to the problem are the Radical programme of 1885 and the Liberal programme of 1906.

The third school of thought was of less importance, because its influence was declining. It was that of those Conservatives who thought that there was nothing seriously wrong with the economic system and that the main concern of government should be to see that it had every facility and encouragement to continue its good work. If everybody worked hard, cared for their children, and saved up for sickness and old age, the volume of cases requiring, and deserving, outside help would be small. Public social services, except for a strictly administered Poor Law, were likely to diminish the incentive to work and save. Therefore it would be best to leave as much as possible of the welfare work to the voluntary agencies. This was the basic philosophy of the Charity Organisation Society, the most important voluntary agency of the time. It rested on the belief that England was a rich and prosperous country, and that, where wealth abounded, poverty must be unnecessary. Mrs Bosanquet, a leading exponent of the doctrine, asserted that all who were not genuinely incapable of work should be held responsible for their own maintenance and that of their dependent relatives. It may be asked, she said, 'what if the social conditions will not permit them to meet the responsibility?' And her answer was—'It is a vain and idle hypothesis. The social conditions *will* permit them.'[22]

These three points of view are deeply rooted in the very nature of modern society and the issues they raise have therefore remained alive to this day, though in a setting that has gradually changed. The dividing line between the first and the second—the 'revolutionary' and the 'reformist'—came to fall, not between the Socialists and the rest, but within the Socialist movement itself. On the one hand were those who continued to maintain that the only policy acceptable to Socialism was one that aimed at the elimination of the capitalist system. Social welfare measures were merely palliatives, which sapped the strength of the attack on capitalism. On the other side were those who became increasingly interested in, and favourable to, social legislation that humanized the capitalist system without overthrowing it.

The second point of view, which favoured welfare measures, was of course held also by many non-Socialists; by Radicals in general and by those Liberals who had escaped from the strait-jacket of nineteenth-century dogmatism. They had been given a lead by the distinguished economist Stanley Jevons, who argued in favour of judging practical issues on their merits and not by appealing to the authority of some doctrine. 'In social philosophy,' he wrote, 'or rather in practical legislation, the first step is to throw aside all supposed absolute rights or inflexible principles', even the principles of liberty and property. 'I conceive,' he continued, 'that the State is justified in passing any law, or even in doing any single act which, without ulterior consequences, adds to the sum total of happiness.'[23] The view was also held by many Conservatives for humanitarian reasons, and by some, perhaps, for the rather more subtle reason given by Arthur Balfour. 'Social legislation, as I conceive it,' he said, 'is not merely to be distinguished from Socialist legislation, but it is its most direct opposite and its most effective antidote.'[24]

The third point of view carried diminishing weight as the social policy of the twentieth century developed, but it reappeared in a modified form as a result of the alleged arrival on the scene of the Affluent Society. It was argued that amid so much affluence poverty can be only an exceptional phenomenon, and that now it really is possible (as Mrs Bosanquet wrongly believed it to be half a century earlier) for all but a few to win for themselves all the amenities of a civilized existence.

3 | The problem of poverty

It is not surprising that most countries of the Western world should have felt, towards the end of the nineteenth century, that their methods of dealing with poverty were in urgent need of revision. The new information which was being accumulated revealed not only the true magnitude of the problem but also the great heterogeneity of the company of paupers. Where the Poor Law had been for centuries the only public agency for giving assistance to the helpless and destitute, as well as 'correcting' the idle and insubordinate, it had become a multi-purpose affair without having developed a variety of methods corresponding to the variety of cases with which it had to deal. The relief of poverty, too, was a field of action in which both public and voluntary bodies were active, often with a fairly equal distribution of responsibility between the two. And the public authorities concerned were mostly local ones. Thus there was a need both to co-ordinate the services and to standardize the procedures of the various agencies, and this was particularly necessary where urbanization was changing the nature of the problems and making some of the old methods of dealing with them obsolete.

In facing this task Britain suffered more acutely than any other country from the unhappy legacy of its nineteenth-century system. Nowhere else could you find quite the same combination of harsh deterrent principles, centralized policy control, and administration by an isolated authority, detached from the normal organs of local government, specializing in the treatment of paupers and nothing but paupers, and functioning in regions peculiar to itself. The Poor Law Guardians lacked both the incentive to modify and humanize the ideas which the central government obtained from the contemplation of its overall responsibilities, and also the personal touch that one might expect to find in true representatives of a neighbourhood. In fact it was precisely because the parish authorities had been too weak or too fearful to check the spread of indiscriminate relief in the early years of the century that the Poor Law Guardians and their Unions had been invented in 1834. Although in most countries of the Western world there had at one time been a tendency to lump rogues, vagabonds, and paupers together in a single category, and to treat them all in semi-penal institutions, the concept of pauperism as both an inferior and a shameful status persisted longer and penetrated more deeply into the public mind in England then elsewhere. It was kept alive, and deliberately reinforced, by the bureaucratic machinery created to translate it into action.

The situation was different in countries where the dominating influences were those of voluntary and charitable bodies, especially the Churches, or of the accepted leaders of local communities. In France, for example, the protagonists in the story were the Church and the Commune. It had been declared by Louis XIV that the estates of the Church were the patrimony of the poor, and ideas about poverty were still coloured by this tradition. The central government recognized that the secular power and initiative in this matter should be located in the Commune. At this level there was an Office of Charity (*Bureau de Bienfaisance*), usually headed by the Mayor. It was described as the 'representative' of the poor, and it alone was authorized to receive gifts and legacies on their behalf. This notion of 'representation' of the poor was inimical to the concept of poverty as a degradation, but it was entirely in harmony with the principle that all relief was a kind of charity. Another circumstance favouring a higher status for the paupers than in Britain was the acceptance of the rule that relief should be given in the home, whenever possible, which is almost exactly the reverse of the British practice. The idea was that, if the pauper remained at home, his relatives would care for him; if he was put into an institution, they would wash their hands of all responsibility.[1] We find the same principle adopted later in the Scandinavian countries.[2]

Debates about the problem of poverty in twentieth-century Britain revolved around the notion of 'the break-up of the Poor Law', a phrase popularized by the Webbs to denote the recommendations of the Minority Report of the Poor Law Commission of 1909. But, though the phrase may have been invented by the Webbs, they did not originate the process, which had been going on with gathering force throughout the Western world for some years before the Commission came into existence. It did not, however, at that time aim, as the Webbs did, at the total dissolution of the Poor Law and the authorities that administered it. The purpose of the movement was to provide special services for distinct categories, and to do this outside the ambit of the Poor Law. The categories of persons who were being gradually extracted from the heterogeneous company of paupers were the children, the old, the sick, and the unemployed.

The case for the special treatment of children was an obvious one and had long been recognized in most countries by the provision made for their education and for their exclusion from, or protection in, industrial employment. Measures of this kind applied to all children, whether paupers or not, though the education of the paupers might be given, as it often was in Britain, in special pauper schools. At the same time steps were being taken by the Poor Law authorities to get children out of pauper institutions by boarding them out in families or putting them in cottage homes or entrusting them to voluntary organizations. These practices were encouraged in Britain by the strong recommendations made by Mrs Nassau Senior in her report to the Local Government Board in 1873.[3] The combined effect of these two lines of development was to build up the status of children as a special category among paupers, even when they remained technically in the care of the Poor Law. To them must be added the important legislation which initiated the School Medical Service in 1907 and authorized local authorities to provide meals for school children in 1906. These were clearly seen as an encroachment by the education authorities on the preserves of the Poor Law and were therefore the most definite moves in the direction of its 'break-up' so far as children were concerned.

At the turn of the century most countries of the Western world suffered from a guilty conscience about the aged poor. In Britain a whole series of commissions and committees were set up to study the problem, and a survey made for the government in 1899, with a supplement in 1908, described the action taken in Russia, Norway, Sweden, Denmark, Germany, Holland, Belgium,

France, Italy, Austria, Roumania, and New Zealand.[4] We shall be concerned with the results of this awakening interest in old people in the next chapter. The point to be noted here is that by the end of the nineteenth century it was universally agreed that respectable, 'deserving' old people, who had worked while they could and were now without means, should not be treated as paupers. But the only action that had been taken in Britain by 1900 was to instruct Guardians not to force such people into the workhouse, and to see that the relief given them in their homes was adequate to their needs.[5]

As regards the sick, it had for some time been noticed in Britain that the services rendered to the paupers by the District Medical Officer, the Poor Law Dispensary, and the Poor Law Infirmary were not very different from those offered to the general public by the Medical Officer of Health and the municipal and voluntary hospitals. The government had recognized the special character of medical relief and treatment by enacting, in 1855, that its receipt through the Poor Law should not carry the stigma of disfranchisement; this implied that the sick poor were not necessarily to be regarded as paupers. It went on, a few years later, to state officially that it had no objection to the Poor Law Infirmaries being used as general hospitals for ordinary citizens, when no other equivalent facilities were available. As in the case of school meals and the school medical service, some of the Guardians saw this as an encroachment on their preserves, and complained that it blurred the distinction between the pauper and the independent citizen. In Manchester, in order to keep this distinction alive, they instructed their officers when speaking of Poor Law institutions for the sick 'to avoid using the word "hospital" or "infirmary", and simply to use the word "workhouse" '.[6]

The fourth distinctive type of poverty was that caused by unemployment. We have already seen how sharply public attention had been drawn to this in the 1880s and how substantial were the emergency relief funds raised by voluntary subscription. The first clear indication of a new official attitude came when Chamberlain, at the Local Government Board, issued a Circular in 1886 to Local Authorities and Boards of Guardians urging the former to utilize voluntary funds to set to work unemployed men referred to them by the latter. The wording of the circular is significant. The men selected by the Guardians were to be those whom 'it is undesirable to send to the workhouse or to treat as subjects for pauper relief', and they were to be given 'work which shall not involve the stigma of pauperism'.[7] Chamberlain's successor, Walter Long, revived this policy and prepared a Bill which became the Unemployed Workmen's Act of 1905. This rendered obligatory in towns of over 50 000 inhabitants what till then had been only permissible. The task was to be undertaken by Distress Committees representing the Councils and the Guardians; but the Act was a failure. The experience showed that temporary work could not confer any permanent benefit.

Such, in brief, were the trends leading towards the break-up of the Poor Law which were visible at the beginning of the new century, and they were common to the Western world as a whole. Even in the United States, where the resistance of the States to Federal interference in domestic matters and the passionate belief in individual liberty combined to check the development of social legislation, the same tendency was noted by those devoted to the cause of social welfare. One of these observed that 'the movement to analyse the relief load and to substitute for a general assistance programme appropriate provision for certain groups or categories was making real headway before the war',[8] that is to say the First World War. And we must also bear in mind that, already in the 1880s, Bismarck had initiated in Germany the first programme of compulsory social insurance, covering sickness, invalidity, and old-age pensions, and had thus introduced the world to what was destined to be the principal alternative to the Poor Law as a means of maintaining the personal incomes of those unable to earn.

The Royal Commission on the Poor Laws and Relief of Distress was appointed by the Conservative government in 1905, shortly before it fell, and reported to the Liberal government in 1909. Its creators intended it, we are told, to suggest administrative improvements which might make it easier to keep the 'principles of 1834' in operation. But it issued two reports, the more conservative of which (the Majority Report) recommended a substantial modification of those principles, while the more radical Minority Report called loudly for their total rejection. Both Reports delved deeply into matters of policy concerning every social problem in which poverty was a factor, and made a host of practical proposals about all of them. But the immediate effect of their labours on policy was very small indeed. The Liberal government had planned most of its social programme, and already put part of it (old-age pensions) into effect before the Reports appeared. In fact it was not till March 1911, we are told, that Lloyd George began to read the Reports. By then he was well on with the preparation of his National Insurance Bill and, since both Reports were opposed to compulsory social insurance against sickness and unemployment, they could not help him very much.[9] Nevertheless the two Reports are historical documents of great importance. They give us a picture of informed opinion on the major social problems of the day, and they present most of the arguments that were being advanced for and against new proposals current at the time. In addition the Minority Report, written by Beatrice Webb with the able off-stage help of her husband, planted an idea in the minds of British politicians which was first translated into action when the Poor Law Guardians were abolished in 1929, and finally triumphed— or appeared to do so—when Parliament passed the National Assistance Act (1948) with its opening sentence—'the existing poor law shall cease to have effect'.

The two Reports of the Commission had much in common, as the Webbs admitted. They listed the points of agreement, which included the transfer of the administration of the Poor Law to the ordinary local authorities, the abolition of the general mixed workhouse, the abandonment of the principle of deterrence, the adoption of preventive and curative measures in addition to palliatives (or mere relief), the extension of the public medical services, and the introduction of old-age pensions and some kind of facilities for insurance against unemployment.[10] As a matter of fact they were somewhat over-generous to the Majority. For these, while rejecting deterrence in its old form, with its associations of 'harshness and still more of hopelessness', favoured a mild kind of 'less eligibility' even for the aged, and they did not want medical treatment to be 'so attractive that it may become a species of honourable self-indulgence'.[11] Their view on unemployment insurance was the same as that of the Minority. They recognized very clearly the need for more insurance than was as yet provided by the trade unions and other voluntary

bodies, but they were opposed to a compulsory scheme, mainly
because of the very unequal distribution of the risk among the
various occupations. So they recommended the encouragement
of voluntary insurance by State subsidies.[12] Pensions for the
old and incapacitated worried them a lot, as their instinct was to
rely on personal savings. But the evidence was too strong. They
expressed their final view in the rather odd sentence—'we almost
seem driven to the conclusion that a new form of insurance is
required, which, for want of a better name, we may call Invalidity
Insurance', but they left it to others to work out a plan.[13] They
said it should be contributory, unlike the scheme just enacted by
Parliament, and one must assume that they meant it to be compulsory. The Minority, on the other hand, wanted a more generous non-contributory scheme for pensions at the age of sixty-
five.[14]

There were two major points of disagreement between the two
groups. The first concerned the respective roles of the State and
the voluntary agencies. The Majority wanted the latter to be the
front line of the attack on poverty, with the public service following
behind and taking care of the cases with which voluntary action
could not deal. And public assistance was to be deliberately made
less attractive than voluntary assistance. The Minority objected
strongly to these proposals on two grounds. First, because they
held that full responsibility for policy and its execution must
rest on the public authority, which should make such use of
voluntary helpers and the voluntary agencies as it thought fit.
This reflected the Fabian belief in the virtues of scientific planning
at the centre. Secondly, they could not accept the principle of
discrimination between the deserving poor, who would be the
charge of the voluntary agencies, and the less deserving, who would
be passed on to the Guardians or their successors. This savoured
too much of the attitude characteristic of what Beatrice Webb
called 'my friend the enemy—the Charity Organisation Society—
one of the most typical of mid-Victorian offsprings'.[15]

The second point of disagreement was more fundamental.
While both groups favoured the extension of the special public
services for the care of the old, the sick, the children, and the
unemployed, the Majority believed that there would always
remain a residual class of destitute persons who could only be
looked after by a Destitution Authority, which they proposed

to re-name the 'Public Assistance Committee'. It would not only distribute relief in cash or kind, but would provide for all the needs of those entrusted to its guardianship. The Minority maintained that if the public services were properly developed there would be no such residue, and it would be possible to get rid of both the separate category of pauper and the Destitution Authority. There would be only a temporary and miscellaneous collection of 'omitted cases' deposited through the meshes of the administrative net, which could be disposed of by an official whom they proposed to call the Registrar of Public Assistance, because he would also keep a record of all those receiving assistance of any kind from public funds.

The issues raised here are so vital to our subject that we must look carefully into them and see what arguments were, or could be, advanced in support of the two opposed points of view. It is best to begin with the Minority, because their motives are easier to identify. They had three main reasons for wishing to dispense with a destitution authority. The first sprang from the determination of the Webbs to apply scientific principles to social administration. It was unscientific to treat the poor as an operational category, since poverty was of many different kinds and resulted from many different causes. Scientific administration would split up this heterogeneous mass for purposes of treatment into its distinct component parts.

Secondly, they maintained that social policy should never be satisfied merely to relieve distress; its primary aim must be to prevent it and, failing that, to cure it. A destitution authority could never prevent distress, and could rarely cure it, because it could only touch those who were already destitute; and even the destitute often tried to evade its clutches as long as possible, for fear of the stigma its assistance carried with it. And their third reason was that a destitution authority that catered for all the needs of those entrusted to its care would duplicate the general public services in a wasteful and inefficient way, as indeed the Poor Law services for the children and the sick were already doing.

The Minority envisaged a widely ranging system of public services, co-ordinated at the local level by the Registrar of Public Assistance. For 'Public Assistance' for them had nothing to do with the relief of the poor as such, but referred to every kind of benefit offered to any class of person by a public agency financed (apart from what the recipients might pay) from public funds. It included, as they explained, the case of the paying patient in the County Lunatic Asylum, of the poor man's wife receiving milk at a nominal charge, of the County Bursary to Oxford, and of compulsory admission to an industrial school.[16] They were not offering everything for nothing, nor did they shrink from the need to empower those administering the services to discipline the unruly. The unemployed man, for instance, who could not at once be placed by a Labour Exchange, would be assigned to a Training Establishment, and for the 'industrial malingerer', who kept coming back for relief after he had been given several chances of work, there would be 'judicial commitment to a Detention Colony'.[17] This was the alternative the Minority preferred to the mass assignment of the undeserving to an inferior category and an inferior status.

The Majority were, no doubt, influenced by the natural inclination to cling to the familiar. A dozen of them had been personally active either in the public service or the voluntary agencies and might be expected to defend what they believed to be good in them. It must also be remembered that a proposal to transfer Poor Law functions to the general public services was a proposal to put your faith in what did not yet exist, or what was in the process of being created while the Commission was sitting. When they began their debates there were no old-age pensions, no health insurance, no unemployment insurance, few homes for the aged (except for the workhouses), few general hospitals under public control (except for the infirmaries); the treatment of mental defectives was in its infancy and was being studied by another Commission; free meals for poor school children as offered in London, were a novelty regarded with suspicion (until the Act of 1906); Care Committees under the education authorities were only just beginning to appear; the powers to deal with cruel or negligent parents were quite inadequate (until improved by the Children Act of 1906). The picture drawn by the Minority, or rather by the Webbs, was in fact a brilliant anticipation of the eventual results of a movement which had only just started and of which they sensed the nature, except for their rejection of the instrument of compulsory social insurance.

It is not surprising that the Majority should believe that the residue of cases left untended by the specialized public services would be, at least for a long time to come, a large and important one, and that consequently there must continue to be a general assistance agency to deal with them. When one asks what would be the common characteristics of these cases, one comes to the crux of the matter. And here it is best not to try to establish what actually were the motives that influenced the minds of the Majority but rather to see what their proposals seemed to imply.

One of the common characteristics was, of course, extreme poverty. But there was another, closely associated with it, which we might call helplessness, and the Majority were much concerned about this more personal factor. It must be interpreted as covering not only the old, sick, feeble-minded, feckless, idle, and (if children) neglected, but also the incorrigibles who were apparently incapable of living a decent life but were not criminals. All these needed something more than cash benefits, because poverty was not their only problem, and also something more than a specialized service, because their trouble was aggravated by poverty. They were cases, it might be argued, where it was necessary, either for their own benefit or in the public interest or both, that somebody should take charge of their lives. The Majority made it clear that the authority accepting this responsibility should try, not merely to relieve their distress, but also to overcome their helplessness. They also made it clear that even if helplessness were a common characteristic of these cases, they must also be poor. They did not wish the public assistance authority to extend its range of activities beyond those afflicted by poverty. But they proposed a certain enlargement of the definition of the class eligible for assistance by suggesting that it be described as 'necessitous' instead of 'destitute'.[18]

The Majority were also much concerned that the family, in which several different factors might be at work to produce distress, should be treated as a unit. It was a part of the ancient tradition of the Poor Law in Britain and elsewhere that it should deal with families, and not merely with individuals; hence the basic principle, dating from Elizabethan times, that the resources of the family must be taken into account in deciding whether poor relief should be given and, if so, how much. It is true that this principle had some bad consequences, such as the practice of treating the whole family as paupers if the head became a pauper. But it also had its good side, potentially at least, since welfare work is most effective if based upon the family unit. This was coming to be recognized by the voluntary agencies to which the Majority wished to assign so important a role. They were developing the techniques of 'family case-work', which came to be one of the most highly esteemed forms of social work in the mid-twentieth century. The Minority's plan, with its reliance on specialized services for different individual needs, would, said its critics, militate against family-based welfare work. The Webbs were aware of this criticism, and tried to answer it in a long footnote in one of their books. It might be objected, they said, that in 'directing attention to the fact that it is always an individual who is attacked, not, at first, the family as a whole', they were ignoring the case of families which were 'as whole families, in a state of destitution'. Their reply was that 'each member of such a family requires, for restoration, specialized treatment according to his or her need'.[19] But this really missed the point. It was not only a question of what we should now call 'problem families' but also the much wider one of treating all individual cases with due attention to their family setting. And the fear that the specialized services might fail to do this was not groundless. It is generally agreed that the most glaring defects of the policy of the next few decades was the failure to help parents of large families (by family allowances) and the failure to provide medical care for the families of insured persons.

But all this does not necessarily lead to the conclusion that the old Poor Law Guardians had to be preserved under a new name. What was there about them that the Majority considered to be so indispensable? Was it, perhaps, precisely the fact that they were not a 'service'? A public service is run by public servants who minister to the needs of those who are ultimately, though very indirectly, their masters, and who have the right to demand what the public servants are there to supply. But the person for whom a guardian cares is not his master, but his ward. And a ward is placed, or places himself, in the hands of his guardian, who accepts the responsibility of making decisions on his behalf. Thus the 'wards in poverty', as we might call the paupers, had no clear-cut right to demand any particular benefits or attentions from the Poor Law Guardians. The guarantee that their needs would be met rested, not on their right to insist, but on the Guardian's obligation to provide. The only difference between this and charity was that the obligations of the Guardians were legal and those of the purveyors of charity, moral or religious. It was this relationship of dependence, or of ward to guardian, that the Majority appear to have considered necessary for the proper treatment of the 'necessitous', and it was precisely this feature of Public Assistance that the Minority most intensely disliked and wished to abolish.

What we have touched on here is the whole question of the role and the organization of welfare services in modern society and in particular their relationship with services for the relief of poverty. The British Poor Law had the functions, but not the spirit, of a welfare service, and the authors of the Minority Report were quite right in urging that it must be uprooted. But when the 'break-up' for which they had campaigned eventually took place, it was found, as we shall see later, that in the process something had disappeared which it was necessary to re-create in a new form. The consequence was that in Britain, unlike most other countries, welfare and the relief of poverty were placed in separate administrative compartments, and we shall in due course be concerned to explore the advantages and disadvantages of this solution of a very difficult problem.

When the Reports appeared, the Webbs launched a nation-wide campaign in support of their plan for the 'break-up of the Poor Law', but, as they later admitted, it was a failure. The changes which actually took place at that time amounted to little more than a chipping away of the fringes of the Poor Law, accompanied by a certain humanization of the services retained within it. But a new note was struck by the Liberal leaders after their spectacular victory in the 1906 election. They spoke as the heralds of a new age of social reform, and insisted that their programme, though necessarily introduced piece by piece, was an integral whole whose total effect would be of momentous importance. It was, said Churchill in 1908, a programme that 'marks the assertion of an entirely new principle in regard to poverty; and the principle, once asserted, cannot possibly be confined within existing limits'.[20] He could not know that he would live to see it culminate some forty years later in the creation of the Welfare State.

4 | The coming of social insurance

It was during the first forty years of the twentieth century that compulsory social insurance was generally adopted by the countries of the Western world as one of the main instruments of social policy. Voluntary social insurance had, of course, been practised by Friendly Societies and various kinds of industrial and social clubs for a very long time. Schemes of this kind were often supported by government subsidies and made to conform to regulations imposed by law to ensure their sound administration. In the case of certain classes of workers, such as miners and seamen, regulation by government was common, and Prussia had made the insurance of miners compulsory as early as 1854. But the first decisive step in the establishment of compulsory social insurance on a more general basis was taken by Bismarck in the 1880s. By 1910 it was possible for two American observers to write that 'in all countries of Europe the beginnings are readily discernible of a movement towards a complete and connected system under which working-men will be insured against all contingencies where support from wages is lost or interrupted by any cause other than voluntary cessation of labour'.[1] But, though the principle was universally accepted, it was not used in the same way by all countries, and 'complete and connected' systems did not appear everywhere quite as soon as these authors expected.

Compulsory social insurance was a novelty in three respects. It involved a new kind of interference in the affairs of industry, a new type of relationship between the citizen and the government, and new problems of finance and administration. When introduced by Bismarck it had the character of a request to industry to join with him in making concessions to meet the legitimate claims of the workers, in order to make it easier both for him and for it to resist their illegitimate ones. But as presented by an aggressive figure like Lloyd George it had more the character of an attack, not against industrialists personally, but against the capitalist economy of the nineteenth century and against the 'establishment' which had tolerated its inhumanity. 'No one,' he said, 'can honestly defend the present system.' Side by side with great wealth there were multitudes who were not assured of even a bare subsistence. And the Liberal government aimed at something more than subsistence, namely at an income large enough to maintain efficiency for every man, woman, and child. 'The individual demands it, the State needs it, humanity cries for it, religion insists upon it.'[2] But the economy did not provide it; hence the need for the political power, backed by morality and religion, to interfere and make good the defect.

There is a curious passage in the Majority Report of the Poor Law Commission on this point. They were discussing the need for pensions, and they said: 'the evidence shows that, with very few exceptions, what working-men desire is the "cash nexus"—the bare wage contract uninfluenced by any but purely economic considerations—and the employing classes generally have accepted the situation and consider their obligations fulfilled when they pay the wage'. Most wages, they added, were fixed by collective bargaining, and the result was a 'maximum wage during the prime of life, and no wage at all when the prime is passed'.[3] They were quite right to describe the wage system in this way, but one wonders where they found the evidence that the working-men wished it to be so. It does not appear in the Appendices to their Report, and it is in conflict with what many labour leaders were saying when they denounced a system that treated labour as a commodity. But the passage brings out clearly the exact way in which compulsory insurance interfered in the affairs of industry. It inserted something into the relationship between the employer and employed which was not just the cash nexus; it interfered with the contract of employment, the very keystone of the free market economy, by writing into it a new mutual obligation. The contributions paid by and on behalf of the insured workman, and the benefits he earned thereby, became an integral part of his status as an employee.

Compulsory insurance also created a kind of contractual

relationship between the insured and the State, which was a new political phenomenon. The benefits were due, as specified, because the contributions had been paid, and the government was a party to the contract, being responsible for its terms and for their faithful fulfilment. It was thought that this contractual element in social insurance would prevent it from becoming the plaything of party politics. Governments, out of respect for the sanctity of contract, would not feel free either to cut the benefits in the interest of economy or to increase them in a bid for votes. But in the event mass unemployment between the wars and then the fall in the value of money made constant revision of the terms of insurance necessary, affecting the rights and obligations of those already in the scheme as well as new entrants, so that hardly any subject was more constantly at the centre of political strife. It was also believed that the beneficiaries would be happy to feel that they had won their benefits by their own action (even though they had no choice in the matter), while appreciation of the fact that larger benefits must mean larger contributions would put the brake on extravagant demands.

This emphasis on the binding, contractual character of social insurance had some subtle and probably unforeseen effects. It led people to exaggerate the distinction between social insurance and social assistance, and helped to maintain the flavour of inferiority and shame that clung to the latter. Secondly it caused, or at least was accompanied by, a widespread misunderstanding of the nature of social insurance which bedevilled discussions of social policy for many years. And this brings us to the new problems of finance and administration that social insurance brought with it.

The prominence given to the term 'insurance', with all its associations of security, respectability, and virtuous providence, implied that the schemes were modelled on the current practice of insurance companies, Friendly Societies and others engaged in similar operations. But this was true only to a very limited extent even at the beginning, and it became less true as time went on, as Beveridge explained very clearly in his Report.[4]

In private insurance the income consists of the premiums paid by policy-holders and the interest on accumulated funds. The premiums are assessed in relation to the risks covered, by a process of actuarial calculation. The same terms are offered to those exposed to the same risk, but anyone whose circumstances raise the risk above the average is required to pay a higher premium. The tubercular must pay more for life insurance than the healthy, or 'good-life'. The policy-holder can, therefore, claim that he is paying the true price of the coverage he receives, and if the price seems too high, he is free to take it or leave it. With public social insurance the position is different. If the State makes insurance compulsory for a large section of the community, it has a responsibility towards the insured greater than that of a private company, just because they are not free to 'take it or leave it'. The terms enforced must be such as they can afford to meet and the benefits must bear some relation to their real needs. The only way in which they can protest against terms which they consider unfair is by political action, through Parliament; consequently the fixing of the terms is primarily a political decision and only secondarily an actuarial one. The State can accept this responsibility because it is free to diverge from the strict actuarial principles of commercial insurance. And it enjoys this freedom because it has the power to draw on money other than the subscriptions of the beneficiaries; it can compel their employers to contribute and it can transfer sums from public revenue to the insurance fund. The ultimate guarantee of the solvency of any public scheme is the power of the State to levy taxes.

The part played by the State, and the nature and basis of the rights acquired by the citizen, differ according to the purpose of the insurance and the kind of risk it is designed to cover. A special position was occupied from the beginning by measures for the compensation of workmen for industrial injury, because they involve the legal liability of the employer. British law originally recognized a claim by the workman only where there was proof of negligence on the part of the employer or (by the Act of 1880) of one of his employees. But the Workmen's Compensation Act of 1897 brought British practice into line with that on the Continent of Europe by accepting the principle of 'occupational risk'. This meant that it was not necessary to prove negligence, but only that the accident arose 'out of and in the course of the employment'—since the risk was inherent in the occupation —and the principle was extended in 1906 to certain industrial diseases.

But there are different steps which a government may take to ensure that the workman in fact receives the compensation due to him. In a majority of countries this aim was achieved by making it compulsory for employers to insure their employees, at their own expense, against occupational risks, either in a central State scheme or, as in Germany, in Mutual Associations set up for the purpose by the various industries, or (exceptionally) with such insurance companies as they chose. It followed that the injured workman received compensation, at standardized rates, as a benefit provided by a form of social insurance of which employers bore the cost. It is true that most British employers insured voluntarily, but this was not insurance of the workmen against occupational risk; it was insurance of the employer against his liability to meet such claims as he could not rebut. Consequently the injured workman had to establish his claim for compensation, not with an insurance policy, but against his employer, if necessary in a court of law. It was not until after the Beveridge Report that compensation for industrial injury was included among the social insurance benefits.

In the case of other risks—old age, sickness, unemployment, etc.—it was the potential beneficiary who was compulsorily insured, and contributions were usually levied both on him and on his employer. In some countries social insurance was treated as being fundamentally a bipartite affair, between employer and employed, with the State only supporting the scheme from outside, as it were. Since it had set it up and made it compulsory, the least it could do was to guarantee its solvency. But it might go beyond this and contribute a lump sum annually to the funds (as in France), or add a fixed amount to each benefit paid out (as in Germany), or help to finance some special branch of the scheme which was least able to be self-supporting. But Britain, and some other countries, adopted a tri-partite system in which employers, employed, and the State (or the tax-payer) are all full partners, and all make regular contributions, though not necessarily of the same amount. In British thinking this partnership was not simply an administrative convenience, but a matter of political principle, because it reflected truly the distribution of responsibility in the society.

Whatever system was adopted, it is evident that social insurance lacked the qualities that gave to private insurance its respected status as an expression of personal thrift, since the contributions of the beneficiaries were neither voluntary nor sufficient to cover the benefits. But this did not prevent people, dazzled by the magic word 'insurance', from asserting that they had a right to their benefits because they had paid for them. Or, rather less crudely, they might claim that they had paid their fair share of the price. This was true, provided that it was realized (as generally it was not) that their 'fair share' was not something that an actuary could calculate, since he could estimate only the total income needed to cover the risks. The decision as to what proportion of that total should be charged to the beneficiaries was a purely political one. The contribution of the insured person should, in fact, be regarded, not as paying for the benefits, but as qualifying him to receive them, and the State is entirely free to fix whatever qualifying conditions it may think desirable. And it has generally fixed them, for political, fiscal, and psychological reasons, in such a way as to create the appearance of some logical relationship between contributions and benefits, although in fact no such relationship exists.

This is true in particular of statutory old age pensions to which it is peculiarly difficult to apply the principles of insurance in their classic form. For old age is not a misfortune which may fall at any time on any member of an insured population; it is a normal phase of life to which people can look forward and which they may hope to enjoy, and it comes to all, at the appointed time, provided they live long enough. So, whereas one *insures* against sickness or unemployment, one *saves* for old age, and the saving process must continue throughout one's working life. In the case of insurance against a risk, like sickness or a motor accident, what one draws out in return for a given premium depends on the extent of the damage suffered, and may be more than one had paid in; those on whom the misfortune falls benefit from the contributions of the lucky ones who escape it. And this is for the 'mutual benefit' of all, because all are equally protected against the risk. But in the case of saving for old age one can draw out, when the time comes, only what one has paid in together with the interest it has earned, and perhaps a share in the capital appreciation. This gives rise to special problems.

First, it is difficult to persuade people to keep up their payments continuously over a long period, so there is a strong case for compulsion. Secondly, the value of money may fall and make the pension, when eventually it falls due, quite inadequate. And thirdly, when a new scheme is introduced, those who are already in middle life would, if they were allowed to join it, have to pay much larger premiums than younger men in order to earn the same pension. It is in order to overcome these difficulties that the State has so often found it necessary to 'boost the benefits' to a level above that which corresponds to the contributions made by, or on behalf of, the insured.

Voluntary insurance for old age had been practised for some time in most countries, but because of these difficulties the societies had run into trouble. In France there were so many cases of insolvency that in 1850 a ban was placed on private insurance for pensions, and public savings banks were set up instead to receive the contributions of individuals and of societies, and the State added a subvention to guarantee their stability. Belgium and Italy followed suit before the end of the century.[5] In Britain, although Gladstone had expressed alarm at the number of companies that failed and of policies that lapsed, and had established the Savings Bank and a Post Office insurance scheme for the benefit of small savers,[6] no proposal was made that private savings should be subsidized by the State until Joseph Chamberlain put forward this idea in the 1890s. Its attraction for the Victorians was that the State would be helping only those who helped themselves; but it was pointed out that unfortunately the most urgent need was that of those who were far too poor to save anything at all. The suggestion was not adopted.[7]

By this time Germany had, in 1889, introduced a fully-fledged scheme of compulsory contributory insurance for pensions. It covered practically all wage-earners and other employees earning less than the equivalent of £100 a year, and it provided pensions for old age (at seventy), for invalidity (i.e. permanent disability), and for widows and orphans. Employers and employees contributed equal amounts, and the State added a fixed sum to each pension. Both contributions and benefits were scaled to correspond to some extent to the level of earnings, the insured being divided for this purpose into five income classes, each with its own rates. German policy, in deciding that pensions should reflect economic inequalities, underlined the difference between insurance and assistance. In the former, the more you had the more you would receive (and also contribute), but in the latter, where a means test was used, the more you had the less you would be given.[8]

In spite of the German example, British opinion was on the whole opposed to a contributory pension scheme. The Minority Report of the Poor Law Commission had been emphatic on this point. 'The insuperable difficulties inherent in contributory schemes of Old Age Pensions', they said, had been expressed in the reports of previous Commissions 'in a manner and with an authority that we take to be conclusive'.[9] Even Bismarck himself had not intended that the employees should be obliged to contribute towards their pensions.[10] But when the Act was passed he was no longer in power, and by then all the machinery for compulsory insurance had been created to deal with sickness and accidents, and could be used for pensions. Also, since the total pension (including the State subvention) was something between 2s. 6d. and 3s. a week, the contributions could be small.

There had been so much discussion in Britain about the needs of the aged poor that the Liberal government had to put pensions in the forefront of the programme it announced in 1906. But, argued Asquith when he introduced the Bill, it was not possible to have a contributory scheme. In the first place the administrative machinery for this did not exist. Secondly, the immediate task was to save old people from falling into the clutches of the Poor Law, and a contributory scheme could not do that, because 'none of its benefits would come into actual enjoyment until after the lapse of twenty or more years'. Finally a regular insurance scheme would antagonize the private agencies already engaged in the business. The government had therefore prepared a non-contributory scheme, to be financed directly out of taxes. By caring for the needs of the old in this way they would make insurance against other risks much easier. But if pensions were not to be given as an insurance benefit there must be 'some kind of discrimination' by which to select the pensioners, and the possible criteria were age, means, status, and character. The qualifying age was to be seventy, the qualifying income (for the full pension of 5s. a week) was fixed at £21 a year and the status was that of a British subject who had not suffered imprisonment during the last ten years and was not in receipt of poor relief. As to character, Asquith thought that the less said the better, but he was overruled and the Act stated that the pensioner must have worked to the best of his ability to maintain himself and his family. In New Zealand, where a similar scheme had been introduced in 1898, the pensioner had to be 'of good character and have for five years preceding application led a sober and reputable life'; so great was the anxiety lest the stigma of pauperism be lifted from those who did not deserve to be free of it.[11]

We have examined two ways in which the State can, in its management of social insurance, deviate from the orthodox principles of commercial insurance—namely by participating in the basic contributions, and by 'boosting the benefits' above the actuarial level. A third method (to which we referred briefly above) may be called the 'pooling of risks'. It is best seen in health insurance and in unemployment insurance. While all health insurance schemes at this time included cash benefits to compensate for loss of income during sickness, their major task was to bring medical care to the insured. In the period we are considering the concern of the State with the health of the people was being extended from the environmental to the personal services. This was in part a result of the growing sense of public responsibility for the welfare of the citizen, but there were special reasons for it as well. The evidence that was being accumulated made it clear that, although it was certainly true that bad sanitation and slum conditions were a potent cause of sickness, it was undeniable that the inadequacy of the medical services for detecting and treating illness, and for teaching people how to look after their own health and that of their children, made things worse than they need have been. If steps were to be taken to provide the cost of medical service for a large part of the population, it was essential that thought should be given to the question of how that service should be organized. A start had been made in England with the school medical service, and there was a great interest in the possibility of fighting tuberculosis by individual treatment in special institutions. Professor Mackintosh in fact claimed that 'the cause of the tuberculous was the spearhead of the campaign for a personal service at the beginning of the century'.[12] And Lloyd George, when preparing his plans for health insurance, was deeply impressed by what Germany was doing for the tubercular.[13]

At the same time the Friendly Societies and Clubs which provided medical treatment as an insurance benefit were in trouble, and this was true of many European countries. The doctors whom they employed complained that they were not paid enough, that they often had to provide the medicines themselves, and that they were being expected to treat, not only the insured persons, but their whole families, as well as many well-to-do people, who, they said, ought to come to them as private paying patients. In many places these disputes broke out into open warfare. As early as 1895 the *Lancet* had appointed a Special Commissioner to study the matter at home and abroad, and it published his reports under the general title of 'The Battle of the Clubs'. He had found, not only that there was much discontent in England, but also that 'the situation across the Channel is identical with what exists in Great Britain and Ireland'.[14] In Germany the conflict continued to rage between the doctors and the Societies operating under the health insurance scheme. Each such Society negotiated its own terms of service with the association of doctors, and one of the main points of contention was the principle of the 'free choice of doctor', which the Societies were unwilling to concede. In Leipzig in 1904 mounting grievances drove the doctors to go on strike, and 'blackleg' labour of very dubious quality was brought in to take their place. After a settlement of a sort had been reached, the association of doctors closed its ranks and called on its members to 'accumulate a heavy war chest' in readiness for the next battle.[15] The German Act of 1911 did not exaggerate when it said that 'for many years keen dissensions have occurred between the doctors and the sickness insurance authorities, resulting in many places in bitter disputes and a state of open conflict'.[16]

It is perhaps not surprising that Lloyd George should have come to the conclusion that the voluntary societies must not be entrusted with the provision of medical care for the insured. But he decided to let them handle the cash benefits. Those that satisfied his conditions would be listed as 'Approved Societies' and authorized to seek the custom of those covered by the Act. The government would hand over to each Approved Society the appropriate proportion of the contributions received in respect of its clients, and the Society would undertake to pay them the statutory benefits when they fell sick. We have here an example of the 'pooling of risks' in one of its forms. It was recognized that the State, when making insurance against sickness compulsory, could not discriminate, in the terms it offered between the sickly and the robust, or between those living in unhealthy conditions and those in healthy ones. These unequal risks must be 'pooled', even though it meant that some people would be getting what was by strict actuarial standards more for their money than others. But the government wanted nevertheless to preserve as much as possible of the spirit of voluntary, or commercial, insurance, and it allowed Approved Societies, if their finances permitted, to give additional benefits, such as medical appliances, dental and ophthalmic services, or extra cash. Some were able to do this, either because they were more efficiently managed than the average, or because they were extra careful in choosing their clients. They could not, of course, demand a higher premium from someone who was a 'bad risk', since the premium was fixed by law, but they could refuse to accept him. The result was that there was a considerable variation in the benefits obtained by the insured, although the contributions were the same for all.

For the general medical service the natural thing to do, one would have thought, was to entrust the organization to the local government authorities which were already in charge of Public Health, but the doctors were strongly opposed to this. They considered it essential, in the interests both of efficiency and of confidentiality, that the real control of the service should be in the hands of medically qualified persons, and they did not trust the local authorities to allow this. Their attitude on this point has not changed. They were even more strongly against a full-time salaried service run by the government, and they insisted that the patient must be free to choose his doctor. In their anxiety about what Lloyd George might do they threatened for a time to refuse co-operation, but the friction was largely due to the cavalier way in which he treated them during the negotiations. In principle they were with him, once he had made it clear that he accepted the three points just mentioned. So the service was organized by special Insurance Committees set up for the purpose, the patients could choose their own doctor, and the doctors who wanted to come into the scheme built up a panel of registered patients and were paid a capitation fee of so much for each patient on their register. The service was free, but it was confined to what an average general practitioner could be expected to give. It did not include specialist services, hospitalization, or dental and ophthalmic treatment and it did nothing for the dependants of the insured, which was a grave omission.

Governments had been much concerned about unemployment ever since the bad days of the 1880s, but their thinking had at first been directed more to finding ways to prevent or terminate it than to measures for making up lost earnings by cash benefits; the trade unions were doing that. The attempt to cure unemployment by getting the local authorities to create work for the unemployed was admitted by everybody to have failed. And little so far had come of plans to fit the unemployed for new jobs by passing them through training centres, though this idea was not dead and was revived after the war. More hope was placed in the device of the labour bureau, which had been imported from the Continent and was showing some promise. It was one of the aims of the Unemployed Workmen Act of 1905 to establish a network of these bureaux, or labour exchanges, throughout the country, but it had achieved its purpose only in the London area. Nevertheless the results were significant enough for the Majority Report of the Poor Law Commission, when drawing up recommendations on unemployment, to begin with the sentence, 'in the forefront of our proposals we place labour exchanges', and the Minority agreed. In this case there is direct evidence of the influence of the Commission, because Churchill quoted this sentence when introducing the Act of 1909 which established a national system of labour exchanges under the direct control of the Board of Trade.[17] By 1914 they were filling just over a million vacancies,[18] but looking back on their history in 1930 William Beveridge, who had done so much to bring them into existence, found it disappointing; only one in five of the engagements of insured workpeople was made through the exchange.[19] They were, however, key points in the administrative structure of unemployment insurance.

The system of compulsory insurance against unemployment introduced in England in 1911 was the first of its kind, apart from a disastrous experiment in a Swiss canton. Everybody knew about the 'Ghent System' by which the municipality gave annual subventions to private schemes in order to increase the benefits, and France had launched the first national system on these lines in 1905, with Norway and Denmark following suit in the next two years. But even Germany, the originator of compulsory insurance, had left unemployment out. It was not that there was any exceptional difficulty about applying the insurance principle to unemployment in normal times. On the contrary, one objection to a comprehensive State scheme was that the principle was already being applied extensively and with considerable success by the trade unions, and a State scheme might interfere with their business.

But each scheme as a rule covered only one industry or occupation, within which the risk of unemployment was of much the same kind and magnitude for all. So the principle of 'mutual benefit' could be applied. But a national scheme would have to include industries in which the risk of unemployment differed widely, and the question was how far the principle of the 'pooling of risks' could be carried. The bad risks were not, as in sickness, individual cases, but whole sections of the population to be insured. If contributions and benefits were the same for all, the stable industries would subsidize the unstable, and the efficient firms the inefficient. So the Liberal government decided to keep the inequality of risks to be covered within bounds and to start with a limited scheme confined to seven selected industries. These, as Churchill explained, were industries in which 'the unemployment is due not to a permanent contraction but to temporary oscillation in their range of business, and that is the class of business in which unemployment insurance is marked out as the scientific remedy for unemployment'.[20] Some inequality of risk did exist among these industries, but its effects were kept to a minimum by limiting the number of weeks in any one year in which benefits could be drawn, and consequently also the extent to which the contributions of one industry might be called on to pay for the unemployment in another. The scheme which was eventually embodied in Part II of the National Insurance Act of 1911 covered about two and a half million workers and was financed by contributions from employers, employees, and the State. For those not covered there remained the voluntary agencies, and the Act provided for a small subvention to be available to help these by adding one-sixth to the benefits they paid out of their funds. Beyond this there was only the Poor Law.

Such were the beginnings of compulsory social insurance, and to many people, including Winston Churchill, it marked the

dawn of a new age of social policy. 'If I had to sum up the immediate future of democratic politics in a single word,' he said in
1909, 'I should say "Insurance". If I had my way I would write
the word "Insure" over the door of every cottage, and upon
the blotting book of every public man, because I am convinced
that by sacrifices which are inconceivably small, which are all
within the power of the very poorest man in regular work,
families can be secured against catastrophes which would otherwise smash them up for ever.'[21] And many years later, in similar
vein, he spoke of the Beveridge Report as 'bringing the magic
of averages nearer to the rescue of the millions'.[22] In the first
of these passages Churchill seems to be attributing to private
thrift a power that is found only in public schemes, and in the
second he appears to have forgotten that averages have disadvantages as well as advantages. For, as Professor Eveline
Burns has well said, 'social insurance deals with *presumptive*
rather than *demonstrated* need, and is a social institution dominated by a concept of *average* rather than *individual* need'.[23]
She was obviously thinking here, not of health insurance, which
provides a personal service to meet an individual need, but of
cash benefits. In their case it is true that, whatever the system, the
insured is paid the sum to which he is entitled without reference to
his financial condition at the time. The *presumption* is that this
will be about right. If it is too little, some method other than
insurance must be used to make up the difference—and, as we
shall see, no problem has proved more intractable than that of
finding the best way of doing this. We shall also see that, since
Eveline Burns made that remark, ever more elaborate and ingenious systems have been devised or proposed for tailoring
social insurance to the measure of the individual. Lloyd George
may have sensed some of the troubles ahead when he jotted down
on a piece of paper (in 1911, while preparing his Insurance Bill)
'Insurance necessarily temporary expedient. At no distant date
hope State will acknowledge full responsibility in the matter of
making provision for sickness, breakdown and unemployment'.[24]

5 | The inter-war years

It is tempting to regard the twenty years that elapsed between the two world wars as an interlude dominated by desperate efforts to cope with an unprecedented depression, and to assume that when the depression ended the stream of events we have been describing resumed its course with nothing added to it but unhappy memories. But this view is untenable. It is true that the period was one not so much of great innovations as of the consolidation and expansion of measures already tested. It is true also that the guiding principles which defined the main areas of public responsibility and the rights and legitimate expectations of the citizen remained substantially the same. Nevertheless important progress took place and the scene in 1939 was very different from what it had been in 1914.

The war itself had some effect by fostering a sense of social solidarity among those who had seen it through at home and by evoking a determination to offer a better life to the men returning from hellish experiences at the front. In Britain this expressed itself in the popular slogan about 'homes fit for heroes', but the mood was short-lived. The depression which followed, striking the countries of the Western world at different moments and with differing force, also presented a challenge, to which, in some cases, the response was similar. In France the Minister introducing the comprehensive social security legislation of 1928 said that 'the essential point is that society as a whole should, in a spirit of national solidarity, assist the wage-earners to defend themselves against the dangers by which they are constantly threatened', and he repeated the word 'solidarity'.[1] In the United States the first major piece of social legislation to be passed at the Federal level went through Congress in 1935. It brought that country at one leap, not quite into line with Western Europe in the matter of social policy, but at least within talking distance. In Britain the major effect of the depression was the collapse of unemployment insurance. But in this case the response was not a great creative effort, but a series of attempts to patch up the system. Nevertheless it is clear that the experience of those years prepared the way for the reorganization of social security which was planned during the Second World War and put into effect immediately after it.

In the history of social policy wars and depressions are accidents, however important their consequences may be. But beneath the surface we can discover processes of growth which are the product of the evolutionary forces at work within social policy itself. Before the First War social reform was a political adventure run by enthusiastic amateurs; in the inter-war years social administration became a science practised by professionals. The commissions and committees which sat in Britain before the war, having gathered such information as they could about the past and present (and it was often fragmentary and unreliable), had little but their imagination and *a priori* reasoning to guide them when they tried to peer into the future and gauge the merits of policies which had not yet been tried. And often, as in the case of those studying the problem of the aged poor, they failed to make any recommendation at all, except that another committee should be asked to undertake further investigations. Those which met after the war were set to examine the records of systems which had been working for several years and could base their conclusions on empirical research. Typical of the first phase are the crusading fervour of Lloyd George and the hit-or-miss efforts of the little band of neophytes which he installed, with Braithwaite at their head, to design a system of health insurance under his inspiring but erratic direction. Typical of the second period are the dry matter-of-fact tones of Neville Chamberlain and the highly expert studies by William Beveridge, especially of unemployment, but also of what he called *Insurance for All and Everything*. What strikes one about that hastily written but brilliant pamphlet is the clarity and precision of the thought, and the implied assumption that the level of understanding of the subject was by then high enough to make this very compressed picture intelligible to the general reader.

This new sophistication was a scientific not a political phenomenon. It was concerned with applying techniques, which were of
universal validity, to problems that were an intrinsic part of
modern industrial society wherever the income of the family
was derived from the earnings of labour, and men and women
fell victim to accidents and sickness. Consequently those engaged
in this work used concepts and spoke a language that were not
local to their home country, but international. And they could
meet in conferences called by the International Labour Office
(later 'Organisation') and freely exchange views, pool experiences,
and adopt resolutions.

The result of all this was a marked convergence of social policy
in all countries where social policy could be said to exist, but
we must be careful not to press this point too far. We can see in
the 1920s and the 1930s an emergent consensus about the nature
and extent of government responsibility for social welfare. There
was also general agreement as to the sections of the population
to which social security legislation should apply. In addition
most countries had accumulated much the same equipment of
techniques and administrative machinery for use in the execution
of their social policy. But here the convergence begins to weaken
and is succeeded by a certain divergence of practice in deciding
which instrument should be used for each particular purpose.

In some cases international convergence was the natural result
of consolidation at the national level. Britain and Germany
afford an example of this. Germany's first programme of social
insurance included pensions and sickness but excluded unemployment; Britain's included sickness and unemployment (on
a limited scale) but excluded pensions. It was natural that both
countries, as they gained in experience, should fill in the gaps.
Britain made unemployment insurance general in 1920 and introduced contributory pensions (at 10s. a week) in 1925; Germany
added unemployment insurance to her system in 1927. After that
the two systems matched very closely.

Another symptom of convergence was the movement which
took place in several countries to unify their social security programmes and enclose them in a single administrative framework.
France launched a composite scheme of this kind in 1928, covering sickness, maternity, invalidity, old age, and death (but not
unemployment) and thus advanced at one step from a relatively

backward to a quite advanced position on the social policy scale.[2] The American Social Security Act of 1935 was also a composite measure, and it has been said that Roosevelt had deliberately blocked earlier proposals of limited scope because of his 'desire to combine old-age pensions with a general program of social security and his belief that a unified program should be worked out'.[3] The Act covered pensions and unemployment, but not sickness, and it also provided Federal aid for a wide range of welfare services. But perhaps the most celebrated unified scheme is that contained in the New Zealand legislation of 1938, described by Sir Arnold Wilson as 'the most far-reaching scheme of obligatory social insurance ever included in a single enactment'. It covered old age, medical care, sickness benefit, invalidity, maternity, widows, orphans, disabled miners, unemployment, and family endowment.[4] But only superannuation and family allowances were free of a means test. Schemes of 'all-in insurance' were proposed in Britain by Beveridge, J. L. Cohen, Sir John Marriott, and others and were carefully considered by the government and rejected as impracticable.[5]

A typical system of social insurance at this stage would be confined to employees and would cover practically all industrial wage-earners, possibly—but by no means always—agricultural workers, and salary-earners with incomes below a fixed maximum (except those otherwise provided for, like civil servants). This gave the impression that society was divided into two layers: the independent, self-sufficient tax-paying layer and the compulsorily insured, benefit-receiving layer. The acceptance of benefits from these public services did not carry the stigma of pauperism, but had become an index of social class. And, for the first time in its modern form, the issue was raised whether social services should be used as an instrument for the redistribution of income between one class and another. Poor relief had never raised this question, since it was a kind of public charity which had no effect on society at large. But the system of social security as it had developed was a quite different affair. It was, indeed, difficult to calculate in what proportions it was returning money to those who had contributed it, transferring income on the 'mutual benefit' principle between members of the same economic class, or redistributing income from the richer to the poorer sections of the community. But it was certain that this last operation was taking place to some extent, and the question was whether it should be treated simply as the natural and inevitable consequence of services designed to satisfy real needs wherever they were found, or regarded as being an end in itself. The full-blown controversy on this point belongs to the period after the Second World War, but the situation that gave rise to it took shape during the inter-war period.

So far we have been taking note of the international convergence of social policy. When we turn to look at the techniques used in dealing with particular problems we are struck by the differences we find. In the Beveridge Report there is an Appendix that summarizes the position in 1938 in thirty countries, other than Britain, scattered over Europe, Asia, the two Americas, and Australasia. It shows that twenty had compulsory insurance against sickness, twenty-four had some form of contributory pensions, all more or less made provision for industrial injury and diseases, but only eight had compulsory unemployment insurance (not counting Germany, where it had been discontinued by the Nazis). Only three (again not counting Germany) covered all three risks of sickness, old age, and unemployment, as Britain did, and they were, rather surprisingly, New Zealand, Bulgaria, and Poland.[6] It would be quite wrong to imagine that the absence of a contributory scheme meant refusal to accept any responsibility for meeting a particular need. It indicated rather a difference of method. The responsibility towards the unemployed, for example, was frequently met by subventions to voluntary insurance supplemented by a well-developed system of social assistance, as in France. In this way the private efforts of the trade unions were stimulated, compulsion was avoided, and the objection to pooling in one scheme risks that were very unequal was met by basing the insurance on individual industries or occupations.

But arguments about principles and theories were soon overwhelmed by the catastrophic impact of the great depression and the mass unemployment that accompanied it. In Britain hardly had the decision been taken in 1920 to extend unemployment insurance to all industrial and commercial workers, in spite of the inequality of incidence of the risk, than the blow fell. By March 1921 the number of unemployed had nearly doubled, and in the 1930s the total rose perilously near to three million. In Germany the peak figure was about five million, and in the United States probably nearer ten.[7] Insurance benefits were soon exhausted, and the choice had to be made between abandoning the relationship between contributions and benefits altogether or passing the burden on to the Poor Law, that is to say on to the local rates. The latter was impossible, so the compromise was adopted of abandoning the principle of insurance but retaining the apparatus and as much as possible of the terminology. Relief was paid far beyond what contributions had earned by means of a succession of so-called 'transitional', 'extended', and 'uncovenanted' benefits, into the nature and fortunes of which it is not necessary to enter here. The result was summed up by Beveridge in 1930. Social insurance, he said, was originally contractual in character, in that it conferred a right that was conditional on the payment of contributions. Now the obligation to pay the contributions had lapsed, but the right to benefit was still acknowledged. Consequently 'the insurance scheme of 1911 has become a general system of outdoor relief to the able-bodied, administered by a national in place of a local authority, and financed mainly by a tax on employment'.[8] He was speaking in terms of the sharp antithesis between insurance and assistance, which events had so dramatically outstripped.

An heroic attempt was made in 1934 to restore the integrity of insurance. Benefits, in the true sense, were once more to be paid only in so far as contributions warranted, but a new Limbo was created between the Heaven of insurance benefits and the Hell of poor relief over which ruled a national authority called the Unemployment Assistance Board. No stigma was to be attached to the acceptance of aid from this body but, as its payments were subject to a 'means test', which took account of the income of family members living at home, it looked just like the Poor Law under another name. Nothing in the history of social policy, except perhaps the old mixed workhouse, has inspired such hatred and detestation as this household means test. This was due partly to the inquisition necessary to make the assessment, and partly to the humiliation it caused to a man who expected to support his family, and not to be supported by it. But the more fundamental cause of humiliation was the enforced idleness and the necessity to go, week after week, to draw money that had not been earned by labour. It is significant that all those in this position, whether the money they were drawing was insurance benefit or unemployment relief, were said to be 'on the dole'.

In the United States the storm broke more suddenly and was even more devastating. A vast programme of relief for the unemployed was developed, including the invention of tasks to be performed at public expense by all classes of person, including writers, scholars, and artists. But in the midst of this an attempt was made to build a permanent piece of machinery into the administrative systems of the Federal and State governments for the maintenance of the unemployed. By the Federal Act of 1935 a pay-roll tax was imposed on all industrial and commercial employers of more than seven persons, with the provision that any State which established an unemployment insurance scheme approved by the Federal government would receive the proceeds of this tax and assign them to the scheme. The practice of unemployment insurance spread gradually over the economy, but a quarter of a century later there were still fourteen million jobs not covered.[9]

The survey of foreign policies attached to the Beveridge Report said nothing about family allowances, because he treated them as an 'underlying assumption' of his plan and not as an integral part of it. Their introduction in Europe was one of the most important innovations of the inter-war period. The pioneers in this adventure were France and Belgium. Voluntary systems by which wages were supplemented for the benefit of dependent children had existed for some time in both countries, and the practice was made general and compulsory by legislation in Belgium in 1930 and in France in 1932. At first this caused a divergence of policy between the countries that adopted them and those that did not. But this was a passing phase. A movement of convergence soon developed as the example set by the pioneers was generally followed, until family allowances became as common a feature of social programmes as pensions.

Family allowances differ from the other services we have so far examined in that their primary purpose is to supplement the earnings of those at work, not to maintain the income of those unable to earn. They are a means by which an individual wage is converted into a family wage by being adjusted to the number of persons who must live on it. It was natural, therefore, that these early schemes should place the whole burden of the cost on the employers. The allowances were treated as a sort of employer's liability, and the principle of insurance entered, as in the case of industrial injury, only because the employers covered their liability by sharing it among themselves. They paid a contribution proportionate to the number of their employees into an 'equalisation fund' by which the allowances were financed. This destroyed any incentive there would otherwise have been to employ bachelors in preference to fathers of families.[10] One aim of the policy of family allowances was, of course, to check and if possible to reverse the fall in the birth rate. But another, and more permanent one, was to sustain the family, as the vital nucleus of the social order. The emphasis, therefore, was on the satisfaction of need, not on the sanctity of contractual rights won by insurance contributions. In Britain the campaign led by Eleanor Rathbone on behalf of what she called the 'disinherited family' had not yet succeeded, when war broke out, in convincing the government of the merits of family allowances. Payments adjusted to family needs were an accepted feature of public assistance. It was true that they had, of dire necessity, been extended in 1921 to the unemployed in receipt of insurance benefits, but there was opposition to introducing them as a permanent feature either of the wage system or of social insurance. And when they were eventually adopted after the war, they were not placed in either of these categories, but in a special one of their own.

Meanwhile the campaign for the break-up of the Poor Law continued, both in Britain and elsewhere. The crucial question faced in all countries was, as we saw earlier, to decide whether the transfer of functions from the Poor Law authorities to other agencies could be carried to the point where the Poor Law as such would cease to exist. As far as relief in cash was concerned, its functions were being transferred to social insurance but, as we have just seen, not quite completely in the case of old people and widows and very far from completely in the case of unemployment. This movement was general. But national practices differed with regard to the services, in the fields of health, education, and welfare, which Poor Law authorities everywhere had administered for the benefit of those dependent upon them. British policy, true to the spirit of the Minority Report, aimed at their progressive absorption into the appropriate general services provided for the population at large. But these processes of transfer and absorption could not proceed freely as long as the Poor Law was administered by special authorities outside the local government apparatus. So in 1929 the critical step was taken of abolishing the Guardians and handing over the residue of their functions to Public Assistance Committees set up by the county and county borough councils. The Poor Law was not abolished, but it was placed under new management with a view to its eventual disappearance.

The Act provided for the transfer of the Poor Law hospitals to the Public Health Authorities, but this happened only to a limited extent and the Poor Law Medical Officers continued to visit and treat the poor.[11] The Public Assistance Committees also became responsible for the old people, children, feeble-minded, and others who needed institutional care, because there were no institutions to put them in except those handed over by the Guardians. We have here the germs of some of the more important modern welfare services. It was obvious that the Poor Law medical services should be taken over by specialized medical authorities of some kind, and the delay in making the transfer was due to the fact that there was, at the time, general dissatisfaction with the way the medical services were operating, but as yet no clear idea what their future structure should be. Once it was decided to set up a National Health Service. the residue of the Poor Law in this field created no problem. But there was no obvious specialized professional authority to take over the embryo welfare services, and they remained where they were until after the war. Other Committees (Education or Public Health) might lend a hand, but the Public Assistance Committee was still responsible and it still operated under the Poor Laws. It is not easy for welfare services to shake off all association with pauperism, for they do in fact deal to a large extent with cases in which a particular misfortune is aggravated by poverty. And anybody obliged to live in a public institution at the public expense is likely to look, and to feel, like a pauper. British policy tried to achieve the transformation by means of a clean break with the past. But the replacement of the Guardians by the Public Assistance Committees was little more than the announcement of a break that could not yet be made, and British social policy suffered for some time the natural consequences of having given the dog a bad name and failed to hang it. The reputation of the Poor Law was blackened, but it was not killed, and it continued to leave its mark on everything it touched. Eventually, as we shall see, the policy succeeded in creating welfare services for citizens, not paupers; but it got there the hard way, by wiping out the past and starting afresh.

Other countries pursued a different course. They did not condemn the Poor Law to death by dismemberment, but tried to humanize and modernize it. In France and Germany, for instance, public assistance continued to function as a multi-purpose service meeting all the needs of the very poor, who were treated as a distinct category, but one which should become smaller as social security measures became more comprehensive. The French *aide sociale* and the German *Fürsorge* provided not only maintenance of all kinds, but help in paying rents, medical and maternity services at home or in hospital (with choice of doctor), education, and vocational training of the handicapped. Thus, while the destitute were set apart from the rest of the population, it was intended that they should be served in the same spirit as the others, an ideal that could not always be realized.[12] In Scandinavia a rather similar development took place, which has been described as 'the transformation of poor relief into modern social assistance'. The sharp separation of the category of the very poor from the rest of the community seems to have been absent, and it was possible to bring under one authority the idle and obstreperous poor, who needed to be subjected to deterrent discipline, those whose main trouble was extreme poverty, and those for whom poverty was only a subsidiary factor in a situation dominated by some misfortune or affliction.[13]

In the United States public assistance, which had been modelled on the English Poor Law, was indeed broken up, but mainly by a process of internal specialization rather than transfer to the general public services. In the nineteenth century the practice had grown up of giving 'preferential assistance' to specially deserving cases; such assistance was both more generous than the average and was supposed to carry no stigma of pauperism. Several States then started special programmes for selected classes of persons—mothers of young children, the aged, and the blind. This so-called 'categorical assistance' spread slowly and was attacked as unconstitutional on the grounds that it involved the 'payment of public funds to persons who were not in need'. In a sense this was true, and it did imply a radical departure from traditional Poor Law principles. The Social Security Act of 1935 standardized the system by offering Federal aid for schemes on behalf of the old, dependent children, the blind, and the permanently disabled, while recognizing, but not aiding, a fifth category of 'general assistance', which was the old Poor Law under a new name. Thus the area of public assistance was expanded, both as regards the needs provided for and the population covered, but it remained 'assistance', in that the services were non-contributory and the benefits were granted subject to a means test.[14] But these measures did much to change the harsh spirit of what Edith Abbott called 'our un-American American Poor Laws'.[15]

If family allowances were the most important practical innovation in social policy during the inter-war years, housing was the most important item to be added to the list of things with which social policy had to deal. Speaking of Britain before the First World War Marian Bowley says that at the time 'the housing problem was the slum problem, the problem of people living in insanitary conditions'.[16] It is true that the main emphasis had been on housing as a branch of Public Health, but the idea that government, both central and local, had some responsibility for what another writer on the subject calls 'house building as distinct from slum clearance' had been translated into legislation in 1890 and 1909, and the distinction was reflected in the regulations governing the two operations. But, although 'housing became a burning question of municipal politics', very little was done to provide houses outside the slum-clearance areas.[17]

The war gave to the housing question a new urgency. Building had been suspended, and rents had been frozen in order to prevent the exploitation of the housing shortage. And the men at the Front had been promised 'homes fit for heroes' on their return. It would hardly have been tactful to greet them with a big rise in rents, and yet, at the level at which they then stood, there was no incentive to private firms to build houses to let to working-class families. And people were beginning to regard their controlled rents as representing the true value of their houses. It was in these circumstances that British housing policy first appeared in the guise of a social service. The responsibility for coping with the crisis was placed firmly on the local authorities; they were to make surveys and prepare plans to meet the needs that they revealed. They were to let the houses they built at rents which bore no necessary relation to their cost, but were assessed in the first instance by reference to the controlled rents for similar accommodation in old houses, and then adjusted to the tenant's capacity to pay. Any loss suffered on the transaction in excess of the yield of a rate of one penny in the pound would be made good by the Exchequer. Under a scheme of this kind both the local authorities and their tenants would receive aid in proportion to their needs. But this policy, which set no limit to what the local authorities could spend, proved too costly, and also failed to deliver the goods, and was abandoned in 1923. Thereafter the subsidies paid by the Exchequer to the local authorities were limited to fixed amounts, and the trend, if we ignore the oscillations of policy associated with changes of government, was towards relying mainly on private enterprise for new building, while concentrating public expenditure on special tasks, such as slum-clearance and the reduction of overcrowding. At the same time attempts were made to bring rent restriction to an end by gradually lowering the maximum value of houses whose rents remained controlled, but the operation was never completed, and at the outbreak of the Second World War about one quarter of the rents were still controlled.[18]

The experience of the other European countries involved in the Second War was very similar. Some of them had started to evolve a housing policy, and the machinery with which to implement it, even before the war. France in particular had, by 1906, developed the whole apparatus of public loans, cheap land, guaranteed interest, and tax relief to help Housing Societies to build houses and let them to working-class families at rents which they could afford.[19] Between the wars there was a convergence of policy in Europe, in the sense that all countries took steps to control rents and stimulate building, but they differed as to the extent to which they subsidized rents. In Scandinavia rents rose as much as the cost of food, but in France, Germany and Italy considerably less. European policy also differed in certain points from British. There was less inclination to adjust individual rents to incomes than to adjust incomes to rent; governments preferred, as Alva Myrdal says of Sweden, to subsidize families rather than houses.[20] More use, on the whole, was made of tax remission as an encouragement to build, perhaps because there were more taxes that could conveniently be remitted, especially taxes on land. But most significant was the multiplication of housing associations, co-operatives, and semi-official, autonomous institutions for financing the building of houses on a non-profit basis. The methods varied but the purpose was the same, namely to provide dwellings which could be let at moderate rent to families with incomes below a certain fixed level, with the minimum of administrative intervention by the local authorities.[21]

The inter-war years saw, finally, two developments of lasting importance which affected the whole character of social policy. The depression, and above all its devastating effects in the areas most heavily hit by it, caused the whole picture of social problems to change. It was realized that social policy must be conceived as allied to general economic policy, and not as a separate area of political action governed by principles peculiar to itself. The vital necessity was to restore the volume of employment, and the relief of the unemployed was a subsidiary matter. In fact, care had to be taken to see that relief was not administered in such a way as to discourage efforts to end the slump. Thus the way was prepared for the Beveridge doctrine that there could be no effective system of social security without a policy of full employment.

In what came to be known as the 'Special Areas' the task confronting the British authorities was nothing less than the rescue of community life in all its forms. Efforts were made to set up new industries, to organize emigration, to devise 'sub-economic' occupations and provide land for 'subsistence production' by which men could be given something to do and could earn a small profit without sacrificing their status as unemployed, and it was equally essential to offer entertainment, recreation, and ways of using leisure which might stimulate the faculties and engage the attention of men and youths condemned to idleness.[22]

The second important development was in the role of the voluntary societies. It was probably in the nineteenth century that the boldest and most imaginative pioneering work was done by private individuals, after which there came a period when some of the leading voluntary organizations were associated with reactionary and conservative views, while the public services embarked on new enterprises, often following a lead that had been given them by the most effective private individuals and agencies. In the inter-war period the pioneering role of voluntary societies was once more conspicuous, while new forces began to stir in some of the older and more conservative bodies. But this time the public and private sectors advanced together so closely and in such harmony that the characteristic feature of the age was partnership between the two. In the early years of the century, says Bourdillon, the question was whether a service should be voluntary or statutory, but by the end of the 1930s the answer clearly was that both were needed, and the problem was 'not whether to co-operate but how to co-operate'.[23]

Many examples could be given. Public services for maternity and child welfare began to be systematically developed on the basis of two Acts of Parliament. The first, in 1915, made it compulsory for the doctor or midwife to notify every birth within thirty-six hours. This gave an infinitely better basis of information for health visitors than the obligation on parents to register the birth, which had existed since 1874. Secondly, the Maternity and Child Welfare Act of 1918 authorized and en-couraged local authorities to develop services for expectant and nursing mothers and for children under five. In this large field, which included health visiting, maternity and child welfare clinics, children's homes, nursery schools, and day nurseries, the volun-tary and statutory agencies went forward side by side and hand in hand. The Blind Persons Act of 1920 empowered local authori-ties to carry out the duties imposed upon them through the medium of voluntary agencies, and this was extensively done.[24] Voluntary youth organizations had existed since the middle of the last century, but it was only in 1916 that the government made its first attempt to set up central and local machinery to co-ordinate the whole range of voluntary and statutory activities, recreational and educational, that were concerned with youth.

One of the most significant developments in this period was the creation of the National Council of Social Service, and its supporting regional or local councils, with the task of smoothing the way to co-operation between voluntary bodies of all kinds, and between them and the public authorities. It was primarily, said G. D. H. Cole, 'not a charitable agency, but a fosterer and co-ordinator of communal activities among ordinary people, and not merely among the "poor" in any narrow sense'.[25] It was the moving spirit behind the drive to establish local Community Centres run on democratic principles by Community Associations which attracted so much attention and aroused such high hopes in the years immediately before the Second World War. It was felt that this represented the vital change from services offered and institutions created by benevolent outsiders, to reliance on self-help and mutual aid. And the National Council also dispensed about a million pounds of government money for the foundation and management of 'occupational clubs' for the unemployed in the depressed areas.

Little or nothing has been said in this chapter about the health services. Had the story been told here it would have consisted largely of growing evidence of dissatisfaction with the state of affairs and tentative proposals for reforms and additions, on which no action was taken. It is more convenient to treat of these matters in the next chapter.

6 | The war and the Welfare State

A modern total war has certain predictable effects on the social problems of the warring nations. It absorbs the unemployed, it stimulates health services in both their technical and their organizational aspects, and it creates a housing shortage, either by destroying houses or preventing them from being built, or both. In a more general sense total war obliges governments to assume new and heavier responsibilities for the welfare of their peoples, especially by controlling the production and distribution of scarce necessities, like food and fuel, and by looking after those who have been made homeless by invasion, evacuation, or aerial bombardment. The experience of total war is therefore bound to have an effect on both the principles of social policy and the methods of social administration. But the nature of this effect will depend to a considerable extent on the fortunes of war—on whether a country is invaded or not, on whether it is victorious or defeated, and on the amount of physical destruction and social disorganization it suffers.

Britain's experience in the war was unique. It was the only sovereign state that fought right through from the beginning to the end, enduring attacks on the homeland but not invasion, and finally emerged victorious, without having at any time suffered social or political disorganization. These circumstances help to explain why the concept of the Welfare State first took shape in England. The magnitude of her war effort and her vulnerability to attack called for sacrifices from all and equally for help given ungrudgingly and without discrimination to all who were in need. 'The pooling of national resources,' said Titmuss, 'and the sharing of risks were not always practicable nor always applied; but they were the guiding principles.'[1] And the political stability of the country, combined with its unshaken confidence in victory, account for the most remarkable feature of the story, namely the way in which the people and their government, in the middle of the war, set about drawing the designs of the new society which was to be born when the fighting stopped. It was to be a society governed by the same principles of pooling and sharing that governed the emergency measures of the war. So the idea of the Welfare State came to be identified with the war aims of a nation fighting for its life. It is not surprising that, in England, it wore a halo which is not to be found in other countries when, in due course, they undertook the task of social reconstruction. And it is not surprising that, when it came to be examined in detail, with the cold eye of reason, its more fervent champions strapped on their armour and declared a holy war on its critics.

As early as 1941 the Ministry of Health announced as 'the objective of the Government, as soon as may be after the war', the creation of a comprehensive hospital service available to all.[2] In 1943 the Board of Education published a report of the Youth Advisory Council (set up for this purpose in 1942) on *The Youth Service after the War*. In 1944 Parliament passed an Education Act which was intended to give full equality of opportunity to all, regardless of family income, and the government published its plan for a National Health Service. But the boldest attempt to set down on paper the nation's peace aims in terms of a new social order was the Beveridge Report of 1942. The government had already committed itself, through the mouth of Anthony Eden, to the principle that 'social security must be the first object of our domestic policy after the war',[3] and had insisted on writing 'social security' into the Atlantic Charter. So Beveridge was fully justified in saying, at the end of his Report, that 'statement of a reconstruction policy by a nation at war is statement of the uses to which that nation means to put victory, when victory is achieved'.[4] And it was as a blueprint of the social order for which the country was fighting that the Report was received and acclaimed.

Yet, when one reads it, one finds that it was in the main, as the government had intended it to be, a technical analysis of the problems and methods of social insurance, with some drastic and often very ingenious proposals for unifying the whole system and making it simpler and more efficient. In these respects it is a remarkable document which had a deep effect on social policy not only in Britain but in other countries as well. But this alone cannot account for its immense popular appeal. There was, in fact, in the social insurance plan itself only one really arresting innovation, namely the extension of the compulsory insurance scheme to include the entire population. But the main cause of the enthusiastic reception of the Report was no doubt the picture it drew—or in parts merely sketched—of the total social programme of which the Beveridge plan proper was only a part. The Report expressed a great idea and presented a grand design which seemed to proclaim a social revolution. In a famous and much-quoted passage Beveridge declared that social insurance was indeed 'an attack upon Want. But Want is only one of the five giants on the road of reconstruction and in some ways the easiest to attack. The others are Disease, Ignorance, Squalor and Idleness.'[5] His Plan for Social Security was a plan to abolish Want, but it could only succeed if the other giants were attacked at the same time. So he listed three assumptions which underlay his proposals, namely that provision would be made for allowances for dependent children, for comprehensive health and rehabilitation services, and for the maintenance of employment.[6] And he might have added, with an eye to the two giants Ignorance and Squalor, education and houses for the people.

Did all this amount to a social revolution? Beveridge himself answered this question. 'The scheme proposed here,' he wrote, 'is in some ways a revolution, but in more important ways it is a natural development from the past. It is a British revolution.'[7] This is true. For what we see here is the final phase in the process described in the second chapter of this book, by which the logical development and natural evolution of ideas and institutions led ultimately to a transformation of the system. The transformation, or revolution, consisted in the welding together of the measures of social policy into a whole which, for the first time, acquired thereby a personality of its own and a meaning that had hitherto been only vaguely glimpsed. We adopted the term 'Welfare State' to denote this new entity composed of old elements. The total ultimate responsibility of the State for the welfare of its people was recognized more explicitly than ever before, and the choice between the three political philosophies described in Chapter 2 was clearly decided. The social services were not to be regarded as regrettable necessities to be retained only until the capitalist system had been reformed or socialized; they were a permanent and even a glorious part of the social system itself. They were something to be proud of, not to apologize for. But even here there were reservations. When the National government presented (in 1944) its version of the Beveridge plan of social insurance, it prefaced it with a statement which contained a tactful warning. National policy, it said must aim to secure 'the general prosperity and happiness of the citizens. To realize that aim two courses of action must be followed. The first is to foster the growth of the national power to produce and to earn, with its accompanying opportunities for increased well-being, leisure and recreation. The second is to plan for the prevention of individual poverty resulting from those hazards of personal fortune over which individuals have little or no control.'[8] The government was anxious not to spread the idea that social security is a substitute for productivity, but it was referring at this point to social insurance only, and not to the whole programme of the Welfare State. Education and health may well be regarded as contributing more to the increase of productivity than to the prevention of poverty.

Beveridge set himself the task of consolidating the various social insurance schemes, standardizing the benefits where appropriate, and adding new benefits where necessary so as to cover all needs caused by loss of income, or the incidence of exceptional demands upon income, such as those arising from marriage and death. He proposed to bring Workmen's Compensation (or Industrial Injury) within the scope of social insurance so that compensation would be received as a benefit, instead of having to be claimed from the employer, if necessary in a court of law. This was done. He proposed to convert old-age pensions into retirement pensions, payable only when the claimant gave up regular work. Those who preferred to go on working, and contributing, beyond the minimum age of sixty-five for men and sixty for women would receive proportionately larger pensions when they retired. This was also done. Next, he proposed to fill the two most serious gaps in the pre-war benefits. Allowances for dependants had so far been given only to widows (in respect of their children) and to the unemployed (in respect of their families). They were not given to the sick or to pensioners with 'dependent' wives under pensionable age. Beveridge insisted that all benefits should include all members of the family, unless they were otherwise provided for. And he wanted husband and wife to receive a 'joint benefit', so as not to insult a wife by calling her a 'dependant'. This typical touch was ignored. Secondly, unemployment benefit was limited to a maximum number of weeks in each year. He wished to pay it without time limit, subject to the condition that, after a certain period, the unemployed man must attend a training centre. This bold proposal, showing great confidence in the possibility of maintaining full employment, was rejected.

Of the new benefits proposed the most important was children's (or family) allowances, beginning with the second child. The case for these had long been unsuccessfully urged, and it had now become clear that one could not refuse to do for the employed what had already been done for the unemployed, or the latter might sometimes find themselves better off than the former. The allowances, though an essential element in the total plan, were not to be given as an insurance benefit, but financed out of taxes. Of the six other new benefits recommended by Beveridge, only two were eventually accepted, maternity and funeral grants. His idea of adding a grant for marriage, benefits for deserted wives, home helps for sick housewives, and training grants for the self-employed were either too ingenious or too complicated to win political support. Home helps did indeed materialize, but as part of the local health service.

Our main concern here is not with the details but with the basic principles of the Beveridge Report, and on this subject its author was quite explicit. We can group them under three heads. First, the plan must be one of universal, compulsory, and contributory insurance. Secondly, contributions and benefits must be at the same flat rate for all, the benefits being fixed at subsistence level. And, thirdly, statutory benefits should be supplemented by voluntary savings, which should be encouraged by positive measures. These three principles are interlocked and interdependent.

Universal coverage was the boldest innovation in the Beveridge plan. And yet he had little to say in defence of this departure from generally accepted practice. He seemed to assume that, given the spirit of the times, it was inevitable. And so, perhaps, it was but it had its critics, of whom one of the most vehement and effective was the economist H. D. Henderson. He declared that the extension of compulsory insurance to the middle classes could not possibly do anything to further Beveridge's 'proclaimed objective of abolishing want'. The logical way to do this was to locate and measure the want and to raise and dispense enough money to relieve it.[9]

But Beveridge could not consider this for a moment, because it was not insurance. It resembled the New Zealand scheme, which was later described by one of its administrators as one in which 'each citizen would contribute according to his means, and from which he could draw according to his need'.[10] And that was public assistance financed by a tax. The essence of insurance was the interdependence of contributions and benefits, and it was contributory insurance, so he believed, that the people of England wanted. They wanted it as the only alternative to the hated means test of the inter-war years. His aim, therefore, was 'to ensure at all times to all men a subsistence income for themselves and their families as of right; that is to say without any form of means test or enquiry about other means they had'.[11]

In stressing the idea that benefits must be granted 'as of right' he was, of course, expressing correctly the central aim of European social policy since the beginning of the century. It had been internationally endorsed in 1925 when an ILO Conference resolved that social security for the workers 'can best be attained by means of a system of social insurance granting clearly de-fined rights to the beneficiaries'.[12] But it did not follow that these rights could be established only by contributions. Beveridge had himself argued, in his book *Insurance for All and Everything*, that insurance is simply the 'collective bearing of risks', irrespective of the source from which the insurance fund derives its income. A scheme ceases to rank as social insurance only when 'the receipt of the benefit depends in any way upon the discretion of some authority'.[13] And a French Deputy went still further and maintained that social differs from commercial insurance pre-cisely because the worker 'is insured not by personal contribution but by society, which gives him rights and guarantees them in the prevention, relief, and compensation against loss arising out of social risks'.[14] That is the point; it is society that gives the rights, and it may attach them to contributions or not, as it pleases.

But, although he insisted on the contractual character of contributory insurance, Beveridge recognized, and clearly explained, the differences between social and other forms of insurance. In social insurance, he said, there can be a 'pooling of risks'. We have already seen how this worked for sickness and unemployment, where in each case risks of the same kind but of different degree were covered by equal contributions. In devising a comprehensive plan in which a single contribution on one card covered all benefits, he extended the 'pooling' over the whole field and over risks of different kinds. Secondly, although contributions must be related to benefits, the relationship could, he said, be whatever seemed desirable on general grounds; it need not be based on actuarial calculations. The contributions should 'be high enough to give the insured person, because he has contributed substantially without reference to means, a justifiable claim to receive benefit without reference to means'.[15] But what level of contributions that indicates is anybody's guess.

There are also grounds for questioning, or amending, Beveridge's sharp distinction between a benefit received 'as of right' and one that is subject to a means test, or dependent 'upon the discretion of some authority'. For the means test, as used between the wars, was not really discretionary. The benefit was adjusted to the family income by a fixed scale; there was inquisition (which was resented), but not much scope for discretion. Discretion enters when one begins to assess needs. Means can be measured by rule of thumb and arranged along a scale, but needs cannot, because each case is unique. A means test is an appropriate instrument for assessing what somebody should pay for a service, like a university education, but not for assessing what somebody, who *ex hypothesi* is on the verge of destitution, ought to receive. In such cases it is liable to be used to check extravagance and to detect malingering. What is really required is a 'needs test', which, in the broadest sense of the term, is the foundation of every benevolent welfare service.

Beveridge's second principle, of the flat rate and the subsistence level, was also, as he well knew, one that few other governments favoured. 'In most other countries,' he wrote, 'the benefits are percentages of the wages, and vary, therefore, from

.

one man to another.'[16] Here we see most clearly the influence of his political philosophy, the philosophy of twentieth-century Liberalism. The State, he argued, was entitled to compel people to contribute to the cost of guaranteeing for themselves the absolute minimum income necesssary for subsistence. There was no room here for individual preferences in expenditure. But 'to give by compulsory insurance more than is needed for subsistence is an unnecessary interference with individual responsibilities'. He called this 'the principle of a national minimum, above which all citizens shall spend their money freely'.[17] Subsistence benefits must be flat-rate benefits, for the subsistence level, however you calculate it, is the same for all citizens. And if the principle of contributory insurance is to be adhered to, flat-rate benefits imply flat-rate contributions. In so far as it was desirable to depart from this principle and transfer income from the richer to the poorer, this should be done through that part of the total cost which is met out of the proceeds of progressive taxation. That is why Beveridge favoured the tripartite system in which employers, employed, and tax-payers all contribute, and decided to increase the share of the tax-payers.

'Subsistence' was for Beveridge both an advance on the past and a limitation on the future. In the inter-war years benefits were not meant to provide a living, but merely a substantial supplement to other resources. Subsistence in Beveridge's plan meant an adequate income, even when there were no other resources at all. He envisaged a national assistance service, centrally administered, to take over the functions of the old Poor Law with respect to outdoor cash relief, but it was basic to his plan that nobody should have to ask for national assistance simply because his insurance benefits were inadequate. National assistance would be chiefly concerned with caring for the anomalies, including those who, whether by their own fault or not, were not qualified to receive benefit. It would give relief, subject to a means test, and it 'must be felt to be something less desirable than insurance benefit; otherwise the insured people get nothing out of their contributions'.[18]

Could such a scheme really work? The subsistence level of Beveridge looked suspiciously like the 'poverty line' of Rowntree, and the calculations on which the former was based owe much to those used for the latter. But whereas Rowntree's 'poverty line' was an instrument of social research which could, in accordance with the definition of a 'line', be without breadth, the subsistence level was an operational concept which must provide a margin of safety and some room for manoeuvre in a changing world. When the value of money steadily falls and prices rise erratically and unevenly from place to place and commodity to commodity, a universal subsistence benefit becomes unworkable. And if the benefit is raised for all above the danger point, the flat-rate contributions which correspond to the new level become higher than the poorest members of the society can afford. It was on these grounds that the National government, in its White Paper of September 1944, explicitly rejected Beveridge's proposal. It would, they said, mean tying the benefit to the cost of living, and either varying benefits according to individual needs (which is not insurance), or raising contributions to an impossibly high level.[19] The scheme later introduced by the Labour government did aim at subsistence but failed to achieve it, for the government was driven more and more to supplement the benefits of those who had no private means by allowances from national assistance. For this they were denounced by Beveridge in the House of Lords, who called on them either to raise the benefits or to state 'that they formally abandon security against want without a means test and declare that they drop the Beveridge Report and the policy of 1946'.[20]

On that occasion Beveridge was defending his beloved child, and he may be forgiven for passing lightly over its possible defects. But did he, when making subsistence the guiding principle of his plan, foresee the difficulties it would encounter? In one respect he certainly did, for he discussed it at some length. This was the matter of rents. Rents vary from place to place and may represent a large item of expenditure in small budgets. And it is not always possible to reduce the expenditure by moving to a cheaper home. Could a uniform subsistence benefit absorb this item? In the case of national assistance it was found that it could not, and the practice was followed of fixing the standard allowance exclusive of rent, and adding what was needed to pay the rent afterwards. Beveridge carefully considered arrangements of this kind and rejected them as inconsistent with his basic principles. His whole attitude to this question, and to the problem of rising prices, now seems to have been short-sighted.

Perhaps he anticipated more effective measures to check inflation than were actually adopted. Undoubtedly he relied very much on his hope that most people would add to the statutory benefits by voluntary insurance.

And this brings us to the third of his major principles, the importance of leaving room for private saving. He wanted positive steps to be taken to encourage this. He had two suggestions to make, which he put forward, not as integral parts of the plan, but as 'eminently desirable'. He had decided against continuing to use 'approved societies' to operate sickness insurance as independent agents because of the inequality of benefits that resulted. But he wanted them to act as channels through which standard, statutory benefits were distributed, so as to give them an opportunity to persuade people to take out additional policies voluntarily. Secondly, he proposed that the Industrial Assurance, or 'Collecting', Societies, which were run for profit, should be replaced, and their business taken over, by a national Board having a statutory monopoly in this kind of insurance. Neither of these proposals was adopted.

As a result, the balance of the plan was upset. Beveridge spoke of it as 'combining three distinct methods: social insurance for basic needs; national assistance for special cases; voluntary insurance for additions to the basic provision'.[21] The third of these methods was left to take care of itself, but action was taken to institute the second. The Act of 1948, which set up the National Assistance Board, opened with the words (already quoted in an earlier chapter) 'the existing poor law shall cease to have effect'. The clean break with the past was made at last, and it involved two important innovations which distinguish the British from most other systems. First, relief in cash was shifted from the rates to the taxes, that is to say, from the local authorities to a national body. The ancient tradition of the Western world that the relief of the poor is the affair of their neighbours was brought to an end. Secondly, assistance in cash was, as a result, separated from the welfare services, which remained a local responsibility. This meant that, as these developed, they had a better chance of avoiding the taint of pauperism which clung obstinately to the National Assistance Board. On the other hand it can be argued that, had the two not been separated, the humiliating character of cash assistance might have been neutralized by association with the more humane atmosphere of the personal services. This was the pattern adopted, apparently with some success, in the Scandinavian countries.

The second main supporting pillar of the Welfare State was the National Health Service. When the Labour government introduced the Bill which became the Act of 1946, its spokesman stressed the fact that it was the 'outcome of a concerted effort extending over a long period of years', and achieved what responsible people had been advocating since before the war. Nor was it 'the preserve of any one party'.[22] This was perfectly true, but it cannot be too strongly emphasized that a National Health Service is something essentially different from a system of health insurance. The survey made for the Royal Commission of 1924–6 of fourteen foreign countries showed that medical care was treated in all of them as an insurance benefit, as it was in Britain. In some countries the schemes were still voluntary, but there were clear signs of a trend towards the introduction of compulsory schemes covering specified classes of the population, again as in Britain. Most of them were administered by local bodies—either 'approved societies' or semi-autonomous statutory bodies representing the locality. These negotiated with the local doctors and made arrangements with the local hospitals and clinics for the medical care of their clients, the insured families. They tried to cover as many types of treatment as possible, and they generally offered at least some of them to dependants. Patients usually had to pay part of the cost of the treatment they received. But, as we have seen, systems of this kind do not always function smoothly. Friction often develops between the local agencies and the medical profession. One way of reducing this, used extensively in Germany and as the general practice in France, was to leave the patient to pay the doctor and to reimburse him subsequently for the prescribed proportion of the amount. This, however, involved retaining that direct financial transaction between patient and doctor which it had been one of the main objects of national health insurance to eliminate. The other weakness of a locally based health insurance system is that it does not lead to, and may even hinder, the creation of overall plans for the distribution of medical resources and services throughout the country and for their systematic development.

The pre-war British system was a compromise. General

practice by 'panel doctors' had something of the character of a national service, and it was claimed that the distribution of practitioners in relation to population had greatly improved, as well as the quality of the service provided.[23] But there was no local authority to co-ordinate the medical services; hospitals, general practice and public health were separately administered. And, as in Europe, the operation of the whole machine was clogged by the paraphernalia of insurance. This can be illustrated by a few random quotations from a description written during the war. 'The inside of an Insurance Committee's building is a gigantic filing system. . . . Every insured person is indexed both according to his doctor and according to his Approved Society. . . . Changes of doctor give endless trouble to the staff. . . . The scheme suffers because it is geared to the obsolescent organisation of general practice in this country. . . . The trouble with the National Health Insurance is that it is not "national". Administrative emphasis is on the word "insurance". The sick are considered not as citizens but as insured persons.'[24]

The case for a planned national health service was foreshadowed by two Reports published between the wars. The first, the so-called 'Dawson Report', was prepared by the Consultative Council set up to advise the government. It approached the subject from a strictly practical and professional angle, and not with any preconceived theories about the principles of social policy. 'The changes that we advise,' it said, 'are rendered necessary because the organisation of medicine has become insufficient, and because it fails to bring the advantages of medical knowledge adequately within reach of the people.'[25] The general practitioner was cut off from modern facilities for diagnosis and treatment and from contact with specialists and consultants. To remedy this the Report proposed to set up health centres at two levels, local ones as bases for the general practitioners, and regional ones for specialists. The latter, it seems, would in fact be miniature hospitals. The existing voluntary hospitals, which had 'fallen on evil days', were to be resuscitated and worked into a general service directed by local health authorities. The Royal Commission of 1924–6 saw things in much the same light, and had visions of a comprehensive medical service. 'The ultimate solution will lie,' they said, 'in the direction of divorcing the medical service entirely from the insurance system and recognizing it along with all the other public health activities as a service to be supported from the general public funds.'[26] But the time, they thought, was not ripe. In view of the mounting burden of public expenditure, 'the State may justifiably turn from searching its conscience to exploring its purse'.[27] So nothing of importance was done.

The war conquered these inhibitions, and the Beveridge Report paved the way for action. It is interesting to compare the plan put forward by the National government with the Act passed under the Labour government. The former left the hospitals much as they were, but created new Joint Authorities, formed by amalgamating contiguous local government areas, to run the rest of the services. The aim was to rehabilitate and reintegrate general practice, and make it the backbone of the service, which was what all the inter-war experts had recommended. But the doctors were alarmed. They saw this as the first step towards converting them into 'a service of technicians controlled by central bureaucrats and by local men and women entirely ignorant of medical matters'.[28]

Aneurin Bevan, for the Labour government, turned this plan upside down. He left the general practitioners much as they were, except that the old Insurance Committees were replaced by Executive Councils, half of whose members represented the professions, and new and far more effective means were devised for controlling the distribution of practices. But he took the drastic step of nationalizing the voluntary hospitals and putting them, and the municipal hospitals, all under Boards appointed by, and responsible to, himself. The teaching hospitals had each its own governing body directly under the Minister, while the rest were grouped geographically under Regional Boards. And, in due course, it became clear that the hospitals had become the backbone of the service, while general practice struggled along in a state of intermittent dissatisfaction both with its remuneration and with the conditions under which it had to work. An optimistic general practitioner wrote in 1949, having described what was then wrong with the service: 'The new order of things may alter this. The liaison between health centres and hospitals, the idea of general practitioner hospitals, the growing feeling that it is absurd to train students in modern methods and then to deny them the use of these methods when they go into practice, are likely before long to ease the general practitioner's task in curative medicine enormously.'[29] In the 1960s people were still discussing how these hopes might be realized, but that is a subject that belongs to a later chapter.

But Bevan's great achievement consisted in the creation of a genuinely universal, free medical service, wholly detached in its administration from the contractual apparatus of insurance (though receiving a portion of the contributions) and aiming at a standard of performance as high as the medical resources of the country were capable of achieving. 'The field in which the claims of individual commercialism come into most immediate conflict with reputable notions of social values,' he wrote, 'is that of health.'[30] And he was determined that no trace of commercialism should creep in between doctor and patient in his service. He agreed later to a charge of one shilling for each prescription, but when the Labour government introduced further charges he resigned, saying that it was the 'beginning of the destruction of those social services in which Labour has taken a special pride and which were giving to Britain the moral leadership of the world'.[31]

The three pillars of the British Welfare State were the Education Act, the National Insurance Act, and the National Health Service Act. They are associated with the names of Butler, Beveridge, and Bevan—a Conservative, a Liberal, and a Socialist. When one remembers the mixed origins of social policy at the beginning of the century it is not surprising to find that the Welfare State, when it eventually saw the light, was of mixed parentage. And when in the following decade it was subjected to reappraisal, its critics were to be found in all three parties. Some attacked its principles, others its practices, while others again rebuked it for not living up to its own ideals. It is a curious fact that in no country which had accepted its basic ideas and methods was it as strongly challenged as in that of its birth. It survived these attacks, and went on to face the more deeply considered and constructive criticism of the 1960s.

Two | Beyond the Welfare State

7 | Re-assessment of the Welfare State

The purpose of this short chapter is to serve as an introduction to Part Two of the book by bridging the gap between past history and the present situation, and in particular by describing the changes of mood that took place in England during the twenty years or so following the legislation of 1946–8.

The British Welfare State was, as we have seen, the culmination of a long movement of social reform that began in the last quarter of the nineteenth century. But the final product was something that the originators of the movement had not envisaged. The forces of growth within the movement itself, combined with the influence of historic events like the great depression and the two world wars, had given this product of an evolutionary process a revolutionary character. That was how Beveridge saw it, and he was quite right. But the culmination of an evolutionary process marks the end of a past phase of history, whereas a revolution is likely to mark the beginning of a new one. Anybody surveying the scene in 1950 was bound before long to ask himself to which of these two categories the Welfare State really belonged.

There is no doubt at all that those who were preparing, during the war, the measures on which the Welfare State was to be built believed that they were laying the foundations of a new epoch in social history, and this mood persisted during the years of creative legislation after the war. Some questioning voices were raised, but they were shouted down. When, however, the period of critical appraisal began in or around 1952 the opposite view was widely expressed, namely that the Welfare State belonged to the past from which it had emerged. Future historians will probably decide that both were right, and that it contained within itself elements of both past and future and provided a stepping stone from the one to the other.

In examining the criticism levelled against the Welfare State at this time one must remember to distinguish between its two principal parts, the social security system or Beveridge plan, with its guarantee of the minimum, and the National Health Service, with its promise of the optimum. Both came under attack, but for different reasons. The social security system bore clearly upon it the marks of its origin and history. It had been constructed of measures designed to wage war against poverty, and it was in order to complete the victory over poverty, or Want, and the other four giants in the path that Beveridge had elaborated his plan. When the laws that it inspired were being debated it seemed that the giants were still there; they had not vanished with the coming of peace. Times were still hard. The war had drained the country's resources, laid waste great areas in its cities, and its end was followed by a period of economic strain. The principal controls were kept in force, including the rationing of food and other consumer goods which was not finally abolished till 1954. The nation had chosen to submit to a regime of austerity in order to prevent the reappearance in large sections of the population of the extreme poverty that had befallen them in the worst of the inter-war years. It was not unnatural to imagine that the principles on which the social security system had been built had lost nothing of their relevance in the post-war age. The methods that had been designed to conquer poverty should still be appropriate for holding poverty at bay.

But this judgement underestimated the differences between the situations before and after the war, in both their economic and their social aspects. The most obvious of these was the contrast between the persistent large-scale unemployment of the 1920s and 1930s and the continuous state of full, and at times 'over-full', employment of the 1950s. This was accompanied by a rising standard of living for the bulk of the wage-earning class and a shift of interest from unemployment benefits to retirement pensions as the item in social security that mattered most. A system obsessed with the ideas of poverty and subsistence began to look out of place in a society enjoying the first-fruits of a new prosperity. But before these changes of circumstances and of mood became fully apparent, a weakness of a different kind had been revealed in the Welfare State and provoked the first wave of criticism that struck at the very roots of the system.

In February 1952 *The Times* published two articles on 'Crisis in the Welfare State'. It associated the crisis, the first the new system had to face, with economic insecurity and a need for retrenchment in public expenditure.[1] It had become necessary, it said, to re-examine the principles upon which the whole system was based. About the same time two future Conservative Ministers, Iain Macleod and Enoch Powell, produced a pamphlet entitled *The Social Services—Needs and Means*. Here too the theme was that the Welfare State had been trying to do more than it could afford, and had failed. Benefits had fallen below subsistence level, and those without other resources had to apply for additional assistance to what was in effect the old Poor Law under another name—assistance given not as a right, but at discretion and subject to a means test. This is what Beveridge himself denounced in the following year as abandonment of the 'policy of 1946'. The most economical way of abolishing want was not to distribute standard cash benefits and free service to all and sundry, whether they wanted them or not, but to concentrate scarce resources at the points where they were most needed, with the help of a test of means. 'The question therefore which poses itself', they said, 'is not "should a means test be applied to a social service?", but "why should any social service be provided without a test of need?".'[2] This came near, as Titmuss asserted in his broadcast commentary, to advocating 'a new version of the nineteenth-century poor law', as far as cash benefits were concerned,[3] a return, one might say, not to the pre-Beveridge but to the pre-Lloyd George situation. If applied to the National Health Service (the principal target of those attacking extravagance) it would mean, as *The Times* rightly pointed out, 'a reversion from Bevanism to Fabianism',[4] for the Fabians had held that everybody should pay as much as he could afford for the public services. The scrapping of social insurance and its replacement by national assistance and a means test, though this seemed to be logically implied by the remarks of some of the critics, was hardly ever explicitly proposed, and certainly not by the authors of the pamphlet. But the idea of charging for services, including both health and education, was definitely favoured by many Conservative writers, and even more emphatically by the Liberals.

In this phase, then, the background to criticism was the urge to economize in the face of economic stringency, and the Welfare State was found to be at fault, not because it was over-obsessed with poverty, but because it did not concentrate on it enough. The typical charge was that of extravagance and the typical question: 'can we afford it?' Then the mood changed. With remarkable speed the conviction spread that the time had come to give the Austerity Society decent burial and to welcome the Affluent Society in its place. And an Affluent Society should not need to maintain a complicated and expensive apparatus for waging war on poverty. To apply the Beveridge principle in 1960, said a Conservative MP, 'is to swallow the drug after the disease has gone. For primary poverty has now almost disappeared. Full employment has lifted the mass of our working population to a level of affluence unprecedented in our social history.'[5] This estimate of the economic situation was over-optimistic, and it seemed to overlook the fact that one factor in the reduction of primary poverty was precisely that system of social security of which Beveridge was the chief architect. Without the 'drug' the 'disease' would have been even more widespread.

The proposal to which this line of thought generally led was that as much of the burden of social provision as possible should be passed over from public to private shoulders. People should be released from the system of compulsory insurance and given the freedom to exercise personal responsibility and provide for themselves. And when they used the public services they should be charged according to their means. For a time little attempt was made to discover what the effects of such a transfer would be, either on the public services which would still have to function or on the private institutions which would in part replace them. The emphasis was still on the negative side, on how to get out of the false position in which the country had placed itself by carrying the legacy of the past into the present. The one thing that seemed to emerge clearly was that the critics wanted to cut down the public social services, though whether this was because the country could not afford to keep them up or because it could afford to do without them was not always obvious. What did appear certain was that, in some influential political circles, the tide was turning against the view, which had grown in strength from Lloyd George to Beveridge, that the public social services must be regarded as a permanent part of the national culture of which the people should be proud. Such statements as the following struck a different note: 'the true object of the Welfare State, for the Liberal, is to teach people how to do without it' (by a leading Liberal economist),[6] and: 'Conservatives must strive for a large reduction, in the long run, of the public social services' (by a member of the Conservative Bow Group).[7]

Meanwhile events elsewhere did not seem to be moving in this direction. It is true that in France the proposal, made in 1946, to extend insurance to cover all risks and all citizens met with so much opposition that the government was forced to modify its programme, while the reliance, for unemployment insurance, on private schemes and collective agreements continued unchanged. But there was no move to reduce the role of the State, and when de Gaulle tried to launch a campaign for economy, he had to bow to the protests of the champions of the public social services. In the United States too, where Federal social policy always had to contend with stubborn individualists and defenders of State rights, the trend was towards a shift in the balance between statutory and voluntary services in favour of the former. News was coming in of interesting developments in Sweden, in health, housing and pensions, but probably the strongest impact was made by reports of the German legislation of 1956 which replaced a wage-related pension scheme of standard pattern by a system of universal superannuation. The German scheme was announced with a great flourish of trumpets as a decisive step forward and away from traditional practices. Finally, when Britain began to negotiate for entry into the Common Market it was natural to compare the levels of social provision at home and in the six European Member States. Some thought that Britain might be under pressure to lower her standards if she joined. But a survey of expenditure on social security and health services published by the ILO in 1961 showed that the proportion of the national income devoted by the United Kingdom to these purposes was lower than the lowest in the Community and not quite three-fifths that of the highest.[8] The authors admitted that the figures could not be entirely reliable and must be used with caution. But, when all allowances were made, the headline in *The Times*, 'Britain lagging behind in Social Security Spending', seemed to be justified.[9]

By the end of the 1950s the emphasis in discussions of British social policy had shifted from curtailment to expansion. Local authorities had been developing ways of meeting the responsibility for welfare services placed upon them in 1948, and much attention was being given to ways of providing more intelligent and intensive treatment of the problems of old people, 'deprived' children, the mentally disabled and others in personal need. All this involved an increase in public expenditure. In January 1962 the government announced a plan for spending £500 million in ten years (and eventually £700 million) on hospital building and improvement, while decisions were taken in rapid succession for the founding of seven new universities in England alone. This was not exactly parsimonious. Finally, as the prospect of a general election drew nearer, there began to emerge from the political parties, or from semi-official groups within them, blueprints for the social services of the future bolder and more grandiose in conception than anything that had gone before.

The feeling of affluence had put an end to the economy drive and restored the kind of consensus which had been originally engendered by the Beveridge Report and then shaken by political and professional disputes over the measures to be taken to implement it and by the 'crisis' of 1952. But the object of consensus can be better described as the Welfare Society than the Welfare State, because it was not so clearly committed to the defence of an inviolable package deal of statutes and administrative arrangements establishing the powers and the responsibilities of the central government. The agreement was about a kind of society in which a high priority was accorded to welfare, and in which 'welfare' was not the relief of social and economic casualties, but the provision of benefits and services available to all, through agencies and institutions the general pattern of which had by then been absorbed into the social structure. This left plenty of room for argument about the inner priorities, the level of provision, the methods by which the service should be brought to the beneficiaries and the respective roles of government, central and local, voluntary organizations and private enterprise. It was no longer a matter of choosing between the three schools of thought described in Chapter 2 of this book—whether to abolish capitalism, to humanize it, or to leave it to cope with society's problems in its own way. For events had been moving in all three directions at once, and had created a state of affairs in which a mixed economy functioned through markets subject to adjustment by a government which at the same time made full-scale provision for (minimum) social security and (optimum) health and welfare, with the co-operation of industry and commerce. It is a system which Richard Crossman once referred to as 'Welfare Capitalism', hinting thereby at its inherent instability, while others hoped it would establish itself firmly as the mid-twentieth-century version of social democracy.

For something more than twenty years after the passing of the Acts which established the Welfare State the consensus about fundamentals was sufficient to prevent changes of government from driving social policy along a zigzag course. Political conflict was, for the most part, either about what might be called the technology of social policy (sometimes referred to as 'social engineering'), or about priorities, levels of provision and the speed of advance towards goals which each party claimed to be pursuing in its own way. But when the full significance of the so-called 'rediscovery of poverty' in the 1960s made itself felt, this phase of 'consensus politics' petered out. The fact that the various kinds of 'primary poverty' now being revealed were occurring in an affluent, not an impoverished society, made it possible for some to regard them as incidental or accidental phenomena in an otherwise healthy system, which could be put right by appropriate treatment, while others saw them as symptoms of a deeper disease—of a pervasive inequality which violated the basic principles and fundamental values of the Welfare Society as they understood it. When political controversy becomes heated, and when arguments about measures are couched in ideological terms, it is not easy to distinguish the issues which are matters of principle from those which are questions only of alternative practices. An attempt to do this will be made in the final chapter.

8 | Social security

The term 'social security' is used here in its narrower sense of arrangements for providing cash benefits, by social insurance, family allowances in respect of children, and the various grants made subject to means test which we can refer to collectively as 'assistance'. Some of the purposes for which these benefits are provided can also be met by devices incorporated into the system of taxation, and these must be brought into the picture. One major concern of these services is to try to abolish, or at least to reduce the incidence of, poverty. But, since poverty (admittedly an equivocal term) is not a matter only of cash income, we shall look at it as a whole in a separate chapter, confining what is said about it in this one to explaining how grants specifically designed to help the poor fit into the structure of the cash benefits system.

The British Welfare State, we have suggested, belonged both to the past and to the future. Those who looked at it critically in the 1950s against the background of British history were inclined to identify what belonged to the past in it with what it had derived from the Beveridge Report, while recognizing that the National Health Service, in spite of imperfections, represented a step forward into the future. But the picture as seen through European eyes was rather different. For European observers still found in the Beveridge Report elements both of the past and of the future, and regarded the National Health Service, with its strong centralized control over the medical services and the medical professions, as not necessarily the model to be copied by all progressive societies.

In a report of the European Economic Community (the Common Market) published in 1958 the position in the six

Member States was summed up as follows: 'Two different conceptions underlie the systems found in the countries of the Community: some have retained the notion of social insurance, the others have directed their policy towards social security. At the level of principle, these two notions are very far apart.' But, it added, at the level of practice the differences were not substantial.[1] The report went on to explain the contrast between the two conceptions. Insurance, it said, is built up of contracts covering specified risks. Social insurance covers only paid employees, but social security extends to all citizens. Insurance bases rights on contributions, but social security is based on 'a right directly accorded to the individual by virtue of the protection owed him by society'. Pierre Laroque, who might appropriately be described as the French Beveridge, wrote in the same vein. One of the most important features of social security, he said, was its treatment of the problem 'as one to be solved for the whole population by a general policy and under a general scheme'. He also agreed about the basis of the right to benefits. In a general scheme of social security, he said, one may expect to see the 'disappearance of all connection between contributions and benefits'. It becomes 'comparatively unimportant whether the money has been obtained by means of contributions or drawn direct from public funds'.[2]

A subsequent report of the European Economic Community, dated 1962, added two further points. It distinguished between two aims, one to wage war on want by a policy based on the concept of need, and the other to maintain incomes for those unable to work (through sickness, unemployment or old age) at a level comparable with former earnings, in which case the policy was based on the economic value of the worker. The former established 'a national minimum' by redistributing income between rich and poor; the latter adjusted the flow-through time of earnings of the working population to the mutual benefit of all. Secondly, the report spoke of the sharp distinction which used to be drawn between 'classical' social insurance and 'old-style' public assistance, and maintained that the progressive obliteration of the traditional frontiers between them was 'one of the characteristic traits of the modern evolution of the system of social protection', that is to say, of the evolution from social insurance to social security. As a result of this, public assistance could legitimately be used as a means of filling the inevitable gaps in the coverage offered by the insurance-type services.[3]

Now it is evident that the Beveridge plan, and the British policy based upon it, belonged to the era which emphasized the virtues of insurance and the distinction between it and assistance; an era which Laroque and some other European thinkers regarded as belonging to the past. On the other hand its bold insistence on universal coverage as a right of citizenship gave to it the character of 'social security' as they understood it, and on that account they honoured Beveridge as a great innovator. But what followed in Europe (though not immediately in Britain) has proved to be neither pure 'social insurance' nor pure 'social security', but a blending of the two. The 'connection between contributions and benefits', far from disappearing as Laroque foretold, has been elaborated and built more firmly into systems of cash benefits than ever before. But the idea of 'social security' has not been lost. Governments do aim at solving the problem 'for the whole population by a general policy', but it is a policy which uses a combination of different methods, one of which—and increasingly the central one—is a system of earnings-related contributions and benefits. This looks in many ways very much like ordinary commercial insurance. However there are, as we shall explain, mechanisms built into it which give it the character of a social service fulfilling 'a right directly accorded to the individual by virtue of the protection owed him by society'.

This last point can best be illustrated by reference to pensions. As we have already seen, the original practice in most countries other than Britain was to relate both the contributions and the pensions to earnings. And the new type of pension described in the Common Market report is also related to earnings, but in quite a different way. Pensions of the older kind were small in amount and designed only to soften the blow of retirement. The grading of contributions, and therefore of benefits, was little more than a financial device for increasing the revenue of the pension fund and reducing the burden to be borne by taxes. With pensions of the new type the starting-point of the calculation is the idea of a decent provision for old age, and 'decent provision' is not, like subsistence, an absolute quantity, but is relative to the standard of living enjoyed by a man and his wife before retirement. It will be less than what they had then, but will not imply any catastrophic change in their manner of life. An ILO Convention of 1967 set the minimum 'replacement ratio' of pension to earnings at 45 per cent for a man and his wife, but since then many countries have adopted a *target* of 70 to 75 per cent of a man's average earnings in the last few years of his working life.[4] The Labour government's 1969 plan for superannuation aimed at from 50 to 65 per cent compared to the 40 to 42 per cent of average *net* earnings which the existing system was yielding at the time, as a basic flat-rate pension to which the graduated pension might add 3 or 4 percentage points. But we are dealing here with rough averages and with figures which are not strictly comparable, because there are different ways of making the calculations. The effect of such schemes, broadly speaking, is to apply to the working population in general the principle which has long governed the pensions of public servants, civil and military, and which we may call 'superannuation'. The policy cannot be given any political label, for it is found in both 'capitalist' and 'socialist' countries. It contains in itself elements of both socialism and individualism, because it recognizes a universal social right in a manner that takes account of individual differences.

In its second report the European Economic Community noted the convergence of policies among its members towards the pattern we have been describing and observed that, paradoxically enough, this represented in some of its aspects, not a departure from the 'classical' principles of insurance, but a return to them. For each beneficiary (or insured person) had, as it were, his personal account which determined the size of the pension to which he was entitled. This operated like an insurance policy, with the percentage of his earnings that was assigned to it corresponding to the insurance premium. Secondly, the system was essentially one for employees, since it was based on earnings, which meant that it was rooted in class solidarity, not in national solidarity. Consequently the European system of social security was in reality nearer to the classical model of insurance than was the Beveridge plan.[5]

There is much truth in this, but not the whole truth. To take the last point first, it is obvious that an earnings-based scheme can apply only to those who earn. But this does not mean that it is confined to wage-earners; it can (and generally does) cover all salaried employees up to the highest level. Pre-Beveridge social insurance excluded salaried employees with incomes above a certain ceiling. The income ceiling in superannuation operates differently. It does not exclude the people with high incomes; it excludes from its calculations that part of their income which is above the ceiling. The pension is related to earnings up to that level only. It is true, too, that it is not easy to apply the system to the self-employed in the same way as to employees, because of the difficulty of calculating their pensionable earnings, though it can be done. The only people totally left out of such systems, unless they choose to enter voluntarily, are those who do not earn at all, but live on unearned income or are supported by others. In this respect an earnings-related scheme is not as comprehensive as the system advocated by Beveridge. It is, so to speak, tailor-made for a modern industrial society in which the vast majority of the population work for money, and the great majority of them get that money from an employer, public or private.

It is true, again, that the 'individual account' on which each pension is calculated resembles the practice followed in commercial insurance, and that commercial firms can, and do, run schemes sufficiently similar to public social insurance of the superannuation type to operate in conjunction with it. This, however, is not the result simply of the assimilation of the public to the private, but of a convergence of the two towards a middle point. In the classic form of commercial insurance the customer decides what coverage he wishes to have and pays the contributions necessary to buy it. In a public superannuation system he earns his pension by his work, at the rate laid down in the scheme. As an American social security official put it, 'a person's security and that of his family grow out of the work he does. He earns his future security as he earns his living, and he pays towards the cost of that security while he is earning'.[6] He pays *towards* it, rather than *for* it, because his pension is not assessed on the basis of the money value of his contributions, but of the work they represent and the amount it would have earned at the time of his retirement. There are various ways of making the calculation. The simplest, and roughest, is to relate the pension to earnings in the last few pre-retirement years, so as to give what is called an acceptable 'replacement ratio'. The German scheme has an interesting way of taking account of the whole career. Past earnings are converted to present values by using as index the ratio of a man's earnings in each year to average earnings in that year. His pension then reflects his status in the occupational structure of the society, and takes account, not only of changes in the value of money, but also of changes in the national standard of living. This illustrates very clearly what is meant by saying that the pension is based on work.

When in 1957 the Labour government produced a plan for superannuation on the above lines, Iain Macleod commented that it was 'pleasant to see our opponents being converted to the capitalist system, and to a proposal which, in fact, intends to carry into retirement the inequalities of earnings in working life'.[7] He must have been aware, when he said this, that wage and salary differentials are not a peculiarity of the capitalist system but are found also in all socialist societies, and he may have known that, in the Soviet Union and other countries of Eastern Europe, pensions are awarded on the principle 'to each according to his work'. 'Fair shares' does not mean equal pay; it implies that some inequalities are fair and acceptable, and others are not. So it is important to remember that the most unacceptable inequalities, those at the top and the bottom of the scale, are not, or need not be, carried forward into retirement by a scheme of superannuation. The top ranges of income, as already explained, are left out of the calculation of benefits, and there are various ways of 'boosting' the pensions of the low-paid which violate the strict principles of commercial insurance in the interests of social welfare. Nevertheless the significance of this incorporation, even in a modified form, of the structure of market inequality into the structure of social insurance should not be underrated. It involves government responsibility for regulating that which Beveridge held should be left, like the market itself, to individual enterprise and initiative, and it follows a principle that clearly differs from the strict egalitarianism to which the health and welfare services owe allegiance.

It was natural that the country which had greeted the Beveridge plan as the panacea of all ills should adhere to it as long as possible. But in the twenty years after 1946 events induced the government to depart from it in two important respects. As was pointed out earlier (p. 90), it had soon become clear that a far greater use was being made of national assistance, as against national insurance, than Beveridge had intended, so much so that in 1953 he declared that the government had, in fact, dropped the Beveridge Report. But nothing was done about this until 1966. By that time nearly 30 per cent of those in receipt of social insurance benefits (excluding maternity and industrial injury) were also getting means-tested assistance supplements and, looking at it from the other angle, 77 per cent of all weekly means-tested payments were being made to people already receiving insurance benefits.[8] The action taken in this year did not aim at reducing these proportions; on the contrary, it was designed to encourage more of those entitled to assistance to claim it. The two systems of insurance and assistance were administratively merged in a new Ministry of Social Security, and the invidious term 'national assistance' was abandoned in favour of the innocuous 'Supplementary Benefit' (or 'Pension') which was used even in cases where there was no benefit to supplement. The significance which these changes were meant to have is indicated by the appearance in the pension books of the statement that 'people over pension age have a right . . . to a guaranteed income', followed by instructions on how to claim it. This was in direct contradiction to the Beveridge principle that there can be no right where discretion enters into the making of an award.

The other departure from Beveridge principles occurred in 1959 as a result of what a White Paper of the previous year called 'the large emerging deficits' of the insurance fund. It would be wrong, said the government, to put an additional burden on the tax-payer, and it was impossible to raise the level of the flat-rate contributions, because 'the speed of the convoy is that of the slowest ship', i.e. the contribution must be within the range of the poorest contributor. So the answer was to erect, on top of the flat-rate pension, a modest earnings-related scheme for 'graduated' pensions. Since contributions would begin to come in some time before any payments became due, this would ease the financial pressure.[9] The departure from the Beveridge principle was important, but the effect on the level of pensions, even ten or twelve years later, was modest. What mattered most for future planning was the introduction of a controlled co-operative relationship between the State pension scheme and the private, or 'occupational', schemes run by business firms. Any firm which provided pensions on at least as good terms as the State did could contract out of the graduated part of the pension system on behalf of its employees. By the time the Labour government was preparing its plan for national superannuation there were 65 000 occupational schemes in operation, covering 12 million workers, of which 70 per cent in the public sector and 30 per cent in the private had 'contracted out'.[10] Thus already a big body of investment and of accumulated rights had been built up whose existence and interests future legislation must take into account.

It was in January 1969 that Richard Crossman published a White Paper on *National Superannuation and Social Insurance* (Cmnd 3883), but the Bill based upon it foundered in the general election of 1970. In September 1971 Sir Keith Joseph presented the Conservative proposals in a White Paper entitled *Strategy for Pensions* (Cmnd 4755). The Act to turn its recommendations into law was passed in 1973, but was not due to come into effect until 1975, before which date the government had fallen. So, at the time of writing, neither the 'Crossman Plan' nor the 'Joseph Plan' had ever been in operation, and the future prospects of both of them were uncertain. Nevertheless they are important documents in the history of social policy, and a comparison of their respective provisions can enable us to see what were the issues at stake in the 1970s, as seen by the two major political parties. Both plans have the wide aim of regulating the income structure of the whole working population in such a way as to provide an income when earnings cease, or are interrupted, bearing an acceptable relationship to the income earned before this happened. They are not, like the Beveridge plan, only 'an attack upon Want'. But they set about their task in very different ways. Many of these differences are technical and need not concern us here: others are matters of principle and must be examined.

Both plans envisage radical changes in the existing system. The Crossman Plan abolishes the two-tier structure which had existed since 1959, in which a superstructure of graduated insurance for earners only is erected on a basis of flat-rate insurance for everybody. It puts in its place a single one-tier system of earnings-related insurance to cover all social insurance benefits, both long-term (pensions) and short-term (health, unemployment, etc.). Participation in the scheme is obligatory for all whose earnings reach the minimum PAYE level, including married women, and contributions are payable at the same rate (6¾ per cent) by both employees and employers on all 'pensionable' earnings below a ceiling of about 50 per cent above the national average for manual workers in industry (in 1968 about £33 a week). Benefits are wholly 'dynamic', being based, as in the German system, on earnings throughout life revalued in tune with average earnings at the time that the benefit falls due. In the absence of a guaranteed minimum flat-rate benefit, something had to be done to boost the benefits of low-earners, and for this purpose the device was adopted of taking a higher percentage (60 per cent) of earnings up to half the national average and a lower percentage (25 per cent) of earnings above that level in calculating the pension. This produced a substantial redistribution of income from richer to poorer. The self-employed are to be admitted as flat-rate contributors and beneficiaries only.

On the other major structural issue, the relation between the State scheme and the occupational schemes run by business firms, the Crossman Plan retains the existing pattern which allows for 'contracting out' by occupational schemes which satisfy the necessary conditions—but only partially. It could not contemplate handing over to them total responsibility for the social insurance of sections of the public. Nor were the terms offered sufficiently favourable to encourage industries to use the option offered them. It was not meant to be an equal partnership, still less a shift of responsibility from State to industry. Crossman himself explained later that it had been his hope that in due course, after ten years or so, 'more and more firms would be finding it convenient to take the State scheme and merely add a little on top of it'.[11]

The Joseph Plan, on the other hand, retains the existing two-tier model, but with two important differences. The upper, earnings-related tier is designed to be manned chiefly by independent occupational schemes; the State provides at this level only a Reserve Scheme to serve as a model, or standard, and to accommodate those who are not otherwise catered for. Whereas under the Crossman Plan, as also for the flat-rate pensions in the Joseph Plan, current benefits are paid out of current receipts on a 'pay-as you-go' basis, contributions to the State Reserve Scheme will be funded and invested in the ordinary commercial way. This method is preferred because it does not allow a heavy liability to build up for future generations, but on the other hand it means that the dynamic character of the scheme is linked with the fortunes of its investments and depends on the 'bonus additions' which, it is expected, will 'offset, or offset to a substantial extent, the effect of rising prices on the purchasing power of the pension' (App. 3, para. 17). But this pension, it must be remembered, will be additional to the basic flat-rate benefit which will be annually reviewed and adjusted to the cost of living. The second major departure of the Joseph Plan from the existing system is that these *flat-rate* benefits of the basic scheme are to be financed by *earnings-related* contributions. This is designed to solve the problem of financing flat-rate benefits, which are 'dynamized' by means of an annual review (i.e. kept moving in line with average *earnings*), without putting an excessive burden of contributions on the lower earners; the Labour government of 1974 decided to retain this Conservative innovation. These graduated contributions for financing flat-rate benefits carry no equivalent differential rights, graduated pensions being a quite separate affair. What is being done, in fact, as Sir John Walley has argued, is to impose a progressive tax to finance a welfare service, with nothing of the true character of insurance remaining. That being so, he continues, would it not be both fairer and more effective to levy the tax on all forms of income, not only on earnings, and to make everyone, not only earners, eligible to receive the service?[12] The argument is worth bearing in mind.

It is highly doubtful whether a one-tier graduated scheme for earners on the Crossman model could provide all who retire with an adequate pension as of right. The scheme itself recognizes this weakness in the case of married women whose earnings, because they are often both low and irregular, might well fail to produce an adequate graduated pension; so they are to be allowed, if they wish, to draw a flat-rate pension on the basis of their husband's contributions, as at present, to supplement or replace it. But nothing similar is offered to other low and irregular earners. The Joseph Plan includes a universal minimum, but it is not set at a level adequate for those with no other income. One reason for this, no doubt, is that it is intended that in due course all earners will become entitled to an occupational pension as well. But earnings-related pension schemes take time to mature and the time required is lengthened by changes of government and consequent changes of plan. In the meantime policy is faced by a dilemma. If the basic pension is made adequate for those with no other income, and in addition is kept in line with rising average earnings, the increments will go, as of right, to all those who are already enjoying occupational pensions, and their number is rapidly increasing. If this is not done, reliance on supplementary pensions must remain substantial. We return to this, and similar questions, in Chapter 12.

There is another problem which arises when a national insurance plan relies for its earnings-related pensions extensively, or even predominantly (as in the Joseph Plan), on schemes run by industries. It is the question of how to preserve a man's pension rights when he changes his job. In a state scheme (like the Crossman Plan) there is no problem, nor in a sufficiently broadly-based occupational one where there is room within the scheme for such mobility as normally occurs. The French have evolved a system of this kind for providing supplements to the rather low state pensions. It has been done by collective agreements between firms and between whole industries to create broad schemes which are then federated in a national association and supervised by a national institution.[13] But there is nothing like this in the Joseph Plan, which can only guarantee that a man's accumulated rights should be preserved as 'deferred' fractions of a pension, to be collected and pieced together by him on retirement.

Every kind of benefit raises its own particular problems. This is because entitlement to a benefit is attached to a status, and a status is not an objective fact, but is shaped by the political decision that creates it. Pensions are usually paid unconditionally in old age, but this can mean anything from fifty-five to seventy, and it may be the same for men and women or different. Very often the pension may be drawn at an earlier date, conditionally or at a lower rate, for instance by those in poor health or who have for a long time been unable to find employment. In the British system, since Beveridge, old age begins at sixty-five for women and seventy for men, but the pension can be drawn at sixty and sixty-five respectively on condition of retirement. This also has to be defined. To retire is to give up regular work, but the so-called 'earnings rule' allows a man to continue to earn up to a prescribed limit by casual work, above which the pension tapers away as the earnings increase. This concession has come to be regarded as an imposition, but if there were no limit placed on earnings, the retirement pension would become an old-age pension, which in some countries it is. The tendency elsewhere, as far as there is one, seems to be to lower the age where it was over seventy, as Canada and Norway have done, and to have the same age for men and women, as is now the case in about half the industrial countries. The other complication is the rule that those who postpone retirement and continue both to work and to pay their contributions, eventually receive an increased pension. Beveridge thought this would induce many people to extend their working life, but the effect has been small. The bait is not sufficiently attractive, and what matters most is how the employer organizes his work-force.

Certain other conditions are nowadays treated as the equivalent of retirement and therefore pensionable in advance of the normal age. Invalidity, or permanent incapacity to work owing to ill-health, is a pensionable status which was well established abroad for some time before it was introduced into this country in 1971. Once it is separated from sickness benefit, which is essentially short-term, it can be shaped and expanded to fit the special needs of this very distinctive category of persons. Special consideration is given, for instance, to young mothers with dependent children, and the 1974 Labour government announced its intention to pay invalidity benefit (and other long-term benefits) at a higher rate than sickness benefit (and other short-term benefits). The case of widows is rather different, since what they have lost is not the capacity to work but the support of a husband. But it is assumed that, if widowed in middle age, they might be unable to find employment. So they were granted what is in effect a premature pension if widowed at fifty or later, and in 1970 the age of entitlement was lowered to forty, but with a much reduced pension rising year by year to the full amount at fifty. A widow also receives an allowance (since 1966) for the first six months of her widowhood to help her to settle her affairs, and a widowed mother's allowance if she has dependent children. The pension used to be subject to an 'earnings rule', but this was dropped in 1964. The rights assigned to widows have recently been extended to the divorced, and in some countries separated and deserted wives are given the same status. An Australian Act of 1942 referred to such people as '*de facto* widows', and Norway enlarged the category to include the 'family widow', the woman prevented from either marrying or earning by having to look after her parents.[14]

These are just some examples of the many problems associated with the position of women in systems of social security, to which great attention was given internationally in the early 1970s. Practices differ greatly from country to country.[15] For instance, the British Conservative State Reserve Scheme would give a widow a pension at half the value of her late husband's entitlement, while in Belgium she gets 80 per cent of what her husband could draw for the two of them; in Germany a widow receives a pension whatever her age, income or family responsibilities (though it is smaller if she is under forty-five), whereas in France no provision at all is made for widows under retirement age unless they are invalids. All this is due to differences of attitude towards the dependence of married women on their husbands, to which must be added the effect, in earnings-related insurance, of the fact that women's earnings are on average lower than those of men and, because of marriage and its responsibilities, they are also considerably more irregular. As a result of this the average pension earned in 1970 by women in Germany, which has a highly sophisticated superannuation system, was less than half that for men. It is normal in flat-rate insurance to allow a wife to choose to be treated as a 'dependant' of her husband and qualify for a reduced pension on the basis of his contributions. But dependency is a status which many women resent, and it is particularly inappropriate in an earnings-related system in which wives who work are compelled to contribute and thus establish rights on their own account. But if they are to achieve pensions on a par with men's, somebody must pay their contributions while they are not working. If one takes the view that all wives do in fact work, though not for money, then it can be (and has been) suggested that either they should pay themselves, if necessary out of what they 'earn' from their husband as wife, housekeeper or mother, or be credited with their contributions in the same way as those whose work is interrupted by sickness or unemployment. The Labour government actually considered this latter idea and rejected it,[16] and we have already noted the compromise solution adopted in the Crossman Plan. An Advisory Committee to the German government came up with a different compromise in 1969, proposing that while a mother stayed at home caring for her children the Insurance Fund should pay her contributions, but if she did not find employment when the children were independent, her husband should pay. Two years later the Minister of Labour produced other proposals including one that an insured woman should be credited with an additional year's insurance for each child born to her. In France, since 1972, it has been possible for pension contributions to be paid as an addition to family allowances for the poorer families.[17]

A major change was introduced in 1966 into the system of short-term benefits for sickness, unemployment and widows' allowances. All those for whom these risks were covered for flat-rate benefits, including those 'contracted out' for pensions, were obliged to participate in a State earnings-related insurance scheme through which they could draw a supplementary grant for a limited period, i.e. for six months following the first two weeks after the onset of the misfortune. The rates were calculated quite differently from those of graduated pensions, and the *total* amounts received could be very much greater, partly because the sick, unemployed and widows often have dependent children whereas pensioners do not. An unemployed father of a family of four would probably be getting *in toto* over 70 per cent of his average wage, and could get up to the statutory maximum of 85 per cent. This was very much in line with what many other countries were aiming at. But the limitation of the graduated addition to six months, and of flat-rate benefits to one year, of continuous unemployment means that most of the long-term unemployed are either on flat-rate benefit only or on Supplementary Benefit (SB). There are still many countries in the world which have no State scheme for unemployment insurance, but rely on arrangements made by employers and unions among themselves. This was always the case in France, but since 1958 collective agreements between employers and unions, backed by statutory compulsion on all firms in the industries that make the agreements to join the schemes, have made the coverage of industrial workers virtually complete. The arrangement is very like that for 'complementary' pensions described above. 'Unemployment' is a status which is even harder to define precisely than 'retirement'. A man is not eligible for benefit if he has voluntarily left his employment without just cause, if he does not use the opportunities offered him to find a new job or fails to take up an offer of 'suitable' employment, i.e. similar and at the prevailing rates. After a time he may be required to take up a different occupation at equally good pay, but he will not be obliged to move to another part of the country, though he may be helped to do so. If all else fails there are rehabilitation centres (but only twelve in all, four of them residential); some 2000 a year go to these voluntarily, but only about fifty are sent. Obviously there is scope here for abuse by the 'work-shy', but the Committee which investigated the matter in 1973 did not attempt to estimate it.[18] It seems probable that loopholes or loose provisions in the regulations are a more important cause of unmerited or unneeded payments of benefit than deliberate misrepresentations by claimants.

An important addition to benefits for those out of work was made by legislation in 1963 and 1965 governing redundancy. When economic, organizational or technological changes make certain workers superfluous or unemployable they are not 'sacked' but 'made redundant', to indicate that the causes of their dismissal are structural rather than personal. They are therefore entitled to receive compensation in the form of a lump sum assessed in relation to their length of service. Redundancy payments, and the procedures associated with them, are regulated by the Acts, and payments are made from a Fund fed by employers' contributions. Co-operation between government and industry is very close here, perhaps because of their common interest in overcoming social obstacles to economic progress. In the case of the other principal short-term benefit, sick pay, co-operation might well be closer. Since a very large proportion of employed persons, especially in the white collar and skilled categories, are entitled to receive sick pay from their employers, there is considerable overlap with the State system, and it might be better, it is argued, if there were a clear division of responsibility by which, in the shorter term, sick leave with pay would be as much a right of the employee as holidays with pay.

The major forms of social security which are not provided by social insurance are Supplementary Benefit, family allowances and, since 1970, Family Income Supplement. Family allowances, when introduced, were the only benefits paid to a family headed by a full-time earner, and they are still the only such benefit paid without a means test. Unlike those in Europe, they were never seen as a family wage shared among employers, or as a means of stimulating the birthrate. They were regarded, and still are, as a national contribution to family welfare financed by the taxpayer. As François Lafitte neatly expressed it, 'the Community, having deliberately and rightly made children expensive, must share the cost of child-rearing with parents'.[19] But in recent years they have been discussed chiefly in the context of child poverty. Both political and public opinion were stirred by the report on *Circumstances of Families* published by the Ministry of Social Security in 1967, which showed that 7 per cent of families with two or more dependent children (and therefore entitled to family allowances) had incomes below the national assistance level; this may seem to be a small proportion of the total, but it included nearly a million children, and it did not include families with only one child. So there was constant pressure to raise the allowances, combined with a determination not to subject them to a means test. An increase given to all families, irrespective of need, was obviously very costly, but this obstacle was at least partly removed in 1968. On that occasion when the allowance was increased, the increment was taken back again from those paying income tax by reducing by an equivalent amount the remission of income tax on the tax-free allowance in respect of their child. This ingenious device came to be known as the 'clawback', and we discuss it further in Chapter 12.

That is also the place for discussion of Supplementary Benefit and Family Income Supplement, both of which are selective measures devoted wholly to the relief of poverty. Nothing need be added here to what has already been said about the former, but the latter requires some comment. The Family Income Supplement (FIS) acts in some ways like an extension of Supplementary Benefit to persons in paid employment who, as earners, are not eligible for SB. But it differs also in two respects: it is payable only where there are children (it is a form of family relief), and there are no additions to cover rent and rates or to meet special needs. The sum paid is half the difference (subject to a maximum, originally £4) between the actual income and the standard income 'prescribed' for a family of that size. So it is not easy for the potential claimant to calculate whether he is eligible, and if so for how much. In spite of this, though the 'take-up' rate in the first two years was very low where the benefit was small, it rose to 75 per cent when the benefit was £2 a week or over.[20] FIS is admittedly an unsatisfactory measure. It is objectionable both as being a direct subsidy to wages and because it is subject to a very rigid kind of means test and, one might add, because it merely adds another, inadequate, piece to a patchwork. It is most unlikely to become a permanent feature of our social security system.

9 | Health care

All modern governments recognize a responsibility for the
health of their people. They are all moving in the same direction
towards the same objective, but they differ vastly as to the distance they have travelled along the way, and very significantly
as to the route they have chosen. In a country like India, with a
vast population and limited resources, a high priority has been
given to preventive measures and the fight against epidemic and
endemic diseases like malaria, smallpox, cholera and leprosy.
These, and the provision of hospitals, are, under the Constitution,
a 'State Subject'. There is health insurance but in the late 1960s it
covered only 14 million in a population of over 500 million.[1] In
the USSR, too, health care is a state service, but a comprehensive
one, with a salaried staff and a ratio of doctors to population
which is one of the highest in the world. The dominant features
of health care in Western Europe are national health insurance and
an independent medical profession, but the United Kingdom, as
we saw, replaced national insurance by a national service after
the Second World War. The United States government per-
sistently rejected all forms of 'socialized medicine' until 1965,
when it introduced public insurance for the old (Medicare)
followed by public insurance for the poor (Medicaid). Before
this only one quarter of the total expenditure on health came
from public funds. The main support for health care was provided by voluntary private insurance. In this case policy reflected the prevalent national philosophy. 'Experience has
shown,' said President Eisenhower, 'that American medicine outstripped the world on a voluntary basis', so it should continue on
the same lines.[2] And the doctors wanted it so, just as British
and European doctors have clung to their form of independence.

The fact that a policy for health care must operate through members of one of the proudest of the ancient professions accounts for many of its characteristic problems. It is not easy to harmonize political with professional authority, nor bureaucratic with professional procedures, yet all are essential and must be respected.

There are other ways in which the planning of a policy for health care is peculiarly difficult. It is important when resources are scarce to use them in the most effective way, and it is relatively easy to see that, for India, this points to a high priority for epidemiology and hospitals. Where a health care system is already well developed, the allocation of resources to it and within it presents subtler problems. It is generally agreed that medical services are costly, that the level of service achieved always falls short of that which, with unlimited expenditure, could be achieved by the application of current knowledge and skills, and that advances in medical science and technology are continuously improving and adding to the means for treating sickness and promoting health. This constant striving for something that is always just out of reach engenders both strong demands for a general expansion of the service and a complex of pressures on behalf of various sectors of it for priority treatment. And there is still very little to go on when assessing the merits of competing claims except the confident assertions of those who make them, that is to say of senior members of the medical professions. And they are not accustomed to having their authority challenged in professional matters.

It has been said that 'medicine is the only enterprise, private or public, in which it has not been considered essential to equate effectiveness and cost'.[3] The first step towards such an equation would be a more serious attempt to establish with scientific accuracy to what extent, and under what conditions, the treatment used produces the results aimed at. Practitioners are well aware that medicine is not an exact science, but in some respects an art. They are inclined to be suspicious of quantitative measurement, and to prefer to rely on the subjective assessment of their personal experience. It is still more difficult to relate benefit to cost, or output to input, and to compare the benefit in one case with what could have been achieved by an alternative use of the same resources. And yet this is the kind of information planning ideally requires. For example, the success of mass X-ray examinations in detecting incipient tuberculosis encouraged the idea that 'screening' would be equally successful for other diseases. But this depends on the accuracy of the test, the severity of the disease and the effectiveness of its treatment at a later stage. All this can be, and has been, measured, showing in some cases that the results obtained by screening would not justify the cost. But eventually one comes up against factors which cannot be measured. Work-days lost or saved can be added up, but one cannot put a value on human health and human life as such.

Much has been done during the past decade to improve the data available to planners, but their position is still a weak one. 'At present,' said an official of the Department of Health and Social Security in 1972, 'there are no means of arriving at scientific assessments of priorities, and decisions are taken mainly on political judgements, or on grounds of expediency or in relation to known public pressures.'[4] Planning was also hampered by the unforeseen and rapid change in the nature of the task with which health services had to grapple. Beveridge had believed that, although costs would certainly rise, total expenditure in 1965 would be about the same as in 1945, because a National Health Service must surely improve the national health, and so reduce the volume of work to be done. The truth was almost exactly the opposite. For one thing, technical progress creates work by making it possible to do what was previously impossible. Surgery offers many examples of this. Secondly, if a service is efficiently organized, it should increase the proportion of those in need of treatment who actually get it. Thirdly, there is the obvious fact that those saved from death in early or middle life must still face a terminal illness, often after a long period of continuous invalidity. The National Health Service, said Rudolf Klein, 'from being conceived primarily as a service for dealing with disease, is becoming a service for maintaining those whom it cannot cure'.[5] A rather epigrammatic statement, perhaps, but the fact remains that in 1970 some 55 per cent of all NHS hospital beds were assigned to chronic cases.[6]

So for some twenty-five years after the end of the Second World War the planning of health services lacked clear directives. British policy had an enthusiastic and adventurous phase when it established the NHS, which was followed by a period of timidity. We believed (not without cause) that we had created the best system of popular medical care in the world, but it seemed to have cost a good deal more than had been anticipated. For a decade or more little or nothing was done to expand the service. The Guillebaud Committee (1955–6) had explained that the figures generally quoted were misleading. For, although the initial cost was more than double some preliminary estimates and rose steeply thereafter, the proportion of the Gross National Product absorbed by the service had actually fallen slightly from 3·51 per cent to 3·24 per cent while cost per head of the population (at 1948–9 prices) had risen only from £7 13s. to £8 12s.[7] However, caution continued to prevail. Expenditure increased slowly and for some time no major developments took place either in the building of hospitals or in the rehabilitation of general practice— two crying needs.

In the 1960s the mood changed. The bubble of complacency had been pricked, dissatisfaction was rife, and there were some who asserted that the service was in danger of collapsing. They pointed to the fact that over 300 doctors—equivalent to about a quarter of the annual entry from the medical schools into the NHS—were emigrating every year, and the hospitals were increasingly dependent on immigrants. A major crisis arose in general practice in 1965 and the doctors threatened to cancel their contracts. The crisis was resolved, a hospital programme was launched and by the beginning of the 1970s total expenditure had risen to about 5 per cent of GNP. It was against this background that, in July 1968, the Labour Minister of Health produced a Green Paper (i.e. a discussion paper) with outline proposals for the radical reshaping of the structure of the health services. It had a bad reception and was withdrawn. In 1970 he issued a revised version, but this died when the government fell in June. His Conservative successor took the matter up where he had left it, and in August 1972 a definitive plan appeared on which was based the National Health Service Reorganization Act of 1973 (Ch. 32).

The central aim of the reorganization was to integrate the three sections of the National Health Service: hospitals, general practice and local authority health services. On this both parties were in agreement. The tripartite structure given to the service at its birth had been something of a makeshift, but the obstacles to its unification seemed for a long time to be insuperable, and such official committees as studied the matter advised against it. When in 1962 the Porritt Committee, representing the medical profession, produced a plan for a kind of unification, or at least federation, this showed which way the wind was blowing.[8] By 1970 certain decisions had been, or were being, taken which greatly simplified the problem. If the local authority *health* services were to be absorbed into the NHS, it was essential to know where the division lay between these and the local *welfare* services, and this was a highly controversial subject. The Seebohm Report had drawn a firm line between them, which had been accepted (see p. 160). The second important development was the reshaping of local government, which created, in the counties and metropolitan boroughs, areas which could also serve as the key geographical units in the administration of the NHS. They were sufficiently substantial to carry the weight of the health services, and sufficiently uniform in size, population and resources to make it possible to plan for a common standard of service throughout the country.

The hierarchy of power in the new structure is composed of three tiers: the Minister at the top, Regional Health Authorities (RHA) below him and Area Health Authorities (AHA) below these. The RHAs are responsible for strategic planning, for the deployment of top-level specialist services and for liaison with university medical schools. They also allocate resources among the AHAs. The latter are the key executive authority. Their areas coincide with the counties and metropolitan boroughs, and they are responsible for co-ordination with local government services. The Areas are divided into Districts which are not an additional tier in the hierarchy, but the operational arms of the AHAs. The District, said one official document, is expected to become 'the basic operational unit of the integrated Health Service'.[9] The government made it quite clear that the whole service was to be run, so far as decisions were concerned, by the Minister and his officers. Members of the Regional and Area Boards, nominated from above like those of the former Hospital Boards, were expected to see that the right questions were asked and that there was full awareness of health needs. 'They are not there to do the work that their officers are trained to do.'[10] The District does not have a Board, but a Management Team composed of officers (in nursing, 'community medicine', finance and administration) and two professionally chosen doctors, (a specialist and a GP). The public's voice can be heard through a Community Health Council representing local government and relevant local organizations. This arrangement, said the government, was designed to avoid the 'dangerous confusion between management on the one hand and the community's reaction to management on the other'.[11] It is clear that the administrative plan is based on the belief that a service of this kind cannot be efficiently run unless control is in the hands of professionals. Consequently, in spite of the emphasis laid on 'community health' (as we explain below), the scope given for community participation is small.

The position of general practice in the service remains virtually unchanged. The family doctors and their colleagues were as determined as ever not to surrender their independence, and they prevailed. The first Labour plan had proposed to bring them directly under the general health authority in each area, but their reaction was such that the proposal was dropped. The Conservative plan was quite explicit. The family practitioners were assured that their status would not be affected by the reorganization. 'They now provide services as independent contractors, and they will continue to do so.'[12] The Family Practitioner Committee with which they would negotiate their contracts, and of which they appointed half the members, was the old Executive Council under a new name. In this respect, therefore, integration remains incomplete.

An integrating operation closes some gaps but almost inevitably opens, or widens, others across which bridges must then be built. This is very obvious in the case we are considering. There were good reasons for incorporating in the reorganized NHS the personal health services hitherto run by the local council. These include domiciliary nursing, health visitors, midwifery, ambulances, maternity and child welfare, the school medical service and, as a new responsibility, family planning. On the other side of the new dividing line are all the personal social services for the aged, for children and for the mentally disordered, including their non-hospital residential accommodation. It is clear that an integrated health service and integrated social service departments must work very closely together; often they would be dealing with the same individuals or families, and in some cases, such as child guidance and health education, the responsibility was to be shared. Important too is collaboration between the new NHS authorities and the health department of the local authority which remains in charge of some environmental health services. One can see what an advantage it is for the Area Health Authority and the county council to have a common geographical base—to be in charge, for their respective functions, of the same community.

'Community' is a word which has figured prominently in discussions of national health problems in recent years, in such compound phrases as 'community health', 'community medicine' and 'community physician'. These are in a sense conglomerates of several ideas current for some little time past and, though rather nebulous, they have practical implications. Community medicine is in effect an expansion of 'social medicine', which was first in vogue during and immediately after the Second World War, as an offshoot of Public Health. In its Report on Medical Schools (1944) the Goodenough Inter-Departmental Committee described social medicine as being concerned with the environmental and communal factors affecting personal health, and as paying special attention to preventive medicine and to the promotion of positive health, rather than only to the treatment of illness. The approach is communal, but the focus is still on the health of the individual. In community medicine the focus is, as the name implies, on the health of the community seen as a whole. For the Royal Commission on Medical Education (1968) community medicine was 'the speciality practised by epidemiologists and by administrators of medical services', and was concerned, not with individual patients, but 'with the broad questions of health and disease in, for example, particular geographical and occupational sections of the community and in the community at large'. This left sanitation, pollution and the physical environment to the Medical Officer of Health, or to the new types of lay specialist who the Commission rightly thought might gradually supersede him. Of particular interest are the 'core subjects' recommended for the training of community physicians: epidemiology, biostatistics, medical sociology, operational research and management.[13] Clearly one task of community medicine was conceived as being to monitor continuously the health of the community, by assembling and analysing statistical and other data. This view was endorsed by a Scottish Working Party which said that 'a community medicine must in our view provide the basic skills to make reliable assessments of the problems and to evaluate the results of different courses of action'.[14] Taken in this sense community medicine is an invaluable aid to the rational planning of medical services.

For others community health is a blanket term which includes all this and pretty well everything else needed to give a global view of the health of a local community and of the activities engaged in promoting and maintaining it. The key concept is that of seeing, and treating, each individual or family case as a whole and in the context of its social and environmental setting. With so broad a view, it is impossible, and would be self-contradictory, to draw a sharp line between health and welfare. Close liaison between the medical and social services is called for, and it is hoped that the integration of each in its own sphere will make it easier to bring them together. A Working Party was set up in 1971 to study collaboration between the NHS and local government, and its reports show how numerous and varied are the possibilities. It is interesting that its second report gave much space to the question of the maintenance of series of statistical data, the location and use of computer services, and the exchange of information.[15] Without the assimilation of the geographical bases of the AHAs and the county councils co-operation would hardly be possible, and it opens the way to new and more sophisticated methods of joint planning in the fields of health and welfare once the new authorities have settled down.

A field in which this liaison is most essential, and most complicated, is that of community care. This phrase, be it noted, does not refer, as do the others we have been discussing, to care for the health *of* the community, but to care for the health and welfare of individuals given *by* and *in* the community. The 'patients' live in families, or alone or perhaps in hostels and are cared for by relatives and friends and social workers, both public and voluntary, with the help of various establishments such as clinics, day hospitals, clubs and workshops. The burden of providing this care and these services lies heavily on the community, which must be prepared and equipped to bear it. The major problems arise in the case of the old and the mentally disordered. The progress achieved in geriatric medicine reduces the number of old people for whom life outside a hospital is impossible, and it has been estimated that now about 60 per cent of those admitted to hospital could be made fit for life outside. For the community and its services, this is more a threat than a promise. The community care of the mentally disturbed is a still more serious undertaking, because their behaviour may be irresponsible, unpredictable and dangerous both to themselves and to others; and many of them need continuing medical attention of a specialized kind. In its early days, as Titmuss pointed out,[16] the campaign for community care was in too much of a hurry and paid too little attention to these matters. However, after many vicissitudes, the official policy on mental health came down in the 1970s firmly on the side of community care.

Modern mental health care could be said to date from the Royal Commission of 1924-6, which laid down that no sharp line of demarcation should be drawn between mental and physical illness; the two should be treated alike. 'The keynote of the past has been detention. The keynote of the future should be prevention and treatment.'[17] It followed naturally that, as we have already seen, the mental hospitals should be transferred from the local authorities to the NHS. In 1959, however, new guidelines were laid down to the effect that, in the care of mental cases, first priority should be given to treatment at home, second to residential hostels, and only third priority to mental hospitals. So the local authorities were asked to take back, in the first two items of this triad, a large part of the responsibility of which they had only recently been relieved; and it proved too much for them. They were supposed to provide residential care for both adults and children, but by the early 1970s only forty-three of the 174 authorities in England and Wales had done so for both categories, and twenty-eight had provided for neither.[18] The policy was not on that account relaxed; it was reaffirmed. The aim was to phase out big mental hospitals, to reduce the number of hospital beds by half and accommodate the remainder inside general hospitals, and to entrust the rest of the cases to community care, in their homes or in hostels, with the help of establishments of the kinds described above. It is intended that this programme should be flexible, because only experience, and careful study of it, will show exactly what should be the respective roles of the hospital, the hostel and day services provided for patients living at home. To cite one example, drug therapy can restore many seriously disturbed patients to apparent health, but their condition is precarious and relapses, with which only a hospital can cope, may be frequent. A policy of speedy discharge can be distressing both for them and for their families. They need a refuge and security, not only when they are acutely ill. Can conditions of life in a hospital be designed to provide this? What is the alternative? Experience and experiment can show, provided plans are not too rigidly conceived and executed.

Of the three constituent parts of the old NHS it is the province of the Medical Officer of Health that has been most deeply affected by reorganization. It had been stripped of its hospital services in 1946 and was deprived of its personal health services in 1973. The environmental services which were left to it then had their responsibility removed for water and sewage, which was transferred to a national water council. Even so, what remained was of great importance to community health, especially at a time when anxiety about pollution was growing. It included such matters as clean food, clean air, refuse disposal, slaughter-houses, public lavatories, home safety and so forth. These, however, were no longer regarded as specifically medical matters, and the office of Medical Officer disappeared. But the profession survived and was quick to see, and to seize, new openings for its members in medical administration and in the role of 'community physician', for which their training fitted them. Had they not, in anticipation, rechristened their Institute's journal *Community Health* in 1967?

The position of general practitioners in the NHS had been an uneasy one from the start, partly because of the dominating position in the structure given to the hospitals, and partly on account of developments in the science and practice of medicine. It was inevitable that, in an age of rapid scientific and technological advance, the specialist should forge ahead of the generalist and make inroads into the areas of his acknowledged competence. And both specialists and technologists were concentrated in the hospitals, through which flowed the main stream of progress in medical knowledge and skills. The GP felt he was being cut off from this vital stream and baulked in his efforts to bring up to date the qualifications which had originally entitled him to practise. The faster things moved, the more contact he needed to have with his colleagues, and he was getting less. The universal provider of consultant services was now the out-patients department, and his relations with it were impersonal. Consultation, in the old sense of a conference between doctor and specialist about a difficult case, was being replaced by 'referral', the arrangement by which a doctor could get an appointment for his patient to attend a particular hospital unit for the examination and tests necessary to make a diagnosis and a recommendation as to treatment. This transfer of responsibility to an institution in which he had no place made it look as if the doctor was acting simply as a go-between, and masked the importance of the decisions he had to take.

In the early days of the NHS it had been assumed, rather than decided, that general practice would retain its traditional place, but the issues involved in this assumption were not squarely faced. Then in 1961 the Gillie Committee was set up 'to advise on the field of work which it would be reasonable to expect the family doctor to undertake in the foreseeable future'. The basic question was whether, in this age of specialization, a 'generalist' could still give a service of the quality that his patients were entitled to expect. The family doctor is the purveyor of 'primary care'. This denotes two things. First, provision of an easy and familiar point of entry into the health care system, from which the patient can, if necessary, be directed to any other part of it. Secondly, treatment—at home or in the surgery—of such ailments as do not need the services of a specialist or the facilities of a hospital, and supervision of the continuing treatment prescribed by the specialist. The first is dependent upon the second because there must be a fairly solid basis of personal service on which to build the relationship of trust and mutual understanding between doctor and patient on which primary care depends. That solid basis was in danger of erosion. In order to preserve and enlarge it the Gillie Committee made the following recommendation: 'It is essential to overcome the professional isolation of the family doctor by such methods as group practice, hospital work and continuing education, and the doctor himself must be active in these respects.'[19]

His initial training was investigated in depth by a Royal Commission in 1968. It told the family doctor, rather unkindly, that he must learn to rely less on 'charismatic authority' and the 'mystique of his calling' and more on proven expertise, which the better educated patients of today are well able to appreciate. But did the generalist have any expertise, or was his work only, as was sometimes said, the 'sum of a number of specialities practised at a lower level of competence'? This old idea, if not yet quite dead, was dying, and an attempt had been made to replace it by the conception of general practice as a specialism in its own right. This had gained support from the foundation in 1952 of a Royal College of General Practitioners, devoted to the maintenance of high standards in the profession and the advancement of knowledge and skills. The conception was well-founded, but it was not an easy one to sell. The gravest problem for a doctor, as for most other professional people, is that the training by which he qualified becomes rapidly out of date; continuing education, theoretical and practical, is essential. For the GPs there were refresher courses in graduate medical schools, and some part-time clinical posts in hospitals. These were very valuable, but not enough, unless the conditions under which they worked allowed them the time and the opportunity to keep in constant touch with current medical progress.

In the early days of the NHS this was far from being the case. The doctors, in their determination to retain their independent professional status, had accepted an arrangement which, in the words of Enoch Powell (ex-Minister of Health), 'combines private enterprise and state service without the characteristic advantages of either'.[20] This was particularly galling because hospital specialists enjoyed the characteristic advantages of both: security, salary with increments, premises, equipment and assistance provided at public expense, holidays with pay and freedom to continue their private practice, even within the walls of the hospital. The family doctor, by contrast, had to provide, equip and staff his surgery, and be on duty (in person, or through a locum) round the clock throughout the year; for this he received a fixed income in proportion to the number of patients he enrolled, not to the amount of work he did. Conscientious doctors complained that they could not make a living without excessively enlarging their practices. It is not surprising that when the crisis broke in 1965 over a pay award the British Medical Association presented, not a pay claim, but a 'Charter for the Family Doctor Service'.

The most important innovations that followed, and restored the peace, were the recognition of the doctor's right to annual and weekend holidays, the provision of funds to meet the cost of these, and the taking-over by the government of the major part of the surgery overheads.

But even under these improved conditions a single-handed practice would only exceptionally be able to give an up-to-date service. The doctor has little time for study and lacks the stimulus of continuous contact with colleagues and through them with a wider range of specialists than he is likely to have dealings with on his own. It had long been official policy to encourage and assist the formation of partnerships and group practices, but in 1970 20 per cent of principals in general practice were still working single-handed, compared with 43·6 per cent in 1952.[21] It will be remembered that in 1920 the Dawson Committee had recommended the establishment of a system of health centres, local and regional (see p. 93). The local version was like a group practice set up by a public authority, as part of the planned development of local health services. It provided, like group practice, a stronger base for the generalist in which he could benefit not only from collaboration with colleagues but also from the work of auxiliary staff, of the secretarial and the social worker type. There might also be attached to the centre practitioners of professions lying outside the normal range of the generalist, such as a psychiatrist, an orthopaedist and possibly a dentist. It was not till the middle 1960s that any progress was made in setting up such centres, but then it became very rapid, and by the end of 1971 there were over 600 of them, operating or in preparation, in the United Kingdom.[22]

The regional health centre in the Dawson plan was, by contrast, a team of specialists, but it never caught on in this country. Centres of this kind are a basic unit in the Soviet Union. They are sometimes called 'polyclinics' and resemble hospital out-patient departments brought nearer to the public. Something similar has been tried from time to time in parts of the United States, where the generalist has almost disappeared in face of the advance of the specialist. One such is the 'internist' to whom patients will probably take any ailment which does not obviously fall within the province of another specialist, but he would deny that he offers comprehensive primary care in the manner of a British GP. The question is: can a team of specialists collectively replace the generalist as the purveyor of primary care? Some American doctors clearly doubt this, and have expressed anxiety at the fragmentation of medical care, wishing to bring the disjointed parts back into what they call the 'main stream'. The situation is fluid, but in Britain at present primary care remains firmly with the family doctor, or groups of family doctors continuing to practise as generalists.

Whatever may be done to strengthen the position of the general practitioners, there are obvious reasons why the system as a whole is inevitably dominated by the hospitals. First, the whole system must be planned around them. In the reorganized NHS, for example, there is to be a district general hospital as the focal point of each District, and a teaching hospital and medical school in each Region. Secondly, the top levels of medical science and technology must be concentrated within them. Thirdly, and in consequence of this, their senior staff are the élite of the profession, in terms both of pay and of prestige. Unfortunately they have not been prone to conceal their sense of superiority from their colleagues in general practice. There has been some improvement of late, but a committee of the Royal Colleges reporting in 1972 on ways of improving relations could say no more than that 'the causes of mutual frustration and irritations between hospital doctors and general practitioners are slowly being removed'.[23] Finally, hospitals are immensely expensive. At the end of the Second World War all countries had too few hospitals, and many of those they had were obsolescent. In the course of the next twenty-five years a great effort was put into the building of hospitals, which meant that they were everywhere given high financial priority. It began in America with a presidential inquiry which showed that the country had less than half the hospital beds it needed. Action followed in the form of Federal subsidies, and by 1960 the number of beds had risen to 80 per cent of requirements. According to the World Health Organization this stimulated a similar effort in Europe 'to renovate the whole hospital scene'.[24] The British government paid tribute to the importance of hospitals in a national health service by nationalizing them, but did not do anything to develop them until the 1960s. It then produced two plans in 1962 and 1966 involving an expenditure of £1000 million in ten years. This may seem a lot, but it was not exceptionally high compared with what other countries were doing.

It cannot be said that the demand for hospital beds has been met; there are long waiting lists in some departments. But the shortage would be much more serious if it were not for two developments. Owing to efficient management of the use of beds and a remarkable shortening of the average time spent by a patient in hospital, the number of patients treated in a given number of beds over a given period has nearly doubled. At the same time, as we have seen, it is hoped to reduce drastically the number of hospital beds occupied by geriatric and mental patients.

We turn now from the organization of the services to the principles on which they are based, and which determine the relation between the service and the citizens. When the National Health Service was established, Aneurin Bevan, for the Labour government, made it perfectly clear what those principles were, and in 1970 the Labour government recalled them in its Green Paper; the first two, in this recapitulation, were: 'The health service should be financed by taxes and contributions paid when people are well rather than by charges levied on them when they are sick; the financial burden of sickness should be spread over the whole community.' Secondly: 'The service should be national in the sense that the same high quality of service, but not a standardized service, should be provided in every part of the country.'[25]

The second principle indicates the advantage which a national service was expected to have over a system for covering medical costs by national health insurance, such as we had before and the countries of Western Europe have, basically, retained. It was thought that, even if family doctors were independent contractors, they could be prevented from setting up practices in over-doctored areas and induced to set them up where they were most needed, and that by this means a more even distribution would be obtained throughout the country. The improvement was at first considerable, but it has not been wholly maintained. This is the price paid—and paid quite deliberately—for preserving the independence of the doctors. In a country in which, as in France, the general practitioner service is organized by negotiation between the local insurance Funds (*Caisses*) and the doctors in the area, controls cannot be exercised in this way. A comparative survey published in 1973 showed that there were six times as many doctors per thousand of population in and around Paris as in some rural areas, which is only marginally better than in America, where free enterprise prevails.[26] In a national service the hospital system can be planned totally, and manned, as in the NHS, by a salaried staff. The first concern of an insurance system, by contrast, is not to build hospitals, but to cover the cost of the treatment given inside them. However, so vital is the role of a well-developed hospital system in modern health care that countries retaining the insurance system have increasingly evolved ways in which the Funds, the local authorities or the central government can engage in hospital planning and production. A survey made for the ILO at the end of the 1960s showed that in Western Germany most of the hospitals were run by the local authorities. In Belgium, although 60 per cent of the hospitals were private, 90 per cent of all hospitals were co-operating with the national health insurance system by taking its patients on acceptable terms.[27] In France a Hospital Reform Act of 1970 established what is in effect a public hospital service, embracing both public and private hospitals, supervised by representative regional councils.[28] In this respect, therefore, there seems to be a convergence between the health insurance and health service alternatives.

The first of the two principles cited above asserts that there must be total pooling of risks among the citizens. Collectively they pay for the system as a whole; individually, what they pay is unaffected by the cost of what they receive, and what they have a right to receive is unaffected by what (if anything) they may have contributed, whether as insurance premiums or as taxes. No money passes between patient and doctor, and no sum is mentioned; the service is not even costed. It makes no difference, either to the doctor or to the patient, whether the treatment prescribed is cheap or expensive. Even in those cases where charges have been imposed, for medicines, dentures and spectacles, the charge is at a flat rate and is remitted for those to whom it might cause hardship. This was the system also for dental treatment until, rather surprisingly, in 1971 the flat-rate charge was replaced by a proportion of cost.

The Continental health insurance systems work differently. Doctors are paid on the 'fee for service' basis: i.e. the rate for the job. The patient pays and claims reimbursement from the Fund, exactly as happens with a private contract of insurance. The service, therefore, is costed, and the doctor's earnings are affected by the character of the treatments he prescribes. That he might, therefore, be tempted to go above and beyond what was really necessary was recognized in Germany when it was laid down that the treatment must be no more than 'adequate and appropriate' and carried out 'with reasonable economy as to the means used'.[29] But the effect on the patient is more important, because the practice is to make the patient himself bear a proportion of the cost. This is called in France the *ticket modérateur,* and it was increased in 1967 from 20 per cent (a common rate at that time in Europe) to 30 per cent. So the more expensive the treatment, the more the patient has to pay. The fee for service charged to the patient, in addition to the prepayment of his insurance contribution, is explicitly designed to act as a deterrent against frivolous and unnecessary demands on the doctor's time. In 1971 Germany tried the experiment of substituting the carrot for the stick, by paying a bonus to those who had not consulted their doctor during the year, but the principle is the same, and it is totally at variance with the spirit of British policy. It is true that many calls made on the doctor are unnecessary, and this has given rise to quite a volume of complaints. But it would be inconsistent with the principle of a free service to use a financial deterrent, and illogical to discourage the reporting of minor symptoms while stressing the importance of early diagnosis.

For the *ticket modérateur* system to work properly there must be some control over the level of fees charged, and this has caused much trouble, notably in France. Attempts to regulate things in 1958 and again in 1960 were not wholly successful, and a new agreement was concluded in 1971 which was meant to 'determine in a lasting manner the relations between the medical profession and the sickness insurance institution'. It called, significantly, for 'the application of self-discipline' by the doctors, but it did not impose complete standardization.[30] It still allowed higher fees to be charged in certain circumstances, including when the doctor involved was one of high professional standing. This had produced an awkward loophole in the system, but it also contributed to the greater freedom of choice which the Continental system gives as compared with the British. It is the patient who pays the doctor, with the money he gets from the insurance Fund, and he can, subject to any restrictions imposed for administrative reasons, take his money where he pleases. If he chooses to employ one of the physicians or surgeons who is authorized to charge higher fees because of his greater eminence, he can pay the difference himself without forfeiting what the Fund has paid him, though he may, as in Belgium, be charged a *ticket modérateur* of 50 per cent instead of 25 per cent.[31] There is, in fact, no sharp division between the public and the private health services. But this freedom is bought at the price of introducing a 'commercial' element into the relation between doctor and patient.

It has been suggested from time to time in this country that patients ought to be obliged to pay something, in addition to what they contribute as prepayment through taxes or insurance, for the service they receive. This would, it was said, strengthen their position vis-à-vis the medical profession, make them recognize the value of what they are getting, and increase the income of the service without increasing the burden of taxes. Any such arrangement would clearly violate the basic principle of the NHS, by treating sickness, to that extent, as a personal liability and medical care as a consumer good, instead of treating sickness as a misfortune and medical care as a community service. At the time of writing, however, the main issue is a different one, and concerns the conditions under which public and private health services can co-exist. General practice is not the problem, since only about 3 per cent of the population go exclusively to private doctors. It is quite different with the hospitals, which in 1970 absorbed 50 per cent of the total current expenditure, central and local, on the health and welfare services combined. These are organized in such a way that the public and private elements are not merely interdependent but even interlocked. Something like half the consultants (it used to be 75 per cent) are now engaged part-time and continue to run substantial private practices, and they can treat their patients in the private (paying) beds in public hospitals.

The costs of specialist and hospital services are so high that few people could afford them if it were not for the fact that organizations now exist which offer an alternative system of prepayment through voluntary private insurance. The largest of these is the British United Provident Association (BUPA). So the issue turns on what is to be the future of this and similar organizations, which in 1974 together covered about 2·5 million persons. In the United States they dominate the scene, and it is generally admitted that since the coverage they give varies according to the amount subscribed the result is a very unequal distribution of medical care. And the bills incurred by those not qualified to use Medicaid or Medicare, and not rich enough to pay the maximum subscriptions to Blue Cross and Blue Shield, can be quite crippling. The NHS is far too firmly established for this to happen in Britain, but the number of people using private insurance could, and probably, will, increase, with the help of the nursing homes, clinics and 'mini-hospitals' which BUPA is establishing. Some people welcome this, on the ground that the citizen should have the right to spend his money on buying the health care he prefers, if he wishes to do so. They also argue that the existence of private practice has a stimulating effect on the medical services as a whole, and that in particular it benefits the hospitals to have part-time consultants working in their out-patients departments and treating patients in the private wards. If the system that allows this were abolished, they say, the hospitals would lose many of their best staff.

Others totally reject the idea that wealth should be able to buy superior health care: in this, they say, all should be equal. But the immediate question is not whether private medical practice should be prohibited, but whether it should be allowed to continue within public hospitals. This is objected to on the grounds that it amounts to a subsidy to the doctors who practise there and deprives the public of accommodation which ought to be used to shorten the waiting list. A 1972 White Paper, reporting on a rather sketchy study of this matter, argued that the abolition of private beds in public hospitals would have no significant effect on the length of the queues.[32] Though it sounds improbable, this may well be true, because many of the former private patients would join the queues, and experience has shown that in those departments in which pressure is greatest increase of provision promotes increase of demand and the queues soon become just as long as they were before. In any case the closure of private beds would not solve the problem of the co-existence of public and private medical services, and might merely stimulate the growth of facilities for institutional health care outside the NHS. So many people who feel unhappy about allowing private practice in NHS hospitals feel nevertheless that the practice should be allowed to continue, at least for some time to come.

Some of those who believe strongly that private medicine should be not only permitted but encouraged, and who realize the difficulty of unscrambling the public and private systems, as far as the hospitals are concerned, have recently come out with a new plan. It offers a three-tier arrangement: the cost of caring for chronic sickness, including geriatric and mental cases, would be paid directly out of tax revenue; compulsory insurance would be maintained at a level sufficient to support a service at the present NHS standard; and those who wished could pay additional voluntary contributions to earn additional or superior services either within the NHS or outside.[33] The result would resemble in certain respects what happens in most European countries. It could be argued that it would only be applying to health what we already do for pensions—namely, run a state insurance system in conjunction with private insurance schemes, both of which give differential benefits in return for differential contributions. But, as was pointed out in the Introduction, income maintenance and personal welfare services are not, and cannot be, governed by the same principles.

10 | The welfare services

In a book about London government in the 1960s S. K. Ruck defined the welfare services as those 'provided by local authorities to give assistance, other than medical and financial, to those needing such assistance through handicaps of age, or physical, mental or social infirmity'. The catalogue of the people receiving this kind of assistance includes the old, blind, deaf, dumb, permanently disabled or mentally handicapped, children deprived of a home life, unmarried mothers, the homeless, problem families, and 'down and outs'.[1] The common characteristic of the welfare services provided for all these various cases is that they are personal. This was reflected in the terms of reference given in 1968 to the Seebohm Committee: it was instructed to study the 'personal social services'. The word 'welfare' was not used. For definition of services by their objective it was too vague; for denoting an administrative area it was too narrow, for at that time welfare departments did not even include work with children let alone other more peripheral relevant services. Instead the Committee's task was defined by reference to the nature of the activities themselves, to the method of operation common to the services to be reviewed. The key word is 'personal'. This does not mean merely that there is a face-to-face meeting between client and agent, since this occurs even when pensions are paid out at a post office. It means that the two meet and communicate as persons, that the agent seeks to understand and interpret the needs of the client, and is prepared to exercise some measure of personal judgement, based on his knowledge, skill and experience, in rendering his—or more usually her—service. This relationship is characteristic also of such professions as medicine, law and teaching, but the addition of that invaluable, if imprecise, word 'social' indicates that these are not to be included in this category. 'Personal social services' well describes the subject of this chapter, but the term in common use before 1968 was 'welfare services', and we shall continue to use it till we arrive at Seebohm.

The welfare services as we know them took shape only in comparatively recent times, following the whittling down and final transformation of the Poor Law and public assistance which took place during this century, more especially in the inter-war period. The break with the past was more complete in Britain than in many European countries, where the trend was towards developing the welfare element within the social assistance services. There had also been abortive signs both in America and in Britain of an urge to advance along these lines. As far back as 1929 New York renamed its Poor Law 'Public Welfare Law', and gave it the task of doing everything necessary for those unable to maintain themselves, in order to 'restore such persons to a condition of self-support', and also to help those 'liable to become destitute' to escape this fate.[2] But this was not the pattern that was destined to prevail. Similarly in the late 1930s the London County Council proposed to rechristen its Public Assistance Committee 'Social Welfare Committee' and to call its Relieving Officers 'Welfare Officers'.[3] But here too events took a different path, and when the new name was eventually introduced, it was given, not to the old committee and officers, but to new ones, with the express purpose of breaking completely with the old tradition—particularly with that which clung to the Poor Law institution, or workhouse.

The consequence was that 'the welfare services department is as it were the residuary legatee of the old public assistance department'.[4] The term 'residuary' is particularly appropriate, because the heritage consisted of those bits and pieces of a welfare service which could not be assigned to specialized agencies when the Poor Law was broken up. And these bits and pieces were not even handed over as going concerns; the charge given to the welfare authorities was virtually to create services of a quite new kind, partly to replace those which were marked with the stamp of pauperism, and partly to supplement them. In its Report for 1944 the Assistance Board, which had been instructed to perform its task 'in such manner as may best promote the welfare of pensioners' observed that in doing this it was breaking new ground, and that 'there was no common body of doctrine or practice indicating the kind of services required'.[5] After 1948 it became necessary to evolve one, and as the shadow of the Poor Law and the workhouse receded, the features of a modern welfare service gradually emerged, together with its characteristic problems. These arose chiefly from the change in the relationship between the provider and the receiver of the service, as the latter, once classed as a pauper, came to be treated, and in due course to be generally referred to, as a client. The sphere of operation of the service was to be extended in principle from 'the poor' to the public. It was to be available to all, without regard to means. Of course most of the clients would still in fact be poor, but they would no longer be classed as such. This was bound to affect both the content of the service and the way in which it was administered.

Poor Law administrators are expected to discourage applicants for relief in order to restrict their operations to what is absolutely necessary and to put their mark of shame only on those quite unable to avoid it. A welfare authority, on the contrary, can publicize its wares, because its policy is to see that all who are in need of its service ask for it, and it hopes that publicity will help to cleanse it of the taint inherited from the Poor Law. So those in charge of the disabled were enjoined, as their first duty, to spread information widely about the new services. The new regime also required a redefinition of the powers and responsibilities of the new authorities, designed to fit the status of their intended clients. This was provided by legislation for the three major categories of beneficiaries, the children, the aged and the physically and mentally handicapped. The initial regulations were embodied in the Children Act of 1948 and in Part III of the National Assistance Act of the same year. When a blanket clause (such as had once fitted relations between guardians and poor) is replaced by a specification of rights and duties, inevitably there are gaps. The authorities responsible for the care of old people, for example, were authorized to provide residential accommodation for them, but not to do anything else for their general welfare. This frustrated the good intentions of many councils until the deficiency was made good by fresh legislation in 1968.[6]

Change in the status of the client posed new problems as regards 'the authority vested in the service and its agents. Referring to the services for children, Noel Timms writes: 'The child care worker has to come to terms with her authority (her statutory obligations) and her power (her forceful position in regard to both parents and children).'[7] In Poor Law times the authority over the pauper was limited only by responsibility to the officer's superiors and to the law. In a modern welfare service these responsibilities are still there, but there is also a direct responsibility to the client. There is vested in the service the power, and the duty, to prescribe in general terms what can be done, or given, to what categories of person and on what conditions, and the worker has the authority and the duty to decide, or at least recommend, what, within these limits, should be done to meet the claims and the needs of the client in each particular case. The power is very real, as always where someone has control over much-needed benefits, and the task of balancing obligations is a delicate one. This is particularly so because clients vary in character from the perfectly clear-headed person wanting help in obtaining that to which he has a right, to those of 'diminished responsibility', such as a confused old person, or a mentally handicapped one, or (rather different) the parents of a family in which things are going so badly wrong that a child is at risk. It is indeed true that his or her authority is something with which the social worker 'has to come to terms'.

We now turn from these general reflections on the nature of welfare services to survey briefly their development in this country since the last war, beginning with services for children. The right of a public authority to enter the home in the interests of the child had long been recognized in the case of education and of infant health; recognition came more slowly when the question was one of the vaguer notion of welfare. The approach lay through action to punish cruelty. The story can be traced back to the Select Committee of 1871 on 'the best means of preventing the destruction of the lives of infants put out to nurse for hire by their parents', and through a series of not very effective measures to deal with deliberate crime and gross neglect, to the Children's Act of 1933, which took the crucial step across the gap that lies between the punishment of crime and the promotion of welfare. This Act contained, in addition to a formidable array of penal clauses, a section providing that children 'in need of care and protection' could be brought before a juvenile court (without being charged with an offence) and placed in care of a 'fit person', who might be, and generally was, the local authority. Thus judicial procedure could be used, not only to punish parents for cruelty, but also to take their children away if they could not be trusted to look after them properly.

In 1946 there were 13 000 children (in England and Wales) 'in care' under this law, in addition to over 32 000 necessitous children maintained by the public assistance authorities.[8] But there was evidence to show that the new welfare approach had not fully prevailed over the old penal one. A voluntary committee under Mrs Hubback, which investigated the situation at that time, reported that in practice it proved difficult to do anything for the child until steps had been taken to prosecute the offending parent or guardian, and this was possible only if it could be shown that the neglect or ill-treatment of the child was 'wilful'.[9] This was equally true of the work of the National Society for the Prevention of Cruelty to Children, whose officers also operated by prosecuting or by threatening to prosecute. How closely the responsibilities of the social worker and criminal prosecutor are related is well illustrated by the cases of 'battered babies' of which so much has been heard of late.

Meanwhile the Curtis Committee had been given the task of inquiring how best to provide for 'children deprived of normal home life with their own parents and relatives'. It had interpreted its assignment as being confined to the study of the various ways of disposing of them after they had been removed from their own homes and had not felt 'called upon to deal with children who though suffering from neglect, malnutrition or other evils, are still in their own homes under their parents' care'. It hoped others would consider this important question (para. 7). In its recommendations as to treatment the Report (1946) followed the line of thought generally current at the time, namely that children taken from their homes should be put to live in conditions as much like a home as possible. Adoption and 'boarding out', or fostering, were probably the best solutions, provided the host families were well chosen. The Committee summed up its thoughts on this difficult issue by saying that, although there might be a greater risk of 'acute unhappiness' in a foster home, 'a happy foster home is happier than life as generally lived in a large community' (para. 422). This was no doubt true of the typical 'community' as it existed then, namely a big barrack-type institution, but the Committee looked with some favour on the intermediate solution of putting the children in smaller Homes or groups of cottages where more of the atmosphere of family life could be created.

There was considerable concern in the early 1970s about both fostering and adoption, brought to a head by the publicity very properly given to some tragic cases of maltreatment and unhappiness. Apart from the difficulties inherent in the tasks of selecting or approving foster or adoptive parents, and of supervising children in foster homes, there is a potential clash between rights and welfare. Since adoption has been, since 1926, a legal process which is permanent and irrevocable, the critical point is that at which it must be decided whether the transfer of full parental rights is, in the particular case, in the best interests of all concerned. As the Departmental Committee on the Adoption of Children (1972) said, there is here great scope for skilled case-work in investigating and counselling on both sides, and it recommended that there should be a statutory obligation on local authorities to provide a comprehensive adoption service. It also wanted a firmer declaration that, when rights and welfare clashed, the interests of the child must be paramount. But it is not easy to achieve this when parental rights are invoked to carry through what is judged to be a quite unsuitable transfer or to prevent a highly desirable one. In fostering the difficulty is the opposite, namely that foster parents have no firm rights and foster children no security. The natural parents can claim the child back, and the foster parents, who have been urged to treat the child as if he were their own, must be ready at any time to give him up. In a small but significant number of cases, some of them very distressing, the child has had to be given back even though the responsible agency thought it would have been better for him or her to stay with the foster parents. But the conclusion reached by a Home Office survey was that 'foster parents seem generally to have co-operated with the agency in plans for the child, even when this entailed parting with the child after a considerable period of time'.[10]

One of the most important recommendations made by the

Curtis Committee concerned administration. They insisted that the whole responsibility for children 'in care' should be entrusted to a single committee of the local authority, with a Children's Officer of senior rank as its executive agent. Opinions differed, they said, as to which committee should assume the responsibility, but 'the one point of agreement is that it should not be the Public Assistance Committee under another name' (para. 439). This recommendation, which was accepted, marks one of the last stages in the break-up of the Poor Law before its final liquidation. And it was a break-up in a form of which the Webbs would have approved. For although the children's department was to have the whole responsibility for the welfare of the children, it was not to be, like the old Poor Law, a general purpose authority. For the specialized services of education, health and the rest the 'deprived child' would use the same agencies as all other children. But the Curtis Committee, unlike the Minority Report, realized that, when this specialization had been carried as far as it would go, welfare would still remain as something that needed to have a service of its own, and a very important one.

The main recommendations of the Curtis Committee were put into effect and the advance of policy from that point followed lines which the Committee itself had foreseen. Legislation in 1948 and 1952 gave local authorities the power, not only to accept children placed with them by the courts, but also to receive into care other children found by them to be 'in need of care and protection', and also laid upon them the duty to seek out such children wherever they had cause to believe they might be found. But in these cases, where there was no court decision, the child could be taken from its home only with the consent of its parents or guardian, and this consent could be revoked at any time. In exceptional cases, however, the council could apply to the court for permission to 'assume parental rights' over the child, which meant that the parents could not take it back.

The next step was to develop welfare work in the home in two ways. First, to try to *prevent* a state of affairs from arising in which it would be necessary to take the child away, and secondly, to try to *create* a state of affairs which would allow the child to return to its parents as soon as possible. Preventive action is logically the final stage in the extension of welfare services because the intervention of a social worker in the affairs of a family before an acute need has become manifest can be regarded as—and may even become—interference. The power to engage in preventive action was explicitly conferred by an Act of 1963 which authorized local authorities to give 'advice, guidance and assistance' with a view to 'diminishing the need to receive children into or keep them in care'—which in fact many of them were doing already. A survey made in 1969 showed that 20 per cent of the cases were preventive in character.

The second reason why child welfare cannot be wholly detached from the judicial apparatus is that one of the things that may demonstrate a child's need for care and protection is its disorderly or delinquent behaviour, and the distinction between the two is a narrow one. There is general agreement that, from some points of view, it is best to avoid making the distinction for children below a certain age, and to treat all cases as 'children in trouble', presenting a question of welfare rather than of punishment. The difficulty is that, while this saves many delinquent children from the trauma of an appearance in court, it may make some of the more law-abiding (and their parents) feel that they are being classified among the delinquents. It is also the case that many quite young children suffer a sense of injustice (as do their parents also) if, when charged with an offence, they cannot get the question of their guilt or innocence established by due process of law. This led the British Labour government to drop a proposal made in 1965 to entrust this task in the first instance to Family Councils. So, although the trend here, as in all services with a welfare character, is from the judicial to the social, from the punitive to the helpful, and from confinement in an institution to treatment in the home, the system cannot help remaining mixed, and the judicial element in the mixture increases as one moves from one age group up to the next. The dividing ages in the British system are ten, fourteen and seventeen. Criminal responsibility begins at ten, but up to the age of thirteen the offender is treated as a child. At fourteen he becomes a 'young person', and is treated more formally and can be punished more severely, and at seventeen he becomes an adult. The Children and Young Persons Act of 1969 raised the minimum age of criminal responsibility to fourteen, but the 1970 government did not implement this. The Act did, however, also provide that children deemed to be in need of residential care should all be classed as children in trouble, whether convicted offenders or not, and sent to Community Homes, which were to replace the old Remand Homes, local authority Children's Homes and Approved Schools. Here they would receive, not punishment, but treatment. Four or five years later it was found, not surprisingly, that accommodation and staff were not yet adequate to meet the demand, and in particular that there was little provision for those deeply disturbed or aggressively delinquent young persons who caused havoc if placed in one of the ordinary Homes.

We turn now to the other major area of the personal welfare services, that concerned with those suffering from handicaps caused by old age or by physical or mental disabilities. In these cases the aim of a welfare service is not to cure, because in some conditions cure is impossible and in others it lies outside the competence of the service, but to combat the limiting effects of the disability on the personal and social life of the afflicted. Old age differs from the other disabilities in that the unsatisfied needs to which it is likely to give rise do not stem solely, or even primarily, from diminished physical or mental powers (though these gain in importance as age advances), but from fundamental and often sudden changes in the social situation caused by retirement, widowhood or isolation, accompanied generally by a substantial reduction of income. It is also important to remember that, unlike those suffering from serious physical or mental handicaps, the great majority of old people, especially the married, have no special need of help or service of any kind, statutory or voluntary. It follows that the services rendered affect only a minority of the age group and range from the establishment of what can be called community facilities, like clubs, through personal service in the home, like domestic help or 'meals-on-wheels', to places in which old people can be taken completely into care, in the same way as children deprived of home life.

And, in fact, the story of the development of welfare services for the old resembles in many respects that of the care of children. There is the same original inadequacy of the powers assigned to the local authorities, and their belated increase. And there is the same legacy of Poor Law institutions and the determination to eliminate them as fast as possible. These barrack-like ex-workhouses have, in the minds of old people, an almost penal character. Professor Townsend, who has made the most intensive study of Homes for the aged, tells how a matron in one of the modern Homes said: 'It's the one threat of discipline we have here—to send them back to the old institution.'[11] This is an intolerable situation. After the war the authorities made a considerable effort to build smaller Homes in which some consideration could be given to the special needs of the old. Much can be done by suitable architectural design and furnishing to make the inmates comfortable and help the crippled or rheumatic to get about and look after themselves with the minimum of help from others. It does not need much imagination to realize that it must be made easy for old people to get suitable spectacles and hearing-aids, that they need not only to be regularly seen by a doctor but to have the services of a chiropodist (very important) and perhaps a physiotherapist, and that there should be somebody handy who is a qualified nurse.

All this is well understood, but the translation of these ideas into practice is inevitably a slow business. This is partly due to the sheer magnitude of the task. In spite of the progress made since the war, 37 000 old people were still living in former Poor Law institutions in England and Wales in 1960, and there were very nearly another 37 000 in other types of public authority Homes. The sympathetic management of life in the Homes depends on having enough staff, sufficiently intelligent and willing to stay long enough to understand the problems with which they are supposed to deal. With the employment opportunities now open to women it is difficult to get staff of any kind, and the turnover rate is high. Finally, many of the unhappinesses that come with old age can never be overcome, and none of them without the active co-operation of the old people themselves, which the physical environment, however well designed, cannot of itself elicit. One of the most depressing features of Townsend's study is the picture it draws of old people sharing a house and meeting one another every day without developing any real system of communication between them or any intimate social relationships.[12]

So policy came to be directed more and more towards trying to keep old people at home, where they could live a normal community life, either in a family or on their own. To provide means for the latter, housing programmes today include dwellings specially designed for old people. Opinions differ how far the provision of suitably designed dwellings and appropriate community services (such as home helps, 'meals-on-wheels', cheap transport, social clubs) could make it possible to abolish altogether the 'old people's Home' by making it unnecessary for an old person to go into a residential institution unless and until he required such medical attention as could best be given in the geriatric section of a hospital. The contention of Peter Townsend that this should be policy's objective is countered by those who argue that the possibilities of community care for old people are being exaggerated, that many old people prefer to live in Homes of some kind, and that the impression gained that most of those in Homes are fit to live outside is misleading. It is only thanks to the conditions of life in the Home and the continuous attention they receive there that they are able to manage so much on their own. It seems probable that the trend in favour of domestic life in the community will continue, but not to the extent of eliminating the other alternatives.

It is true that recent studies have shown both that old people *in general* are less severely handicapped by old age and less consciously deprived of social life than had sometimes been imagined, and also that, even when living alone, they are not usually forgotten or deserted by their close relations. The family is, on the whole, doing its job conscientiously, and real isolation is exceptional.[13] But inquiries have also shown, if that were necessary, how heavy the burden can be for those who look after old people who are physically handicapped or, which can be still more demanding, mentally failing. In one place it was found that one in thirteen of the old people visited 'were causing great strain on the younger generation' and turning somebody into a drudge.[14] In another a daughter wrote to apply for a place in a Home for her mother because her husband had threatened to leave her, taking the children with him, if she continued to neglect them in order to look after her mother.[15] So if old people are increasingly to be absorbed into the community there must be a considerable expansion of the public and voluntary social services which, as we have seen, are necessary conditions for community care.

In the case of the blind, deaf, dumb, crippled, and mentally subnormal, the expansion of the services offered is due at least as much to the increase in our understanding of the nature of their disabilities and the improvement in the techniques of treatment as to the greater sense of responsibility towards the unfortunate. The effect has been to shift the emphasis from taking care of the helpless to overcoming their helplessness by education and training for a special kind of life, which may be tolerable and acceptable, though inevitably limited in scope. This began more than a hundred years ago for the blind when Braille perfected an embossed script that could be read with the fingers, and it has continued with the evolution of methods of training the blind to pursue a variety of occupations in which they can become at least as proficient as those with normal sight, and sometimes more so. Similarly ways were found to enable the deaf and the dumb to communicate, and even to break the isolation of those born deaf, who have never heard the sound of words. In all this much has been done not only by charitable societies but also by the associations of the blind and the deaf themselves. There was a time when it was widely believed that spastics were mentally deficient and mongols ineducable, but the falsity of these beliefs has been exposed, and methods of treatment have been developed which allow these afflicted people to enjoy the fullest life that their disability permits. But the provision made for cases of this kind is still lamentably inadequate.

All these services have both a medical and a social element in them, since there is need both for treatment of the physical condition and for help in adjustment to the demands and the opportunities of daily life. With these personal services goes the supply of special aids and equipment, which again may be both medical (hearing aids, artificial limbs) and social (telephone, radio). For those fit to take jobs the adjustment operates, so to speak at both ends, through training for the disabled man and through adapting jobs to suit the reduced capacities of the disabled, or establishing whole workshops designed to give sheltered employment to the handicapped. The Industrial Rehabilitation Units set up by the Ministry of Labour in 1944 provided a complex of medical treatment, industrial training and welfare services. A corporation known as Remploy was founded to run factories for the employment of the disabled, and it was laid down that all firms, except the quite small ones, should reserve

2 per cent (later raised to 3 per cent) of their jobs for handicapped workers. This last provision however, has not been effectively enforced.

Nevertheless the disabled in general, as distinct from such special types as the blind and the deaf, remained a neglected category among persons in need. Such was the view of those who, in the 1960s, launched an energetic campaign on their behalf, in which a leading part was played by the Disablement Income Group. The campaign had three main objects. First, to get a comprehensive inventory made of the disabled in every local government area in addition to the register of those actually receiving assistance. Secondly, to lay a clear responsibility on local authorities to provide the special welfare services, equipment and appliances needed by the disabled. Thirdly, to institute a special kind of cash benefit for disabled persons of all kinds, assessed, as in the case of industrial disablement, by reference to the nature and severity of the injury, rather than to loss of earnings. The Bill which became the Chronically Sick and Disabled Persons Act of 1970 had included provision for the first, but this was replaced in the Act itself by a requirement only to ascertain how many disabled persons there were in the area—a requirement which, said the critics, could be met by making a sample survey. The Act dealt fully and clearly, in principle, with the second point, but did not solve the problem of finding adequate funds. Progress was made towards a solution of the third point by the introduction of Invalidity Benefit for those whose incapacity to work persisted after their sickness benefit was exhausted, which could be enhanced by a disablement supplement or (as the Labour government of 1974 proposed) set at a higher level than other benefits, and by the adoption by the Conservative government of the Assistance Allowance for the severely disabled which had appeared in the abortive Crossman Plan for superannuation. This did not, however, meet the demand that disabled persons in general should be given the same rights as those injured at work or wounded on military service. But is it obvious that they should? What an injured workman or a wounded soldier receives includes an element of compensation related to risks faced with the knowledge that such compensation was payable. The position of those disabled by sickness or personal accident is different. The relevant criterion in their case could be said to be need only, and not compensation. But the arguments in favour of assessing their needs, as those of the other categories, by reference to the effects of the disablement itself rather than to some average money income are very strong. This question is raised again in the final chapter in the discussion of 'adequacy' and 'equity' as criteria for the assessment of benefits.

It is not possible to cover all the local welfare services here, but a few words must be said about services of a rather different kind from those described above, namely those which try to promote individual welfare through the medium of a social group, such as a youth club. As already noted (p. 83), plans for a post-war youth service were formulated while the war was in progress. It was to be under the education authorities, and would co-operate closely with the voluntary organizations which had been in the field for a long time past. The immediate and pressing need arose, according to the Youth Advisory Service, from the 'background of instability, social and economic, and of changing moral standards, against which the present generation has grown up', but they hoped that the service would not permanently retain the 'therapeutic element' which was inevitably present at the outset.[16] The aim of such a service was to provide a social environment which gave scope for the satisfaction of various needs, even—and perhaps particularly—needs which were not consciously felt by the participants before they joined. But participation must be entirely voluntary, and the young people must discover for themselves the opportunities offered by the group. The enterprise did not flourish. It did not attract enough workers or members, and it lacked resources. The Albemarle Report of 1960 inaugurated a new drive for expansion, and in the following decade youth service activities were developed on free and flexible lines in tune with the spirit of the times. Outside this movement there appeared a service of a different kind: not service *for* youth but service *by* youth, given freely by organized groups of young volunteers or by school children either directly to the old, blind and otherwise handicapped in the neighbourhood, or by being put at the disposal of the local authority. This was symptomatic of a new approach to the social problems of an area, which emphasized the potentialities and advantages of active participation by members of the community, on their own initiative, in what came to be called 'community work'. We return to this subject later in this chapter.

The purveyors of the services we have been discussing are the social workers, who give to them their distinctive character of *personal* service. The core of this company of workers consists of those who have qualified by taking the recognized training and are organized in professional associations. It is true that there are still a great many social workers employed by statutory authorities and voluntary organizations, especially at 'field level' (where the figure is said to be 60 per cent), who are without up-to-date professional qualifications, but it is the principles and standards of the professionals, as expressed in their training and upheld by their associations, that dominate the field. Their position was strengthened when, in 1970, after some years of planning and negotiation, eight specialized professional bodies joined together to create the British Association of Social Workers and in the following year there was established a Central Council for Education and Training in Social Work to cover all branches of the profession. The evolution of the profession of social work began in the closing years of the last century. The pioneers were voluntary organizations, the most important of which in Britain was the Charity Organization Society (COS). Its methods and its philosophy were developed by C. S. Loch who was its Secretary for thirty-eight years. Charity, he said, 'requires a social discipline; it works through sympathy; it depends on science. Its first thought is to understand, and to treat with the reverence that comes from understanding the individual, the family and the community.' It must give, not relief, but service, and its treatment must be 'adequate' to effect a cure by restoring the recipient to a state of self-sufficiency. 'Paupers', in other words, must be turned into 'citizens'. The method was casework and the workers, part voluntary and part salaried, were given a training. This was an innovation, and in due course the COS promoted the establishment of a School of Sociology from which grew the Social Science Department of the London School of Economics, and thereafter similar departments in nearly all the universities in the country.[17]

All this sounds unexceptionable. But in spite of the emphasis on science, training and service, in practice (see p. 39) the focus tended to be on the moral failure and moral rehabilitation of the

individual with, as the goal, his adaptation and willing submission to the conditions imposed on him by society and his
place in it. The first half of the twentieth century saw a significant
change. There began that development towards social democracy
which has been described in Part One of this book, bringing new
ideas about the status of the citizen in relation to his fellows and
to the government. More directly, the academic atmosphere in
which training took place favoured the objective scientific approach
to the subject as against the traditional moral attitude, and the
search for the social as against the purely individual causes of
the trouble. Also, with the expansion of the statutory social and
medical services social workers had a very practical job to do, in
learning exactly what help was available to their clients and enabling them to get it. Case-work was still essential, but it was
concerned less with converting the client to the principles of middle-
class morality than with the management of his immediate social
environment. Then came a shift, largely under American influence, towards the conception of case-work as the therapeutic
treatment of the individual's psychological deficiencies and
disorders. In her scathing criticism of this trend Baroness Wootton
argued that a misdirected ambition to achieve a status equal to
that of the higher professions, particularly medicine, was leading
social workers to attempt to render services beyond their competence. It was better that they should devote themselves to
informing and advising clients about the social services and the
benefit they could obtain from them rather than to 'counselling'
them on how to conduct their personal lives.[18]

It is perfectly true that one ever-present objective of social
work is to ensure that the services provided for the benefit of
those in need are used to the best possible advantage. But
Baroness Wootton seems to underrate the complexity of this
task. It is by no means a mechanical operation; it calls for investigation, interpretation and communication, all of which
require the use of personal skills. It is not enough simply to
know what the services are and how they work. Studies have
recently been made which show how imperfect the communication between worker and client can often be because of differences of social class, education and ideas about the nature of
cause and effect. But these barriers can be overcome, given the
necessary skills and the right approach. In one of the few serious

attempts to evaluate social work it is said that the role of the
worker 'as an enabler, making needs explicit and helping clients
to accept services which they need and to which they are entitled
was an important one among old people whose expectations are
often low'.[19] There is in this an educational element which is
more explicit in some other types of case, as when a disabled
person must be taught how to make the best use of gadgets and
appliances, or 'self-care' in the routine of daily life is taught
to a person who is mentally afflicted.

It is a short step from this to action the aim of which is to
change the client's behaviour. This, sometimes referred to as
'assertive' case-work, is held by many people to lie very near to
the boundary between the permissible and the objectionable. Its
acceptability in any particular situation must vary according to
the degree of assurance or general consensus that exists about the
kind of behaviour towards which the change is to be directed,
the suitability of the methods used and the competence of the
social worker to use them. The Probation Officer tries to induce,
or to help, his charge to behave in a law-abiding manner; that is
his function. But how far should he go in trying to change his
personality or his attitude to society? Preventive case-work
in child care must often involve trying to persuade, or to help,
a mother to manage her home and treat her child in a more
orderly and understanding way. But does this mean that she is
'to encourage certain child-rearing practices and discourage
others'? This is one example given by Olive Stevenson of what
she had in mind when she said, in a talk to the Association of
Social Workers, that: 'It seems unarguable that social workers
are agents of social control, if by that is meant that they encourage individuals to adapt to certain ways of behaviour
which society deems desirable and from which they have devi-
ated.'[20]

This interpretation of the nature of social work, with its frank
(and salutary) recognition of the power vested in its agents,
draws attention to two dangers, of which the speaker showed that
she was fully aware. One is that of encouraging in social workers
an inclination to enter all their cases through a 'diagnostic
doorway', looking for a personality disorder that could be
treated. The other is that, if social case-work is seen as a way of
enabling people not only to make the best of things as they

are but also to 'adapt to' the behaviour demanded by them, the social services themselves may come to be seen as offering a substitute for social reform, when in fact they should be associated with movement for social change. A very different emphasis is offered by Adrian Sinfield when he sums up the functions of a modern social worker by saying that she 'imparts information about rights, makes services available, helps to communicate needs to those in authority, and encourages action by the individual, family and group on their own behalf as well as on the behalf of the community'.[21] Here the stress is on the rights of the client, the services of the worker and the development of the community. But it would be foolish to imagine that anything could be achieved in this way unless social workers were, at the same time, agents of social control, as are all members of all the personal service professions.

In 1965 the Labour government set up a Committee under Frederic Seebohm 'to review the organization and responsibilities of the local authority personal social services in England and Wales, and to consider what changes are desirable to secure an effective family service'. It reported in 1968[22] and its recommendations were incorporated in the Local Authority Social Services Act of 1970. A separate Report was made on Scotland.[23] This move was sparked off by concern about the treatment of 'children in trouble', a category which included those in need of care, those 'at risk' and also young delinquents; hence the invitation to consider especially how to create a family service, an idea which had already been ventilated. The Committee quickly decided that 'family' must be taken to mean 'everybody', including the childless, single, widowed and divorced (para. 32) and proceeded to survey the whole field of work of the children's and welfare departments, as well as the social work elements in the health, education and housing services. But it kept well within its terms of reference as regards making this a study of organization. Its central recommendation, which was adopted, was simple, namely that all these services should be brought together in a single unified social service department. It considered and rejected the idea of creating the 'effective family service' by strengthening and enlarging the children's department, while keeping the welfare department (for the old and handicapped) separate. It also rejected suggestions for merging welfare with health, and possibly with children's services and even education as well, though here there was the qualification that the amalgamation of the health and social services might come at some future date.

When small units are combined to create a large and complex one, two questions arise. Will internal departmentalization develop and break the perfect unity, thus restoring some features of the previous system? The first crucial test came when ten-year plans had to be prepared for submission early in 1973, for nothing reveals divergent or competing interests in an organization more clearly than the discussion of budgetary allocations. Secondly, however comprehensive the enlarged unit, there always remain some areas in which responsibility is split between it and one of its neighbours. Two examples of this can be cited here. The social service department took over the care of the under-fives in day nurseries and play-groups as well as the supervision of child-minders, but nursery schools remained under the education authority. And it so happened that just at this time a certain rivalry developed between private-enterprise play-groups and public-authority nursery schools. More serious were the possible effects of transferring social services for the mentally handicapped from the local authority health department to the new social service department and not to the Area Health Authority of the reorganized NHS. Some critics maintained that this would make it impossible to have a unified mental health service.

The organizational change had implications for the role, and therefore for the training, of social workers, and the Committee gave attention to these matters, but in a carefully restricted way. It was not able to undertake any research into the effectiveness of social work and its methods, or 'to sound consumer reaction to the services in any systematic fashion' (para. 43). But it did nevertheless arrive at the far-reaching conclusion that an integrated social service department should be staffed, for its daily routine work, by generalists. It accepted the widely held view that specialization, both in work and in training, had gone too far, causing a fragmentation of the service and encouraging what it called a 'symptom-centred approach' to cases. A family with several problems might be visited by several workers independently, no one of whom was concerned to assess the situation as a whole. A case is on record of a family which had been visited on behalf of at least six public agencies and six voluntary organizations, and whose members had spent about a dozen periods in various welfare institutions.[24] A reaction against this was already in progress through what an American writer in 1962 called a 'new shift in focus' (or we might say the revival of an earlier one), as a result of which 'both in case-work practice and in recent theoretical articles in the professional literature, the family as a group has begun to emerge as the unit of case-work treatment'.[25] At the same time there was, in the training departments, a movement to create an alternative to post-diploma specialization. It began at the London School of Economics in 1954 with a 'generic' course based on the elements common to all forms of case-work, and suitable as a training for such services as child care, probation, medical social work or family case-work. This fitted very well with the Committee's proposal for a unified service, for its view was that, to get the benefit of an effective family service, 'it is essential that the family or individual should be the concern of one social worker with a comprehensive approach to the social problems of his clients' (para. 516).

On the content of the training, as distinct from its organization, the Committee had little to say, except on one point: this should be reconsidered 'so that attention is paid to work with groups and communities'. The new element here is work with communities, and on this it was awaiting the report of a Study Group set up by the Gulbenkian Foundation under Dame Eileen Younghusband.[26] Community development had already been recognized as an activity of local authorities, and what it signified essentially was active encouragement of and co-operation with groups and societies in the community which were propagating ideas about local social problems and their treatment, and campaigning for action to meet the needs to which they drew official attention. For this purpose some authorities had appointed a special officer for community development. The basic aim, said the Younghusband Committee, was to escape from the static approach of adjustment to things as they are and adopt a dynamic role of helping people to adjust to changes which are taking place, and stimulating joint action to bring about changes which are desired. This conception of participant democracy has repercussions beyond the welfare services, and we return to it in the final chapter.

But the Seebohm Committee recognized two other forms, or aspects, of work with communities. One closely parallels the intended function of the community physician in the reorganized NHS. It consists in 'effort devoted to investigating the needs of an area, and to the overall planning and co-ordination of services and resources, both statutory and voluntary' (para. 478). This is obviously very important, and would presumably include such things as compiling a register of the disabled, referred to above. But the greatest need is for an evaluation of social work and case-work methods and for a clear definition of objectives. The most crucial problems faced in social work arise from uncertainty about aims and still more about the effects achieved by the action taken. This kind of uncertainty is common to most personal service professions, including, as we have seen, to medicine; but it is greater in social work than in most, and will remain so until more research has been done in the field, in which weight is given to the evidence of the clients themselves. The other aspect of work with communities mentioned by the Committee is important only because it illustrates the vagueness of some thinking on this subject. It is said that 'a clear responsibility should be placed upon the social service department for developing conditions favourable to community identity and activity' (para. 483)—surely a formidable task.

The proposals for organizational changes were put into effect by the Act of 1970, but it rested with the authorities to see how best to pursue the objectives set out in the Report as a whole. Naturally the changes caused some confusion, and planning was complicated by the knowledge that the areas of the counties would before long be changed as well. It was soon noticed that in many areas there was a marked increase in the total case-load, due partly to the picking up of cases which had slipped through the interstices between specialized units, and partly to the increased accessibility of the services when all applicants could 'knock on the same door'. It was reported of Cheshire that 'typically, the number of referrals for help doubled in the first few months and departments were left with actual work-loads increased by 20 per cent and still rising'. There was a fear that this might, for a time, threaten the standard of performance.[27]

The success of the scheme depends to a large extent on whether 'generic' social work is both satisfactory for the client and satisfying for the worker, and on achieving a good working relationship between the generalists and the specialists. On the first point, the fact that some workers with long experience in a particular kind of service felt insecure when taking on other kinds does not imply that new recruits would necessarily have the same difficulty. But fear was expressed in some quarters that workers dealing with a wider variety of needs and clients would be less personally involved in their cases and more like agents carrying out the instructions of their superiors, whether professional specialists or bureaucrats.

The need for specialists remains, and their role was seen by the Committee to be that of consultants at headquarters and also perhaps with area teams, though here their function is likely to be more that of supervisors or directors. The place of so-called 'consultants' in the NHS is quite different; they are not supervisors of generalists, but the top echelon in teams of specialists which constitute the operational staff of the hospitals. The Committee anticipated that the present set-up would be subject to change and that new specializations would emerge, but it did not venture to prophesy what these might be.

It is characteristic of the welfare services that every advance made, either by introducing new benefits or appointing more staff, seems to create fresh grounds for criticism or dissatisfaction. 'Each additional social worker appointed,' said a commentator on the first few months of 'Seebohm', 'revealed the need for two more.'[28] It is not only that cases previously overlooked are brought to light, but that with extra staff new possibilities are opened up. When a new benefit is granted to a particular category of persons, like the attendance allowance for the disabled, the boundaries of the category must be defined, and at once it appears that injustice is being done to some who fall outside the boundaries. But this is how progress takes place in an enterprise for which there can be no fixed or final goal.

11 | Housing

Housing may legitimately be included in a study of social policy. A home, or at least a dwelling of some sort, is a necessary condition of health, security and welfare, the three objectives of social policy listed in the Introduction. Modern governments accept certain responsibilities concerning the quality of the commodity (a dwelling) and its availability to the individual consumer, in the discharge of which they intervene in, or interfere with, the operation of the market, in a manner characteristic of social services. But these responsibilities are not precisely defined in terms which would give the citizen a legally enforceable right to be housed. The authorities are under a political obligation to do the best they can with the powers that they possess. The 1971 White Paper *Fair deal for Housing* defined the aim of Conservative policy as 'a decent home for every family at a price within their means'.[1] But this describes a long-term objective, not an immediate responsibility. It cannot be achieved at a stroke. Governments, both central and local, can pursue this objective in any of three ways, or by a combination of all of them, namely by encouraging action which leads towards it, by curbing or preventing action incompatible with it, or by making and managing their own direct contribution to it. Differences between one housing policy and another depend very much on how these three types of action are used and combined. Then there is another level, which we may see as a higher one, namely that of the overall planning of the physical environment. Here what is at stake is not the quantity of housing, but the quality of a culture, and only governments have the power to deal with environments as wholes. Their responsibility is to this extent an immediate one, in the discharge of which they are, in principle, representing the views and the values current in the society.

It should be evident that housing is one of the most elusive and intractable of all the problems with which social policy is confronted. It is not easy to measure even the present need for houses. House-room is a peculiarly elastic commodity. In times of shortage people manage to make do with what they have got. They stay in small homes after their families have outgrown them, and young couples begin their married life in a room in a parental house although they would much prefer to have a home of their own. The volume and urgency of such concealed demand are difficult to estimate. One cannot arrive at a conclusion about the need for houses by setting the total number of rooms in the country against the total population. For houses, once they have been built, are immovable and cannot follow shifting demand; so the geographical distribution of rooms does not coincide with that of people to live in them. And even within one locality the proportion of rooms per person (or of persons per room) differs greatly from house to house. Overcrowding and under-occupation may exist side by side. The 1961 census showed 'houses and households just about in balance overall though unevenly distributed';[2] there were, by then, enough houses in the country as a whole, but there was at the same time a serious housing shortage in many areas, especially the metropolis.

When one turns from an estimate of present needs to one of future needs, the calculation becomes still more difficult. It is not simply a matter of allowing for the increase in the population, since the magnitude of the demand for homes depends on its age-composition and social structure, and policy-makers must try to forecast these, mainly by projecting current trends into the future. It is hardly possible, however, to do this with any degree of accuracy for as far ahead as the buildings they are planning are likely to survive. A movement towards early marriage and small families will increase the number of potential households per thousand inhabitants and reduce the demand for large houses, while a lengthening of the expectation of life of the elderly will increase the demand for small ones. But the most difficult factor to assess and allow for is the geographical shift of the population, or internal migration. It is possible to exercise some influence over this through regional planning, but in general the immediate aim of plans for industrial and urban development is to find ways of absorbing those who are already there or on their way, either by developing areas threatened with decay, or by trying to accommodate the 'overspill' from crowded cities.

Then there is the question what to build. The types of housing now on the market vary so enormously that they hardly seem to be members of the same species—from the bungalow to the tower block, the terrace to the housing estate, the luxury flat to the suburban villa and the commuter's residence. And the whole question of how to deploy the buildings so as to make the maximum use of scarce land, by obtaining an adequate density of people per acre while providing sun and air, open spaces, peace and quiet and easy access to schools, shops, main roads and railways, is the subject of heated and inconclusive debate. In the 1960s high-rise blocks of flats were all the rage; in the 1970s they were fiercely attacked. So the responsibility that rests on the builders, both private and public, is a very heavy one.

Building houses is inevitably a rather slow process, in spite of modern devices for standardization and prefabrication. It may be interrupted by the weather or held back by competing claims for the limited stock of materials and labour available to the building industry as a whole. Successive governments rival each other in their boasts and their promises as to the number of dwellings they have produced, or are going to produce when in power. It is not easy to keep these promises. It must be remembered that the replacement of obsolete houses and the clearance of slums may be, in terms of welfare, an even more urgent task than that of building additions to the total stock of houses. A housing programme must be prepared to destroy as well as to create, so that the net increase in the number of dwellings achieved in a given period will be less than the number of new ones built. When it is decided that an area is to be the object of total renewal, a considerable time may elapse between the scheduling of the area and the commencement of demolition, during which the houses are being evacuated and thereafter standing empty. Some of the houses will be still fit to live in, or capable of being made fit at a comparatively low cost—but only for a short spell until demolition begins. The housing authority must decide whether to invest public money in houses with only a few years to stand, and will be influenced by the urgency of the need for accommodation and the length of the waiting list. If not officially occupied, empty houses may be taken over by 'squatters'. This began to happen in 1969 in a rather haphazard way, but soon came to be organized by various *ad hoc* societies or pressure groups intent on securing the use of empty houses in so-called 'grey areas' as accommodation, even if only temporarily, for the homeless and the ill-housed. The owner of a house occupied in this way could apply for an eviction order, but the courts tended to be sympathetic with orderly squatters, and allow them time to move. Some local authorities, notably in London, accepted the desirability of using empty houses in this way, if it did not mean delaying redevelopment or letting families jump the queue, and came to terms with the squatters' organizations. But it was not an easy relationship to maintain.

Meanwhile a change of policy was taking place as to the best way of dealing with 'grey areas'. At one time slum clearance and urban renewal were seen as a total replanning and replacement of the buildings in an area, and specific powers were given to the authorities to pull down good buildings in order to have a *tabula rasa* on which to create something wholly new. In face of the failure to meet the intense pressure of demand in some areas, and of the discovery that the number of sub-standard houses capable of rehabilitation had been generally underestimated, it was decided that the attempt to solve the problem by 'schemes of widespread, comprehensive redevelopment' was unnecessarily disruptive, and that much more should be done 'to improve and repair houses that can be improved and to get rid of the unfit ones'.[3] This policy of selective renewal can be pursued in part by extending the system, initiated in 1949, of grants to landlords who carry out improvements to their houses by installing the basic amenities needed to bring them up to standard requirements.

When the decent homes have been constructed, they must, said the White Paper quoted above, be obtainable by every family 'at a price within their means'. It is obvious that the capital required to buy or build a house is much more than most people have at their disposal. But their demand can nevertheless become effective if they are enabled to substitute payments out of income for the outlay of capital. This means that they must either borrow the capital at interest and gradually repay it, or else rent a house either from a landlord whose capital is invested in housing for profit or from a public authority which provides houses in discharge of its statutory obligations. None of these processes can fairly be said to be trouble-free, and a large part of housing policies everywhere has been concerned with ways of negotiating loans and regulating rents.

We have already reviewed the problems that claimed attention after the First World War, and the policies that were adopted to meet them, and we saw that some of the measures introduced at that time to cope with what was thought to be a temporary emergency were still in force twenty years later. Then came the Second World War, which revived all the problems created by the First, but in a more acute form. Not only did building cease, but vast numbers of houses were destroyed both in Britain and in many of the countries of Europe, especially Germany. In the boom conditions of the post-war revival the cost of building went steadily up, and land values rocketed in the areas of rapid development. At the same time, in the atmosphere of the Welfare State, the level of expectation and the sense of obligation to satisfy it both rose. But the ingredients of which housing policies were compounded remained essentially the same as before the war: subsidies, cheap loans, tax relief, rent restrictions, and rent allowances. Nobody came to the rescue with any new ideas, unless one were to count as such the British initiative in the creation of New Towns. The difference between the various national policies were caused, rather, by the different ways in which the old devices were employed. Speaking very generally, one might hazard the opinion that in Britain housing policy has been more deeply enmeshed in the wrangles of party politics, that housing legislation is more complicated, and that administration is more fussy and paternal than in most of the countries of Continental Europe.

British policy, unlike that of most European countries, has been based on a sharp differentiation between the public and the private sector, or between council houses and privately-owned houses. In the context of new building this is tantamount to a distinction between houses to let and houses to sell. For economic conditions since the war, combined with statutory rent restriction, have progressively produced a situation in which it is no longer profitable to invest money in building dwellings for letting, except for a small clientèle of well-to-do people who want a temporary home or a *pied-à-terre*. So it is roughly true to say that, while councils build only for letting, private investors build only for occupation or sale.

The political parties differed in principle as to the proportion in which these two methods of production and types of product should contribute to the total national stock of dwellings. The Conservatives favoured private enterprise and house ownership; Labour had a preference for the production by public authorities of houses for letting. Both recognized that any housing policy must give what it considered to be an appropriate place to each. These divergent views have been reflected in the methods adopted to encourage buildings. The standard form of assistance to local authorities is a subsidy to help meet the charges on the capital borrowed to finance the building, but subsidies can be of different kinds, designed to produce different effects. In the aftermath of war it was necessary to run a crash programme to cope with accumulated arrears. Aneurin Bevan, for the Labour government, decided that the operation must be a planned one and that 'the speculative builder, by his very nature, is not a plannable instrument. . . . We rest the full weight of the housing programme upon the local authorities.'[4] Private building was made subject to licence and a general subsidy was offered to local authorities on all domestic building.

The Conservatives, when the situation seemed ripe for it, took the brake of the licence off private building and in 1956 abolished the general subsidy for council houses and replaced it by subsidies for special purposes, such as slum clearance, redevelopment, New Towns and homes for old people. But these 'special' purposes did in fact cover a pretty wide area of cases. In 1961 the general subsidy was reintroduced, at a lower level, and for the first time there was positive discrimination in favour of authorities in greatest financial need. Then in 1972 came the important Conservative Housing Finance Act which once more abolished general subsidies and replaced them by a variety of grants for specific purposes, including some of the former ones, but in principle directed to meeting necessary or, one might say, permissible deficits incurred in executing programmes in conformity with statutory requirements. The most important of these, which we discuss below, were for raising rents to a 'realistic' level and granting rebates to families deemed unable to pay at that level. The intention was that the basic costs of normal housing programmes should be met out of local revenue, primarily that received from tenants in the form of rents.

In the private sector the vital factors are the availability of capital on loan or mortgage and the rate of interest charged on it. Since, as already mentioned, building to rent is no longer profitable, the key figure is the owner-occupier, who builds for himself or buys from another, since it is his ability to pay for his house, whether built to order or as a speculation, that keeps the market alive and house production active. Governments can help him in two ways: by tax concessions with respect to interest on loans, and by enabling him to borrow on terms more favourable than those of the open market. British tax law exempts from income tax money spent as interest on a loan raised by mortgaging house property. It was arguable, when the borrower had to pay tax on the notional income received from the property in which he invested the borrowed capital, that he ought not to pay tax also on the income he had forgone in order to raise the capital. But when the tax (Schedule A) on the property was abolished this argument lapsed; the concession, however, was retained. It can be defended on the grounds that it stimulates the building of much-needed houses and so relieves the pressure on rented dwellings. It also encourages owner-occupation, which many people believe is a socially desirable form of tenure. And some concession of this kind can be justified as long as council houses are being subsidized, from both taxes and rates, to the advantage of the rent-paying tenants. But the sum lost to the Exchequer is very large; at the beginning of the 1970s it was approaching £300 million a year. Also council tenants are in general less well-off than those who buy houses, so that their need may be said to be the greater, though house purchasers are by no means all wealthy people any more than all council tenants are poor. The one really indefensible feature of the system is that, since the larger a man's income the higher his rate of tax, the richer he is the more he benefits from the concession. Consequently most critics propose to amend the system rather than to abolish it. This can be done both by limiting the concession made to the rich and by making easier the terms on which the less well-to-do can obtain mortgages. An example of the latter is the 'option mortgage' introduced by the Labour government in 1967. It offers benefits to people of modest or low incomes who pay income tax at less than the standard rate and cannot therefore receive the full value of the concession. They are able in certain circumstances to get a greater reduction of the interest payable on the mortgage by choosing to receive a government subsidy in lieu of the normal tax concession. Another device, recently proposed by the National Housebuilding Council, is the 'flexible interest' subsidy payable directly to the house purchaser to cover the amount by which the cost of servicing his mortgage exceeds 20 per cent of his gross income. It would be limited to mortgages below a certain maximum and the subsidy would be reduced as the borrower's income rose. It is claimed that this would enable a family with an income of £26 a week to buy a house worth £6000 at a cost to public funds less than that of providing it with a council house.[5] Something on these lines is in use in the United States.

Most European countries have similar arrangements for helping to finance the building and purchase of houses. Tax concessions were exceptionally generous in Germany after the war, so much so that the situation got out of hand and gave rise to some scandals. The Norwegian government which has been providing more than half the funds for house building, has done so to a significant extent by interest-free loans. In Switzerland, on the other hand, the conditions in the open market as regards the interest on and repayment of mortgages have been so favourable that no government intervention was necessary.[6] Of special importance in Europe has been the role of national finance corporations and non-profit housing associations in operating these transactions. It is normal to have one or more public or quasi-public finance corporations or banks through which funds are channelled, as loans or as subsidies, to housing associations, individuals or public authorities according to the intentions of the national housing policy. The terms on which loans and subsidies are granted vary according to the nature or the means of the recipient. In Sweden the execution of the policy is directed and regulated in this way by the Royal Housing Board, which provides some of the funds itself and lays down the terms on which the rest are allocated; for example, the loan could cover 100 per cent of the cost for public authorities, 95 per cent for co-operatives and 85 per cent for private builders.[7] In France the *Crédit Foncier,* the *Caisse des Dépôts* and other similar financial institutions channel funds in much the same way. Important among the recipients are the housing corporations and societies grouped in the so-called HLM (*Habitations à Louer Modéré*) organization. This replaced the pre-war *Habitations à Bon Marché*, and the change of title from 'cheap' to 'at moderate rent' indicates the extension of its operations upwards into higher income brackets.[8] The corresponding Italian organization is the *INA-Casa* and in both countries a part of the money invested in housing is provided by a pay-roll tax on industry.[9] Housing societies and co-operatives occupy a central position in these systems, since they stand between direct public provision of dwellings for letting to the poorer families and the independent buying and building of houses by the well-to-do, and serve in particular the needs of the middle range of families with moderate incomes. It is only recently that British housing policy has made significant moves in the same direction.

Housing trusts and associations had existed in England since the latter part of the nineteenth century as private voluntary organizations to build homes for certain classes of person in certain areas. Some, like the Peabody fund, were charitable (though paying a limited dividend to investors), and others were co-operative. The Housing Act of 1936 had given them a legal status within the category of Friendly Societies, and they were allowed to borrow from the Public Works Loan Board on the same terms as local authorities. After the war scant attention was paid to their interests, and Beveridge, writing in 1948, said of them that 'housing societies today, from the government of the day, get warm words and cold comfort'.[10] The situation remained virtually unchanged until 1961, when a Housing Act authorized the advancement of direct loans to housing associations up to a total of £25 million to help schemes approved by the Minister. This was by way of experiment, and was followed in 1964 by an Act setting up a Housing Corporation to encourage the establishment of non-profit housing societies to 'provide and manage rented houses, or houses on a co-ownership basis'. The Corporation was authorized to devote up to £100 million of public funds in advances to projects of this kind in partnership with the independent building societies, which agreed to put up twice the amount. For some time the success of the project seemed very dubious, but by the early 1970s it was becoming apparent that schemes based on the co-ownership principle, in which members acquire a stake, or share, in the property itself as well as a tenancy on favourable terms, had some prospect of making a significant contribution to the supply of houses and to this extent replacing the vanishing private landlord in the cities. But the movement remains peripheral in relation to government housing policy, whereas in some European countries it has been more fully incorporated into it.

When the war ended all countries agreed that the system of general rent restriction needed drastic revision, but this proved to be easier said than done. The decisive step in British policy was taken in 1957. The Rent Act of that year lowered the maximum rateable value of houses subject to rent control, and thus released at once some 400 000 in England and Wales. And it provided for the decontrol of other dwellings when new tenancies were negotiated—the so-called 'creeping decontrol'—which caused the release of another 500 000 in the first two years. The general effect was not as catastrophic as some people had feared, but neither did it do as much to encourage building houses to let to working-class families as some people had hoped. The Act contained some rather complicated clauses designed to protect the interests of both landlords and tenants. In certain circumstances, such as when repairs were carried out, landlords might raise their rents to a prescribed limit and rules were laid down governing the conditions under which tenants could be given notice to quit. But these regulations have not been very well observed, partly because they were not properly understood, and partly because they were deliberately ignored. Two years after the Act was passed it was found that some 20 per cent of the controlled houses were let at rents higher than those permitted by the law. More scandalous, but fortunately less widespread, was the use made by some utterly unscrupulous landlords of various tough methods, including physical violence, to drive out sitting tenants whom the law protected in order to let rooms at higher rents, a practice which came to be known as 'Rachmanism' after its most notorious exponent.

Old-style rent control simply froze the rent at the current level and gave the sitting tenant virtually complete security of tenure. This meant that, as market rents rose, tenants were to an increasing extent subsidized by their landlords, who consequently had neither a financial incentive nor, very often, the means to maintain their property, still less to improve it. In the furnished letting sector a rather different system had been in practice since 1946. The Act of that year had established Rent Tribunals with power to assess the rents of furnished rooms on the application of the landlord, the tenant or a public authority. They resembled a Magistrate's Court in that they consisted of lay persons serving under a legally qualified chairman. They differed in that they had no legally defined standard to apply in making their assessment. They were told that they could confirm the existing rent, or 'reduce it to such sum as they may, in all the circumstances, think reasonable', or dismiss the case. They could not raise the rent, but they could give security of tenure for a limited period. They operated in a very restricted area comprising only about 2 per cent of the national stock of dwellings, but they were an interesting experiment in rough popular justice, and they marked a step away from crude rent control to the flexible regulation of rents.

Rent regulation was introduced in 1965 for the much larger category of unfurnished dwellings of rateable value not above £400 in Greater London and £200 elsewhere—figures which by 1973 had risen to £1500 and £750 respectively. The system differed in four important respects from that for furnished lets. First, the application went to a professional Rent Officer who gave his judgment: only on appeal from either side against this judgment did it go to an Assessment Committee, a body similar to a Rent Tribunal. Secondly, the Act included guidance as to the standard to be used in making the assessment. The Officer or Committee was to take account of 'the age, character and locality of the dwellinghouse and its state of repair', but to eliminate the effect of a competitive market by acting on the supposition that supply and demand were roughly in balance. The result was known as the 'fair rent': fair to both landlord and tenant. Thirdly, by this procedure rents could be either reduced or increased. At first reductions and increases occurred in about equal proportions, but by 1970 77 per cent of the applications led to an increase of rent and only 17 per cent to a decrease.[11] Fourthly, the new rent could be registered, after which it was the official rent for at least three years, during which time the tenant had full security of tenure. After that a new assessment might raise the rent further, and, if the tenant agreed to pay, his security of tenure continued. In the following year (1966) regulation was extended from rent to rates by the institution of a statutory system of rate rebates. Scales of rebate were drawn up adjusted to the size of the family, its gross income and the total amount of the rates due. The rebate was obtainable whether the rates were included in the rent or not. This could not be called an 'anti-poverty' measure, since those on Supplementary Benefit (whose rent and rates were paid for them) gained nothing, while some rebate could be obtained by an occupier with a large family and high rates with a gross income of £50 a week, or possibly even more.

By the early 1970s rents, taking private and council houses together, had certainly risen from what they had been some twenty years before, not only absolutely but as a proportion of spendable income. Nevertheless, measured in this way, they were not quite as high as at the beginning of the century. It is difficult to make precise comparisons, but it appears that before the First World War the average rent absorbed about 15 per cent of the family budget of the average wage-earner. Shortly before the Second World War the figure was about 13 per cent and it fell rapidly after the war to as low as 7 per cent in the 1950s. Thereafter it rose until in the early 1970s it was again around 13–14 per cent, rising to as much as 18 per cent for very low-income families. These figures may be compared with the 17 per cent in Sweden in the 1950s and 35 per cent before the Second World War. Obviously the conception of what a family can afford is a very elastic one, and in practice the burden varies greatly with the level of income. The value of average figures is very limited.[12]

The 'fair rent' idea was ridiculed by many people as nonsensical, but it proved to be workable. So much so that in 1972 the Conservative government, by its Housing Finance Act, applied it also to council houses. These constituted at that time just under 30 per cent of the total housing stock, or twice as much as private rented accommodation. It has long been clear that the rent situation on council estates was chaotic. The rents had been kept well below the level prevailing in the private sectors by means of subsidies which benefited tenants irrespective of their needs and resources. The system was manifestly inequitable. It had been adopted partly because of the widespread dislike of using means-tested rebates extensively, or even of using them at all. But the rents had been rising step by step for some years past and use was being made of rebates to an extent which many councils disliked. The system was proving ineffective. The 1972 Act brought all council houses under the 'fair rent' system. Councils were to fix provisional rents which would be reviewed by Rent Scrutiny Boards appointed by the government. These would function in exactly the same way as the Rent Assessment Committees. It was assumed that, as a result, rents would be substantially increased—some said they would be doubled—and it was laid down that progress towards the 'fair rents' should begin with an increase of £1 a week in all areas in which rents had not been raised during the previous year. At the same time a general decontrol programme was to start, to phase into the 'regulated' category dwellings whose rents were still frozen; here too, rents would inevitably go up.

It is obvious that this must increase, not reduce, the number of families unable to pay their rent without the help of a rebate, and the Act not only imposed a statutory obligation on councils to reduce the rent for low-income families, but laid down in detail exactly how the rebate was to be calculated. The basis was to be a 'needs allowance' proportional to the size of the family, and a 'minimum rent' of 40 per cent of the actual rent (but not less than £1). If the family income was equal to the 'needs allowance' it would pay only the 'minimum rent'; for every £1 it fell below it the rent would be reduced by 25p, and for every £1 it rose above it the rent would be increased by 17p. This method of assessment was meant to last, though the specific figures mentioned would of course be subject to change. It was impossible to put public and private housing under the same system of rent regulation without giving them the same right to rent reduction. So the Act extended the concession to private tenants in the form of an allowance equal to the rebate which would have been due had they been council tenants. But of course this can be paid to them only if they apply for it, and landlords are therefore required to inform their tenants about the scheme. Even so experience suggests that tenants will be slow to take advantage of their new rights. Finally, by an amending Act in 1973, the same right to a rent allowance, on slightly different terms, was extended to tenants of furnished dwellings.

The effect of all this could be revolutionary. Rent control

halted the competitive market forces in a sector of housing by arresting change. This was bound to be limited either in time or as to the range of housing to which it applied, or both. Rent regulation substitutes for competitive market forces the exercise of human judgment, guided by principles of equity. But it does not wholly eliminate the market element. It takes account of the character of a neighbourhood and of the people who live there, and assesses a rent that is fair for that type of house and that style of tenant. So in principle rent regulation could continue indefinitely, because it is sensitive to economic and social change. Nor is there anything to prevent it covering a very large part of the private sector as well as the whole of the public sector, and in fact the ceiling of rateable value is already set high enough for it to do so.

But it is by no means certain that rent regulation will continue in this form. In fact the Labour government of 1974 was already pledged to repeal the 1972 Act, and it took immediate steps to freeze the rents due to be increased in April 1974. It was estimated that this would affect some 4·5 million public and 3·5 million (furnished and unfurnished) private tenants. This was an emergency measure, and it is not (at the time of writing) clear what will follow. The whole issue raises some very difficult problems. Two of these are of major importance. First: can one accept a system under which a large proportion of tenants on an estate, perhaps in some cases even a majority, are considered unable to pay the full rent, and must therefore be granted a rebate after submitting to a means test? Apart from the strong feeling in some quarters that this is humiliating there is one very practical objection. If the income of a family in receipt of a rebate rises, then the benefit is reduced step by step. This is similar in effect to the levying of a tax on the additional income, and is often described as such. What makes it so serious is that other benefits of the 'negative income tax' type, such as Family Income Supplement, are affected in the same way, and the total result may be to whittle the additional income down to a mere fraction of its original amount. The problem exists already, quite apart from rent rebates, but these add a major item to it (on this point see pp. 191–2).

The chief merit claimed for the scheme is that it is both economical and equitable, since it gives financial aid only where it is needed and to the extent that it is needed. This means that government subsidies can be substantially reduced and also redirected. Under the 1972 Act, as we have seen, they are given, not for building in general, but for a range of special purposes, including the reimbursement of the greater part of the rent rebates and allowances. It is maintained that, under these arrangements, it will be much easier for a council to manage its housing and plan its programme to meet the needs of its tenants and the neighbourhood. But this release from the worst of its former financial worries is bought at the cost of surrendering its control over rents and rebates to the central government and its agents.

The other difficult question to answer is whether 'fair rents' should really be the same in both the public and the private sector. It has been argued, for instance by Anthony Crosland, that 'fair rents' for council houses should be lower, because they should not include an item for landlord's profit.[13] It is true that, although no amount is actually specified for this item in the assessment of private rents, these could not be 'fair' to the landlord unless it was taken into account in a general way— as in fact it is. But it has become extremely difficult, in an inflationary situation, to decide what the rights of the landlord should be. Is he entitled to a fair return on what he paid for the house or what he could sell it for? If the latter, should the value be what it would fetch if offered with vacant possession or as a property occupied by protected tenants? This issue was recently carried right up to the House of Lords which decided, rather disturbingly, in favour of value with vacant possession.[14] On the other hand councils too need to have an income sufficient to service the borrowing of capital and to cover the overheads and liabilities arising from their public responsibilities, which they have and private landlords do not. Even, however, if the whole of any credit balance achieved by charging 'fair rents' were used in this way (and not repaid to the Exchequer), it can still be argued that these are expenses which, if they are to be locally borne, should be met by the rate-payers as a whole and not by the better-off council tenants alone.

But the basic point is this. The provision of council houses has had, since the beginning, the character of a social service for a certain category of persons, namely those unable to obtain a home in any other way. This is reflected in the way the total programme is planned to meet certain specified needs, in the maintenance of rents below the market level, in the granting of rebates to selected low-income families, and in particular in the methods used for allocating houses to applicants. This, like the granting of rebates, is a welfare operation, involving the evaluation of different kinds of need and the determination of priorities among them. Many councils demand a residential qualification, though seldom more than the fact of present residence, some use a points system, all give special consideration to families in sub-standard housing, to large families and to the handicapped. This may prove hard for inadequately housed families which have been trying to move for a long time. A London Director of Housing wrote: 'Our allocation of tenancies in Camden goes four to one in favour of families with particular handicaps, as against those who remain for years on the housing list without the recognized stigmata which win them an immediate consideration. Is this right? We don't yet know.'[15]

It has been urged for some little time past that councils should take a broader view of their responsibilities. The Seebohm Committee expressed this opinion, and went on to say that, in particular, councils 'should be generally concerned with assisting a family to obtain and keep adequate accommodation whether it be in the council house sector or not'. The provision of rent allowances for private tenants has broken through the barrier which separated the two sectors, but there are other possibilities, as the Seebohm Committee pointed out. Families could be helped with their housing problems by advice as to the most advantageous ways of acquiring a home, as tenant or purchaser, in the public or in the private sector, and perhaps by moving from the one into the other. And councils could do more in the way of purchasing houses on the market and adapting them so as to cater for a wider variety of needs and tastes, including, for instance, the officials and professional people whom they themselves have to employ.[16] The implication is that councils should reach out beyond their concern with the social service, or welfare, aspect of their housing policy, and interpret their role in a larger context, as a contribution to a comprehensive and integrated attack on the housing problems of the community.

This is impossible unless policy is also integrated at the centre, and it has not been. A committee set up to study the purposes,

procedures and priorities of council housing, under the chairman-
ship of Professor Cullingworth, made this point at the outset of
its report. 'The most significant feature of housing provision
in Britain,' it wrote, 'is its division into a number of sectors
each of which is affected, aided and controlled in different and
frequently conflicting ways by Government.'[17] The application
of the same principles of 'fair rents' and rent rebates (or allowances) to all rented accommodation would, if it survives, do
much to consolidate policy in that area. But there is a marked
discrepancy, and no co-ordination, between the treatment of
tenants and the concessions given to purchasers of houses by
remission of tax on mortgage interest. Aid for tenants increases the
poorer they are, but for buyers it increases the richer they are.
Operations in the housing market are, in a sense, 'controlled'
by the rate of interest charged by the banks and the building
societies and by the tax concessions, but there is no specific
objective and the results are capricious. Proposals for reforms
current in the political parties include a revision of the system
of tax relief on mortgage interest, to reduce the benefit going to
the rich and increase that offered to those of modest income,
more efforts to encourage housing associations and co-operatives,
the nationalization of land needed for housing development, and
perhaps some consideration of proposals to municipalize pri-
vately rented dwellings.

A comprehensive and integrated housing policy must overlap
at many points with the functions of other departments of
government. There are close associations between housing and
health, between housing, poverty and education, and between
housing and welfare, especially with regard to provision for the
homeless. The latter is a good example of the way in which
responsibilities become divided between service departments, and
sometimes become lost in the process. There are three types of
homeless, only one of which presents a straightforward housing
problem. There are the vagrants, who have no settled way of life:
these are a welfare problem. Then there is 'catastrophic' homelessness, caused by some disaster, such as fire or flood: the immediate need is for shelter as their homelessness may be temporary.
Finally there are those who have had a settled way of life in a
home which they have now permanently lost—and they need to
be permanently housed. Their condition is very often caused by

the break-up of a family, and sometimes by eviction. But, although they present a genuine housing problem, they may, if unable to find shelter for themselves with friends or relatives, become a case of temporary homelessness. So they must be given refuge by the welfare, or social service, department, perhaps in conditions which involve separating the husband from his family or taking the children into care. Friction has often developed between this department and the housing officer to whom it is anxious to pass on the refugees, because he is equally anxious to defend the priorities of his applicants and to avoid putting potentially unsatisfactory tenants (which from a personal or a financial point of view, many of the refugees are) into good houses; so they are sometimes assigned to sub-standard ones. The misfortunes of the clients in such a case arise from the division of a task between two departments, both of which are honestly trying to do their best in the light of their respective total responsibilities. The Seebohm Report proposed, quite simply, that 'The full range of housing responsibilities should be placed upon housing departments. . . . We recommend that housing departments should, as a few already do, assume responsibility for providing accommodation for homeless families [paragraph 401].' This was in fact done in 1974, and there are fears in some quarters that this may encourage a tougher attitude towards the temporarily homeless.

But the problem of obstructive frontiers within the administrative terrain is much more extensive and complicated than this. The powers needed to implement an integrated housing policy, writes David Donnison, exist already, but they are scattered among many departments. 'We need a Seebohm for housing to create a comprehensive service capable of tackling the greater opportunities and heavier responsibilities that are on the way.'[18]

12 | Poverty

When social policy consisted of a Poor Law and little else it is obvious that the focus was wholly on the lowest depths of social life, on poverty. It combined a rescue operation for those whose destitution drove them into its arms with a punitive expedition against those who were able, but unwilling, to work. There was no need for such a policy to define 'the poor', since they simply constituted the immeasurable pool from which was drawn the very clearly defined category of 'paupers'. Rowntree's 'poverty line' marked a step forward, because it defined poverty in terms of the level below which life became a sort of social non-existence, irrespective of whether the poor appealed for help (and so became paupers) or not. This was primary poverty—inescapable, unconditional and, in one sense of the word, absolute. It was not a status, but a condition. A second step forward was taken when the poverty line passed from Rowntree to Beveridge and became the 'subsistence level'. Then, instead of serving only to measure the level *below* which poverty existed, it acquired the positive function of fixing the level *up to* which family incomes must be raised, and thus prepared the way for the recognition of a *right* to welfare. For the subsistence level is, so to speak, the underbelly of the 'national minimum', to which, by definition, all 'nationals' are entitled.

Thereafter, poverty was generally regarded by those concerned with social policy as something which must sooner or later— and if possible sooner rather than later—be eliminated. This was part of the simple philosophy of the Welfare State, and it is vulnerable to sophisticated criticism. Much time has been spent defending the unassailable view that poverty is a relative concept, because the state to which it refers differs from place to place and from time to time. This is obviously true, but preoccupation with it distracts attention from the subtler question: what kind of meaning can we give to poverty when it is used of a particular community at a particular time? One answer given is that, even in this limited context, it is wholly relative in meaning, and can refer only to a position on a scale of inequality, and not to a condition of life. You may say that A is poorer than B, but not that A is poor and B is not. However, the term 'poverty' may be retained (in this view) to denote an arbitrary statistical category, such as the bottom 20 per cent on the inequality scale. This of course implies that poverty is always with us, and can never be abolished unless inequality is abolished too. Others, while still insisting that poverty is relative, not absolute, allow that the comparison by which we recognize it is not just a step in the process by which we compare each level with the one above it right down the scale, but comparison with the *average* standards of the community as a whole, so that 'the poor are those who fall sufficiently far below these average standards'.[1] But how far is sufficient? We can only infer that the comparison made here is not in fact with an average, but with a minimum, and that poverty is a condition of life which lies below the minimum which that particular civilization can accept as part of itself. A minimum is a value judgement, an average is a mathematical calculation. So, though it is still relative, there is a flavour of absoluteness about the concept, in the sense in which we say that something is 'absolutely intolerable'. It is with this meaning that we shall use the term 'poverty' in this chapter.

One obvious objection to this approach is that poverty conceived in these terms is not something whose frontier can be determined by drawing a 'poverty line'. Even its replacement by a band, as in the report by Abel-Smith and Townsend on *The Poor and the Poorest*, though admirable for its purpose, does not dispose of this criticism. But it would be wrong to dismiss such devices for defining poverty as either arbitrary or useless. In the first place they are based on the evaluation of a great deal of evidence about how ordinary people live and what ordinary people think and feel. Secondly, their usefulness is functional rather than purely analytical. A poverty line (as measuring entitlement to Supplementary Benefit, for instance) provides an authoritative standard against which needs can be assessed and is adjustable to changes in the level of living. It can be used to estimate the magnitude of the problems with which social policy has to deal, and to compare conditions in different areas or in one area at different times. Poverty defined as income is an exiguous concept, but it provides a nucleus to which specific kinds of want can be attached to build a much richer concept whose integrity is the product of two qualities present in all its components, deprivation and urgency. Of all these accretions the most important are housing, the physical environment, education and those physical and mental disabilities which exacerbate and are exacerbated by poverty in the narrower sense. These are the poverties of our civilization.

That this idea of poverty as a sub-minimal social condition has been strongly represented since the war among those concerned with social policy, both in theory and in practice, cannot be doubted. It is also true that it has been severely criticized as misleading and dangerous, on the grounds that in theory it encourages the propensity to study poverty apart from its social context, and in practice it may lead to the treatment of poverty as a painful sore on an otherwise healthy body which can be removed under a local anaesthetic. To the first comment one may reply that, if wisely used, this approach may be profitable by directing attention to qualitative inequalities and inter-class attitudes associated with them, and by raising questions about the nature of the social conscience (if any) of the society studied. Those who offer the second comment argue that the real problem on which action should be directed is inequality—in its many different forms—rather than sub-minimal poverty. It is perfectly true that the former represents the context within which the latter must be attacked, but a policy inspired by resentment of inequality can, as has often been seen, be distorted or even frustrated by the strength of its appeal to selfish interests, whereas a policy inspired by resentment of sub-minimal poverty appeals to feelings of altruism, which are not always easily awakened. So the spate of single-minded campaigns directed by anti-poverty pressure groups on behalf of the old, sick, disabled, homeless and generally disadvantaged have contributed something essential to the advance of social policy. It is true that pressures of this kind can be an embarrassment as well as a stimulus to policy-makers who are tackling difficult problems of priorities, but the course of events does not suggest that they have led to the issue of sub-minimal poverty being considered apart from its wider context. The trend has rather been in the opposite direction, away from the piecemeal or patchwork treatment of symptoms towards a systematic and comprehensive view of the problem area of which poverty is a part.

This may be interpreted in two ways which differ significantly. One interpretation leads towards a policy of 'positive discrimination' in favour of impoverished areas which are then treated as total communities, whose whole life must be re-animated and raised to a higher level at which poverty, in the narrower sense, would cease to be an acute problem. The other points to measures attacking the root causes of poverty to be found within the national social and economic system. The War on Poverty declared by President Johnson in 1964 is an example of the former approach. The focal points of the campaign were those 'grey areas' and 'black ghettoes' in which life appeared to be set in a self-perpetuating pattern of material want and social demoralization. The aim was to transform these communities 'by opening to everyone the opportunity for education and training, the opportunity to work, and the opportunity to live in decency and dignity'.[2] The method was twofold. A number of projects were launched dealing with specific questions such as employment, training, health and education, of which the best known is probably Head Start, a programme for 'compensatory education' which tried, by intensive application, to make good what the young had missed, on the assumption that schooling was the key to opportunity. It was criticized on the ground that it merely forced children into a system whose inadequacy was manifest. Secondly there were the Community Action Programs, whose aim was radically to change the administration and the life of the community by encouraging the 'maximum feasible participation' of all its inhabitants in all its affairs. This—the most conspicuous part of the whole enterprise—ran into grave difficulties, for two main reasons. First, it was not fully realized that, though a social problem must be tackled in its social context, the context cannot be substituted for the problem. There was too little contact between the specific projects and Community Action, so that in the latter, it was said, participation tended to become an end in itself, with no clear ideas as to its objectives.

Secondly, although the ultimate aim of participation was a co-operative society, the campaigns were naturally inclined to develop into assaults by the deprived against the authorities held responsible for their deprivation, and some of the organizers of the programme believed and maintained that only by a strategy of 'confrontation', or even of conflict, could the desired structural changes be brought about. The policy was revised and the campaign reorganized in 1969. The specific projects were strengthened, more emphasis was laid on research and experiment, and, while Community Action was retained as an important element, an attempt was made to tame the programmes so that, as the new Director said, they might 'serve as a catalyst for stimulating the broader community to action against poverty, rather than as a lightning rod for discontent'.[3]

Positive discrimination in favour of selected districts has taken several forms in this country. First came the Educational Priority Areas (EPAs) selected as districts within which the problem was 'one of an entire community at social and educational risk'.[4] They differed from the American Head Start in two ways. The plans were based on the idea of equal partnership between action and research, and 'compensatory education' was rejected in favour of the 'community school' as an agency of community development, and of pre-school education as an integral part of the system. This was found to be of vital importance in particular for immigrants hampered by cultural and linguistic obstacles.[5] The Community Development Project launched by the Home Office in 1969 was described as 'a neighbourhood-based experiment aimed at finding new ways of meeting the needs of people living in areas of high social deprivation'. Twelve areas of different character were chosen for the experiment, which, like the EPA projects, included both action and research. The original assumption that urban deprivation was rooted in the characteristics of local populations—a sort of 'social pathology'—was soon abandoned in favour of a more structural approach in which specific issues were chosen for treatment by plans of action which involved participation by the citizens. Much attention was paid to the problem of assessing the merits and defects of different strategies, such as that of local co-operation (or consensus), intra-structural conflict, community organization (to make popular wishes and individual claims effective), and political pressure and planning at regional and national level. Early experience indicated that 'community action' (or 'development') as an end in itself was not enough, and one could not expect a community to pull itself up by its own boot-straps. The question is, said the first Inter-Project Report, 'whether a clear enough awareness of the underlying issues can be developed to stimulate a powerful movement for change from a local base'.[6]

The dilemma of how to strike a balance between problems of acute urgency and the broader long-term issues in which they are embedded arises in all branches of social policy. The easiest way to explain this is to take some examples from British social policy in recent years. The aged poor have been, for a long time, an ostensible object of public compassion, and a valuable item in party political programmes. They were given pensions and then, when everybody got pensions, supplementary pensions, and then, when the depth of the poverty of the poorest was uncovered, they were given allowances additional to their supplementary pensions, and home helps and 'meals-on-wheels' and the services of chiropodists and so forth—a patchwork of aids, subject to constant revision, limited to the relief of poverty, and administered by several different agencies. But increasingly thought has been given, not only to the aged poor, but to the problems of old age in general, and some attempt has even been made to shift the emphasis to the still broader concept of the problems of ageing as a process and an experience. So there is growing up a policy for old age, concerned with the role of each item in the continuum stretching from the geriatric ward, through the Old People's Home, to community care and the various provisions that go with it, and in the relevant areas poverty is absorbed into the general policy.

The case of the disabled is similar. Disablement is not poverty in the ordinary sense, but it is a form of deprivation which poverty exacerbates. It took a vigorous, single-minded campaign to win recognition of the extent and urgency of the needs of those included in this admittedly far from homogeneous category. But categorization was a necessary prelude to action. Then came some piecemeal measures such as new welfare services, attendance allowances for severe cases and jobs reserved for the employable which showed that disablement must be looked at in a wider context because it is not in fact a clearly circumscribed category and its requirements are of very varied kinds. So pressure developed for a policy, or one might say a charter, for the disabled, in deference to which the Labour government of 1974 appointed a Minister for the Disabled. In housing the balance between the particular and the general was different. The major problem which confronts a housing policy is how to ensure that building goes on and that the dwellings built are available to people of all incomes throughout the population; it is concerned with inequality more than with poverty in the absolute sense. Or, rather, slum clearance and provision for the homeless must be harmonized with the demands of the policy as a whole. But the effects of the housing programme on poverty are immediate. 'Housing policy,' said the West London branch of the Family Service Units, 'largely controls where our work will lie.'[7] It is all too easy, because of the peculiar difficulties of this branch of government and administration to allow quite unacceptable conditions of poverty and an alarming amount of homelessness to continue to exist. These have naturally been the object of campaigns by pressure groups, single-minded and even blinkered by their enthusiasm, demanding that such cases should be given top priority and immediate relief. Since this is not always possible without upsetting long-term plans for a more permanent solution, clashes developed between the local authorities and some groups, including those organizing illegal squatting, which succeeded in stimulating action to meet acute immediate needs, but the basic problem of how to devise a policy which can deal simultaneously and effectively both with poverty and with social and economic inequality has not yet been solved.

But the area in which this dilemma presents the gravest difficulties is that of social security, in the sense of cash benefits. The Beveridge plan for social security was an attack upon Want, just as Bevan's Health Service was an attack upon Disease, but both relied for their purpose on universal measures. Selective treatment of the poor was residual in Beveridge's plan and totally absent from Bevan's. But selectivity broke into both, on a large scale in social security through national assistance and Supplementary Benefits, and in a more limited way in the Health Service, through charges (for medicines, spectacles, dentures and dentistry) from which the poor were exempt. A new kind of duality was added with the introduction of graduated insurance:

a duality of purpose. For social security was coming to be directed both at staving off want and at providing for all, when earnings ceased, a pattern of incomes based on the principle of equitable (or legitimate) inequality. The critical question was whether these two aims could be pursued through a single universal system, or whether there must be two distinct but related sets of apparatus to cope with them. For some time no attempt was made at fusion. The gap remained, or even widened, and a new selective aid to the poor was added in the shape of the Family Income Supplement.

Then, as we have seen, both parties decided to produce plans for a comprehensive reorganization of the whole system. The Labour Party claimed for its (Crossman) plan that its universal provisions would of themselves reduce means-tested benefits for the poor to an acceptable minimum, but there are grounds for doubting whether this was so. The Conservatives made no such claim for their new social insurance scheme, which would leave things in that respect very much as they were. But they added a new piece of machinery, tax credits, designed to be both universal in its application and at the same time selective on behalf of the poor. This was still only a project when the government fell in February 1974, but the principle embodied in it is one which can be used in various forms and must be included in our review. But first we must look at the dilemmas which confront anyone who tries to reform the system which current policy and practice have created.

The first may be called the 'dilemma of the gap', that is to say of the gap in value between a social insurance benefit and the larger amount received by those getting the full supplementary pension or benefit, together with an allowance for rent and rates. The dilemma arises because poverty can be seen both as a condition and as a status: a condition of material want and a status of dependence on discretionary aid. Most reformers would like to do something about both aspects, that is, to raise the income of the poor and to reduce the number dependent on supplementary benefits, but it is very difficult to do both at once within the framework of our present system of social security. If you raise pensions without also raising the SB (Supplementary Benefit) rate, you narrow the gap and reduce the number of people dependent on SB, but you do not increase their incomes unless the addition to the pension is more than enough to fill the gap. An increase sufficient to do this would be immensely costly, and it would still benefit least those who need it most. If insurance benefits and SB are increased *pari passu*, there is some gain for everybody (including those who do *not* need it), but the gap remains and the number of people in the *status* of poverty is unaffected. This is the course of action generally adopted, because it seems to be the simplest. It made it possible for the Labour government of March 1974 to announce immediately the biggest increase in basic pensions ever made at one go, because it could add that there would be a similar advance in SB. It also promised that increases in pensions would continue to keep pace with increases, not merely in the cost of living, but in average earnings. So the gap remains, and the number dependent on supplementary means-tested pensions is unchanged until some more drastic reform of the social security system is undertaken.

The second dilemma is that of the 'poverty trap', and it springs from the same source, namely the fact that any benefit or concession given on condition of poverty must inevitably be reduced or withdrawn if and when income rises. The gap is one example of this, but there are others. The most obvious are Family Income Supplement, rent rebates (or allowances) and rate rebates, where the regulations lay down exactly how the benefit is to be reduced as the income rises. The significance of the procedure is greater here than in the case of pensions, because the recipients of the benefit are working and may expect their earnings to rise. The FIS is, in effect, a part of the wage, and, since it is calculated at 50 per cent of the gap between actual earnings and the income prescribed to meet the family's basic needs, any addition to the family earnings is automatically cut by 50 per cent by the corresponding reduction of the supplement. This is called the 'withdrawal rate' and has the effect of a 50 per cent tax on the additional earnings. The withdrawal rates differ as between one kind of benefit and another, and when a family is in receipt of many of these, including rent and rates rebates, free school meals, free medicines etc., the total withdrawal rate is very high, and the situation may further be adversely affected by a rise in insurance contributions and income tax. It is actually possible for an increase in earnings to cause a decrease in net income. Even families above the level for SB or FIS suffer in this way, for example (an actual case), a couple with two children achieved an increase in income from £22 to £24 a week. They lost their rent rebate and free school meals and, when increased national insurance contributions and income tax had been taken into account, the net gain out of a wage increase of £2 a week was 6p—a withdrawal rate of 97 per cent. This is a relatively extreme case, but it is estimated that the withdrawal rate for families of that size in that income bracket runs on average from 50–65 per cent.[8]

While it is true that pensioners are less likely to be affected by the poverty trap than earners because their incomes are static, it does have one important consequence for them. Because any occupational pension is disregarded to the extent of £1 a week, they gain nothing by getting a larger pension than this, unless it is much larger and takes them out of the SB category. This could affect the working of a social security system which assigns a big role to occupational insurance, like the 'Joseph Plan'. Firms might not see much point in running pension schemes for their lower-paid workers. It also discourages the granting of gratuitous pensions to old people by their friends, relatives or former employers, either as allowances or as bequests.

This dilemma is the result of reliance on a host of separate and unco-ordinated benefits, in cash or in kind, for the partial relief of poverty. Estimates of the number of such means-tested benefits in use vary, and one official statement put it at forty-four. But it would be quite wrong to imagine that all these are for the relief of poverty in the absolute sense. They include grants for various kinds of training, for university education and for several sorts of Legal Aid to which people with quite substantial incomes are entitled. There are others where there is most unlikely to be any strict application of a withdrawal rate, such as home helps and 'meals-on-wheels', and others again, like Old People's Homes, where inmates pay what they can afford (retaining a personal allowance), and receive the same treatment whatever they pay. However, the extended use of discretionary, means-tested benefits has produced a situation which is in some respects both chaotic and inequitable.

The third dilemma is that of the discrepancy between economic and welfare values. Here too there is an overlap with the previous category, since one example of this dilemma, and its solution, is the Family Income Supplement, which brings the market value of a man's labour up to a level acceptable by welfare standards. Another is the 'wage stop', and in this case economic value prevails and prevents the welfare standard which is applied elsewhere from being put into effect. The rule is that an unemployed man must not draw in benefits a weekly sum larger than he would be likely to earn if he found work. The same rule applies to temporary sickness. The reason for its introduction was that, since a man in work could not draw any benefit, he might be worse off than his unemployed mate on full SB—which would be unfair. It would also remove the incentive to find work. It is a difficult system to administer fairly for two reasons. First the estimate of an unemployed man's potential earning-power is a matter of personal judgement, which leaves a great deal to the discretion of the responsible official. Secondly, many of the cases are men on the verge of becoming unemployable and thus escaping from the wage stop, which applies only to those registered for work. One of the main conclusions drawn from an inquiry in 1967 was that 'the time has come to examine carefully the whole question of the requirement to register for work as it applies to people who have a combination of disability, age, length of unemployment etc., which makes them virtually unemployable'.[9] When FIS was introduced in 1970 it automatically raised the level at which the wage stop operated. It was officially estimated in 1972 that 20 000 families had benefited in this way,[10] but this did not wholly solve the problem, and the wage stop is still with us.

These three dilemmas all involve the use of benefits which are selective in terms of a means test. Selectivity, or discrimination, can also operate positively in terms of categories for which the existence of a need is *presumed* to exist. We may take as examples the cases of the disabled and of one-parent families. The former has been discussed already, and the crucial point in the demand for a true disablement income is the insistence that this income should be based on the assumption that a certain degree of disablement creates a certain level of need, and that this should not be measured only by loss of earning-power but should also apply to the disabled housewife who had not entered the labour market. A great deal of concern has been expressed in recent years about one-parent families, and especially the father-

less families of unmarried mothers. It is beyond all question
that there is much absolute poverty in this category and that our
patchwork system of social security at present fails totally to
meet its urgent needs. A detailed study of the situation in five
selected areas was published in 1973 which analysed the problem
in great depth. It was found that in all the areas the mean incomes of fatherless families were less than half those of two-parent
families, that the rate of mental trouble was three times as high in
unmarried as in married mothers, and that the mean percentage
drawing SB in the five areas was 2·6 per cent in two-parent families,
15·4 per cent in motherless families and 53·5 per cent in fatherless
families.[11] The case for classing one-parent families as a special
category deserving to be treated with positive discrimination is
overwhelming.

But there is one awkward problem which arises over the definition of the category. For its essential feature is the absence,
not of a marriage contract, but of a family which has the support
of a man and a woman who share the burden between them.
It was therefore laid down in 1966 that, as regards even the inadequate aid now available, a man and woman cohabiting as
man and wife without being married do not qualify. The principle
is reasonable but its application is extremely difficult, and the
inquiries necessary to find out what the situation actually is are
deeply resented. It is even asserted that this is a form of moral
censorship when in fact it is the opposite, in that it allows to
cohabitation the full status—and responsibilities—of marriage.
Another effect of schemes to aid fatherless families, which is said
to be very widespread in the United States, is the break-up of
marriages brought about by the desire to create eligibility for
the benefit paid to mothers bringing up children without the
support of a husband. The break-up may be genuine or a pre-
tence, the husband continuing secretly to support his wife.
There is no obvious escape from this dilemma.

Children are another category of persons whom our social
and economic systems expose to a special poverty risk. It arises
because the family is a closely-knit, self-contained consumer
group whose income from the market is determined without
reference to its collective needs. That is why the problem is
envisaged as one of family poverty rather than simply of child
poverty. The corrective chosen has been, not to institute a

family wage, but to supply financial support to the family independently of the market, as a sort of social, or welfare, service.
In this country, as has been explained in Chapter 8, this support
has taken two main forms, family allowances and the Family
Income Supplement introduced in 1970. The former is not in its
nature an anti-poverty measure, but a modification of the general
system of income distribution in favour of families with two or
more children. In recent years, however, it has come to be viewed
primarily in the context of child poverty. Until the institution
of the 'clawback' it was totally non-selective. FIS is totally
selective and is directed wholly towards the elimination of
family poverty. It is widely felt that these measures have not
given us all that is needed, and that perhaps we are getting the
worst of both worlds, with a selective system which is cumber-
some, invidious and likely to suffer from a low rate of take-up,
and a non-selective cash distribution for whose extravagance, if
raised to a level high enough to eliminate family poverty, the
'clawback' does not provide a permanent remedy.

The search for a solution to this problem of family poverty
is one of the factors which has led to the exploration of some
basically new ideas, the aim of which is to find the answer to
two questions: how to devise a scheme of general application
which operates selectively, and how to unify the systems of
income taxation and income maintenance. A tax-free income
allowance in respect of dependants has the same kind of effect
on family income as the grant of a cash benefit and belongs, as
Richard Titmuss argued in a famous lecture, to the third component of the apparatus of social policy of which the other two
are social security and the personal welfare services.[12] But
tax-free allowances and cash benefits operate independently and
without co-ordination. Parents rich enough to pay income tax
now get both the family allowance and the tax rebate, and the
higher the income the greater the benefit gained from the latter;
whereas those whose net income is below the tax-paying level
get only the family allowance—and this begins with the second
child, whereas tax rebate begins with the first. The plan for
'child endowment', which is now an item in the long-term programme of the Labour Party, is an attempt to answer the two
questions posed above in relation to family poverty only. One
form of this was put forward in 1965 by the Child Poverty

Action Group. They proposed the abolition of both tax-free allowances for children and family allowances (i.e. both income tax rebates and cash grants, presumably including FIS had it existed then) and their replacement by a cash payment, free of tax, in respect of every dependent child, beginning with the first, made to all families. 'Clawback' withdrew from tax-free allowances only an amount equivalent to the increase in family allowances. Child endowment would abolish them, and in so doing would create a sort of built-in selectivity, in that, while the payments received would be the same for all, rich tax-payers would incur a substantial loss, through increase of their income tax, and poor non-tax-payers none at all.

The prototype of the more comprehensive plans is Negative Income Tax (NIT) as first suggested by the American economist, Milton Friedman, in 1963. The idea is quite simple, though the variants which have been suggested are many and the calculation of their effect on personal incomes and on public finance is a highly complicated affair. Everybody would make a full return of income, and this figure would be used as an assessment both of the tax payable by those with incomes above the amount fixed as a tax threshold and for the cash supplements payable to those with incomes below it. If NIT is used for the relief of family poverty, the tax threshold corresponds to the personal allowances in our present income tax. These add up to the amount of income which each family, according to the number, status and age of its members, is considered entitled to enjoy before it is called on, or can afford, to pay any income tax. The tax-free allowances, that is to say, represent an income deemed sufficient to meet the family's needs, and NIT offers an alternative to these allowances to those who do not benefit from them because their income is too low to be taxable. But the tax threshold does not have to be the same as the poverty line (or guaranteed minimum); it can be substantially higher, on the grounds that a family should not be made liable to tax the moment it struggles out of poverty. So the crucial question to decide is to what level in relation to the threshold should incomes which are below it be raised by NIT. On this opinions differ, with some saying about 30 per cent of the way up, others 100 per cent.[13]

There is a rather different approach to this problem which includes what is called the 'social dividend', and also the tax

credit plan proposed by the Conservative government in 1972.[14]
The social dividend method, instead of paying 'negative tax'
as an addition to incomes below the tax threshold, makes a
grant to all, free of tax, in the same way as child endowment but
universally. Taxation then falls heavily on all income other than
this dividend. The grant would replace all the personal allowances
now enjoyed by income-tax payers, and could be so adjusted as to
replace as many of the cash benefits received through social
assistance and flat-rate social insurance as the planners wished.
The effect, as James Meade explains, would be that 'those who
start with Earnings above the average will lose more in tax than
they gain in Social Dividend and those with Earnings below the
average will gain more in Social Dividend than they lose in tax',
and no family's income would fall below whatever is set as the
national minimum.[15] The Conservative tax credits represent a
more modest version of the same idea. The scheme would cover
roughly all employed persons earning more than a given minimum and pensioners, but not the self-employed. All those
covered would receive tax credits in respect of each member
of the family; the figures suggested, by way of illustration only,
were £4 for a single person, £6 for a married man and £2 for
every child, irrespective of age. If tax due on the family income
exceeded the credits given, the balance would be paid to the
Inland Revenue, if credits exceeded the tax due, the balance
would be paid to the tax-payer. The personal tax-free allowances
for man, wife and children would disappear, as would also family
allowances and FIS. It is also anticipated that the need for supplementary benefits would be much reduced, though it is not claimed
that poverty would be totally abolished. The principle is simple,
but the disagreement about the probable effects of the system
are extensive and profound.

There is, however, a fair probability that some scheme of this
kind will at some time be adopted, both to simplify the systems of
taxation and cash benefits and to reduce family poverty. The
advantages claimed for such schemes are that they integrate
procedures for collecting and distributing income in such a way
as to simplify administration and eliminate anomalies; that,
since benefits do not have to be claimed, there is no problem of
'take-up' but everybody gets automatically what he is entitled to;
that the only disclosure of means required is an ordinary income-

tax return, which should not be humiliating; that the assessment
of needs is objective and standardized, not discretionary; that
help is automatically concentrated where it is needed; that it
should be possible through such a scheme to provide a guaranteed
minimum income which would virtually eliminate family poverty.
It is not claimed that any one scheme is likely to have all these
virtues, and some of them are dubious. When, for example,
the Labour government was preparing its pension scheme which
came to grief in 1970, they planned to include a device of this
order to give an 'income guarantee'. It foundered on the rocks
of the Inland Revenue, which found it administratively unacceptable, and in addition, as Richard Crossman related, they made 'the
awkward discovery . . . that the old-age pensioners did not much
like the idea of their stigma being removed by filling up income-
tax forms'.[16]

But the main objection to complete reliance on such systems is
that they are too objective, too standardized. There is always
the old problem of the irregularity and unpredictability of rents,
which are a major element in the family budget. The coverage of
some schemes is limited; the tax credit proposal was to apply
only to those in regular employment or on social insurance
benefits, with a minimum level of earnings to qualify for admission. More fundamental is the fact that any decision on the
income required to satisfy the needs of a family which is applied
uniformly throughout a whole category, is a presumption about
an average. It cannot be totally fair and, unless a very broad
margin of safety is allowed, much of the unfairness will take
the form of deprivation. For human needs and satisfactions are
not an exact reflection of material conditions. There is a point
at which discrimination, discretion or human judgement must
step in.

A scheme of the kind we have been discussing could do a
great deal. It might provide the cash element in that 'infrastructure of universalist services' demanded by Titmuss, above
and on the basis of which discrimination could take place. But
not necessarily discrimination of the kind exercised in the discretionary award of supplementary benefits, which involves a
penetrating inquiry into means and a discretion which is a mixture
of published official regulations, less public and more detailed
instructions and the personal judgement of the man on the case.

Titmuss saw the answer in 'categorical' services, provided as social rights 'on the criteria of the *needs* of specific categories, groups and territorial areas and not dependent on *individual tests of means*'.[17] Another possible development is suggested by an observation made by Barbara Rodgers about a trend she observed in some countries to make use of 'an assistance scheme which emphasizes needs rather than means, and which attempts to meet the individual's needs with service as well as cash allowances'.[18] If the infrastructure looked after all major problems of income redistribution, it is not improbable that most of the unsatisfied cases would call for welfare services as well as cash assistance, which could be jointly dispensed without humiliating effect. Already those administering SB are involved in welfare functions, but their primary concern is with the distribution of public money. There might be a significant difference in approach and in operation between one whose primary task is to dispense cash but with welfare implications as well, and one whose primary task is to provide a welfare service to which the dispensing of cash is a necessary addition. The difference would lie, not in their personalities, but in their responsibilities.

13 | Problems and prospects of the 1970s

British social policy in the 1970s was experiencing the effects of the most comprehensive reorganization of its administrative apparatus that it had undergone since the creation of the Welfare State a quarter of a century before. In the case of local government, the health service and the personal social services, though there was open disagreement on several points, this did not run strictly on party lines, and there was substantial consensus about the basic principles of structural change. Future developments will depend on how the new systems work in practice. The case of social security is harder to judge. Both parties had produced plans for the drastic reshaping of the whole system of social insurance, neither of which had come to fruition by the middle of the decade. The Conservative plan was on the statute book, and industrial firms were busily engaged in adapting their pension systems to the standard set by its Reserve Scheme. But the Labour government of 1974 was so strongly opposed to that part of the plan that it at once declared its intention of suspending it. This does not look like consensus. Yet even here the conflict was primarily about means rather than ends: about the respective roles of the State and private enterprise in providing a universal system of social insurance related to earnings, the standard of which, they both agreed, should be defined by government. But underlying this conflict about means lay differences of social outlook or social philosophy, concerned both with the relations between collectivism and individualism and with the assessment of the social right to welfare. It is therefore necessary, in this final chapter, to ask some questions about the goals which social policy set itself, or at least (which is a more manageable task) about the criteria by which it judged in what direction it should move.

There are many possible ways of classifying the aims of social policy, but the most helpful for our present purpose is that which distinguishes three types, which we may call the elimination of poverty, the maximization of welfare and the pursuit of equality. The first is the most limited of the three and concentrates on the lowest socio-economic stratum of society. The second is much broader, being concerned with the welfare of all, not only of the poor, with the object of achieving an optimum rather than a minimum. The third is the translation into action of a political philosophy whose implications, if pressed to the hilt, are very far-reaching indeed. The three aims are not mutually exclusive; in the first phase of the Welfare State, for instance, policy pursued the first of these three aims in its social security measures, and the second in health and welfare, while believing that in doing so it was making some progress towards the third. But it was an uneasy and impermanent combination of aims between which there are some real differences of principle.

The dominant objective today is undoubtedly the maximization of welfare. This aims at the satisfaction of particular needs without specifying either that the beneficiaries should be in a state of poverty or that the effect should be to reduce social inequality. The former will often be the case and the latter may frequently be the result, but both are secondary to the central criterion by which policy is judged, namely that of need satisfaction.

Although few would today endorse the view current in the nineteenth century that the State, in its social policy, has no business to go beyond the relief of poverty, there are those who believe that developments in the twentieth century have carried social policy, in some of its spheres of action, very near to the permissible limit and perhaps at some points beyond it. Several arguments are advanced in support of this contention, such as that the State is increasingly led on to do things which (though good in themselves) could be more efficiently done in other ways; that its undertakings are often extravagant and wasteful for reasons inherent in the nature of public action; that bureaucracy flourishes where it is least appropriate; that government policy shows signs of lacking a consistent system of values, without which it cannot clearly define its responsibilities, and that this is a natural result of the great range and complexity of its activities. A government may properly commit itself, the argument could continue, to seeing that people get what they need, but not to providing them with what they want. To stray into that area is to run the risk of encouraging excessive expectations as to what public services should supply without any corresponding obligations on the part of the recipients.

It is not possible to examine these highly controversial issues in any detail here. It would not be difficult to produce evidence of questionable expenditures in some social services or to indicate points at which money flows too easily through the interstices of the social system. But the important point is to recognize the danger of assuming that, in social policy, more is always better; to be aware of the staggering contrast between the quality of some publicly-provided institutions and the squalor of many homes and neighbourhoods; to admit the possibility that over-pampering may demoralize; and to remember that it is perfectly consistent to warn against going too far in some directions while denouncing the gross inadequacy of what is being done elsewhere.

The relation between the maximization of welfare and the pursuit of equality is a subtle one. At times they appear to come into direct conflict with one another. One familiar example of this is to be found outside our subject area, in education. It is the mutual recrimination between those who favour selection and streaming and those who want comprehensive schools and 'mixed ability' classes. The former accuse the latter of sacrificing educational potential to their egalitarian faith, and of pursuing the goal of equality by levelling down. Rather similar is the contention that to forbid specialists serving in the NHS to treat private patients in NHS hospitals—or even, perhaps, to have any private practice at all—would be to give effect to egalitarian principles without sufficiently exploring the consequences for the efficiency of the service.

It might appear that we have in the NHS itself the perfect example of a policy in which welfare and equality are successfully and harmoniously adopted as the twin aims of the enterprise. And it is perfectly true that the health of all is the target, and the principle that like cases should be treated alike is the rule of action. But this is only one kind of equality. It was the free services in health, education and welfare that Abel-Smith had in mind when he declared that 'the main effect of the post-war development of the social services, the creation of the "Welfare State", has been to provide free social services to the middle classes'.[1] It is perfectly true that the universal free Health Service did not enlarge the disposable income of those who had a free service already (by national health insurance), while it did enlarge that of the middle classes, by reducing their medical expenses, and thus increased inequality in one respect. But it would be more to the point, and also fairer, to say that the main effects were a great improvement in the quality of the service, especially for the working classes, and the creation of an area of general experience in which the treatment received was unaffected by class distinctions. This is broadly characteristic of British social policy today. The goal is the optimum satisfaction of needs; all operations undertaken in pursuit of the goal must be governed by the principle of fairness; the reduction of inequality is an expected consequence of this and is always present, just round the corner, ready to break in as a positive motive.

The position as regards money benefits, including social insurance, is different. Titmuss has suggested that in analysing the aims of social policy in this area use could be made of the distinction between 'adequacy' and 'equity' as the criteria on which decisions may be based. Adequacy refers to what is required to satisfy measured needs; equity implies conformity with a principle of social justice, which may result in different awards being made to persons with similar needs. He argues that 'concepts of what is "adequate" social security provision are today increasingly entangled with considerations of equity'.[2] A simple example is the case of the disabled, which we have already discussed. The satisfaction given to a man who has lost a leg varies according to whether he lost it fighting for his country, in an industrial accident or by falling down stairs. These distinctions have been held to be equitable, though the need to be satisfied is the same. A similar issue arises in the case of the husbandless woman. Margaret Wynn recently pointed out that the benefit awarded for a fatherless child depended on the status of the mother (widowed, divorced or deserted) and of the child (legitimate or illegitimate) and, if the father was dead, on whether he had died of an illness, was killed in an industrial accident or fell in battle.[3] The differences arose because these individuals had been assigned to different categories, presumably on grounds of alleged equity, and oversight had allowed them to stay there. Today this appears as an injustice to be rectified by giving proper weight to the principle of adequacy, but this does not mean that equity is to be totally excluded or that categories of this kind should be abolished; on the contrary, the tendency is to multiply them—but as a basis to which both criteria can be applied in due proportion.

Social insurance raises some subtle questions. Why, we may well ask, do nearly all governments, including in particular that which devised the 'Crossman Plan', think it proper to incorporate into their arrangements for social insurance systems which reflect, if only up to a limiting ceiling, the inequalities of income created in the economic market? One answer relies on equity. It points to three features of these schemes. There is a contractual element in them, since those who receive larger benefits pay larger contributions; there is an element of merit in them, since they take account only of income earned by the labours of the insured; and they often include some measure of income redistribution from richer to poorer, which may be seen either as the only practicable way of making the awards to low earners adequate, or as a way of somewhat reducing the general inequality of incomes in the society, on grounds of equity—or both. But another approach is possible, which argues that needs vary in relation to income, and that unequal benefits are provided for the satisfaction of unequal needs. This can be expressed by saying that if a man's pension falls below a certain proportion of his pre-retirement income, he suffers hardship, or 'deprivation', because real needs, developed during his more prosperous years, cannot be met. This same entanglement of adequacy with equity also haunts and perpetually bedevils attempts to work out an incomes policy for salaries and wages. It reveals itself when (and this happens) a professional man says, in the same breath, 'I find it impossible to live on £6000 a year', and 'this is a miserable sum in view of my long training and the vital importance of my services'.

It may be added, in parenthesis, that if the concept of need is allowed to become as subjective as this, reflecting the personal reactions of individuals to their circumstances rather than a generalized evaluation of typical and relevant experience, we soon find ourselves involved with the much abused concept of

'relative deprivation'. It was invented for the study of the reaction of American soldiers to the deprivations of war service;
it has been twisted into a term to express the view (as one American writer put it) that 'needs stem not so much from what we
lack as from what our neighbors have'.[4] It may be that social
policy should pay attention to expressions of this kind of subjective need as an aid to the discovery of effects of inequality
which are obstacles in the way of the welfare that it is trying
to maximize. But to do more than this would be to risk losing
sight of its chosen goal. The question of the inequality of incomes
in society at large raises issues far beyond the scope of social
policy as generally understood.

This discussion is not of purely academic interest: it has a
direct bearing on the problem of how to establish and implement
a *right* to welfare. Rights in the full sense of the word can be
attached only to categories of persons (citizens, wives, employees)
or of circumstances (unemployment, invalidity, defamation). The
members of a category, especially a broad one, are never a wholly
homogeneous group. When, as normally in a court of law, the
claimant's right is first established and the damages are then
assessed by an act of judicial discretion, the heterogeneity does
not matter. But when, as in social security, a right is conceived
as determining both the entitlement to be paid and the amount
due, then, in a broad category, only very rough justice can be
done. In the article quoted above Titmuss declares that in some
countries attempts to satisfy more exactly the entangled criteria of
adequacy and equity by splitting up and refining the categories
risk becoming self-defeating. In the first place the tests to which
a person must submit in order to establish his membership of a
particular category may turn out to be indistinguishable from, or
at least as troublesome as, a means test. He instances (rather
laconically) 'income-conditioned entitlement tests within "as-of-
right" programmes' (p. 265). Secondly, the more complex and
precise the system of rules and regulations defining the rights, the
more sure they are, at some points, to curtail rather than enlarge
the services available. For the function of all boundaries is to
shut out as well as to let in.

It is not being suggested here that attempts to establish rights
to welfare are misguided or doomed to failure; far from it.
The point being made is a double one: that rights are not as

absolute as some people think. They are fenced in by qualifying conditions—tests of sickness, unemployment, retirement, age, income, etc. And discretionary awards are not left to the mercy of human caprice, but are governed by principles which may be as powerful as the rules which govern the administration of rights. In the case of both types of service the spirit in which they are administered may well be more important than the form in which they are described. We have it in writing that there is a right to social benefit. This does not mean that it is to be had for the asking, but that, when the qualifying circumstances have been rigorously examined, the basic award will be made according to a scale that is published; on top of this there are 'exceptional' additions, once-for-all or continuing, which are governed, up to a point, by a code (which is not published), and there remains a discretionary margin. One may well ask whether it makes any sense to speak of a 'right' in such circumstances. It is argued here that it can, if three conditions are satisfied, and that if they are not no social rights can be really safe. These three conditions are: first, that the basic principles and aims of the social policy of a country are fully understood and accepted by the great majority of its citizens, and progressively absorbed into their culture; secondly, that the agents who carry out the policy are trained and equipped to accept and to discharge the responsibility which falls on all members of the personal service professions of translating these principles and aims into action in individual cases; thirdly, that all claimants for benefit or service know, or can easily find out, what their rights are in each particular case and are able, of themselves or with the help that is made available, to present and press their claims on those who have the power to meet them.

The first condition is always in the process of being realized, but with an inevitable lag. Great progress has been made in recent years towards the fulfilment of the second, but the effects of the Seebohm reforms have not yet (in 1974) been fully worked out. Success depends largely on maintaining the status and the power of the 'free' professions vis-à-vis bureaucracy. The third presents the greatest difficulty. In an interesting and challenging book, *Social Theory and Social Policy* (1971), Robert Pinker has argued that 'in all industrial societies . . . citizenship is a range of skills rather than a status transmitted from generation to generation'. The rights of citizenship are a reality only for those who have belief in their authenticity and the skills needed to exercise them, and this belief and these skills are developed through experience and socialization in the context of a class society.[5] Consequently to make a claim for a social service as of right can seem to some a mark of status and to others a brand of inferiority. This is one way of describing what is in fact the chief barrier to the fulfilment of the third condition listed above. It is created not only by the stigma or sense of shame attached to any request for aid, which is largely a legacy from the past, but also by dislike of being involved with officials, fear of one's appeal being rejected, ignorance of what one's rights really are and of the procedure to be followed in presenting them, apathy induced by a long experience of frustration and deprivation —in a word, lack of capacity to feel or act as a full and equal member of the community. There is a marked contrast between the power of organized labour and the relative ineffectiveness, when in need or in trouble, of many a working-class man and his wife. One of the outstanding features of the past decade or two has been the spate of activities undertaken by both the authorities and by voluntary associations and pressure groups of many kinds in an attempt to break through this barrier, by spreading information, offering help and stimulating active participation in community affairs.

The form of participation in the field of social policy by persons outside public administration which has the longest tradition is that of the voluntary organizations. They have been, and still are, of many kinds. Beveridge pointed out that the two springs of voluntary action in the field of welfare were mutual aid and philanthropy, both of which originated in personal contacts within small groups or communities.[6] The two differ in three important ways. Mutual aid is a system of help between equals whereas philanthropy has been essentially aid given by the privileged to the under-privileged. Mutual aid is self-contained and concerned only with its internal affairs, whereas philanthropy attacks national social problems and often sees its main task as that of forcing governments to take action. This was obviously the case with some of the great pioneers, like Howard of the League for Penal Reform or Florence Nightingale on behalf of several causes. A good modern example is the Family Planning Association, which has combined active philanthropic work with a campaign (recently crowned by success) for the inclusion of family planning in the National Health Service. Thirdly, when mutual aid expands it develops into large-scale organizations of a business or quasi-commercial type—great national provident associations like BUPA and Blue Cross. When philanthropy expands to national proportions it creates services which run parallel with the public social services, and are well fitted to supplement or co-operate with them. It was the Charity Organization Society that first injected into the rather chaotic world of philanthropy of the mid-nineteenth century those principles of orderly procedure and efficient management which made this development possible.

In due course the voluntary bodies, with their up-to-date administration and their large national federations, came to look and to act more and more like a public service. The way was open for a partnership in which the two sides met well-nigh on equal terms. The principles and practices by which they worked had been shaped more by private than by public influences, and the prestige of the voluntary organizations stood high, while the public services were limited in scope and lacking in experience. The rapid expansion of public service during and after the Second World War made the statutory authorities indubitably the senior partner, so much so that many people thought that voluntary action had had its day and would decline into comparative insignificance. But this did not happen; the partnership continued, taking various different forms. Voluntary action plays an important part in initiating projects, some of which may subsequently be taken over by public authorities. In the case of the care of evacuees during the war, according to Titmuss, voluntary bodies 'helped to hold the line during the period while the official machine was beginning to take efficient action' and handed over to the official machine when it was ready.[7] Sometimes voluntary organizations implement by their services obligations which have been accepted by government, and do so on lines approved of by the government and under its supervision. Examples of this are the Approved Schools and Children's Homes now rechristened Community Homes. Local authorities in the same way entrust cases for which they are responsible to voluntary agencies to which they pay a grant. Very often voluntary bodies offer services similar to those provided officially, but carry them into areas or to types of case which it is beyond the capacity of the public service to reach. Examples, to mention only a few, are clubs for old people, institutional care of mentally disabled children, and help for discharged prisoners. So, broadly speaking, there is no fundamental difference between the types of problem handled by the statutory and the voluntary services.

All these voluntary undertakings are examples of aid given by one class to another, or better, by the secure to the insecure. And pressure groups like the Howard League were also middle-class, altruistic enterprises. Today the situation is different in two respects. First, there has been an enormous increase in the amount of social research going on, and a great deal of it is focused directly on current social problems, with the purpose, not only of collecting and interpreting the facts, but also of suggesting action. Many of the social scientists engaged in this research are in close touch with, or officially advising, governments. In a welfare society with a sensitive social conscience and organs of mass communication which take up and publicize the findings, the effect of social research in providing ammunition for pressure groups of all kinds is much greater and more immediate than in the past.

Secondly, pressure groups have multiplied, and in some cases they form a very direct link between the social scientists and the political activists, who are often the same people. Outstanding examples of this are the Child Poverty Action Group and the Disablement Income Group. Others, like tenants' associations, and pensioners' action associations, are co-operative organs for the protection of the common interests of the members. Acting on a broader front we find the neighbourhood councils which some people would like to turn into statutory bodies which would play much the same part in local government as community health councils are intended to do in the NHS. Of particular interest in relation to the development of new forms of participation is the work of Shelter in the field of housing and more especially on behalf of the homeless. For it combined the normal pressure-group activities of lobbying and propaganda with work among those whose case it was pressing. Through a subsidiary it was instrumental in setting up in Bradford an office 'offering general housing aid service and practical help with house

S.P.—H

improvement, under the improved grant aid scheme',[8] thus helping citizens to understand and exercise their rights. It also helped to finance the Family Squatting Advisory Service, to which most lawful squatting groups in London were affiliated. It was even prepared to give tactical and legal advice to those squatting unlawfully[9]—in all, an interesting, if sometimes embarrassing, combination of the strategies of confrontation and co-operation. Going one step further we come to bodies formed and manned by the insecure and disadvantaged themselves, of which the claimants' unions are a recent example in this country. The movement began in 1968 and was in full swing by 1970. Its main purpose is to help members, all of whom are unemployed and drawing social security, to prepare, present and defend their claims, and also to work for changes in the law.[10] The prospects for the future, as seen in the 1970s, depend very much on how these various forms of participation develop and how successful they are in maintaining their independence of public authority while preserving a constructive and responsible relationship with it. And this, as was briefly explained earlier, is what the community development movement is trying to bring about.

One could say that the problem of race relations, and of immigrants in general, is basically one of participation and community development. This was recognized when the Community Relations Commission was established by statute in 1968 as successor to the non-statutory National Committee for Commonwealth Immigrants. Its task was the positive one of furthering community development in areas with a large immigrant element, while the Race Relations Board tried, by conciliation and if necessary by prosecution, to curb the expression of racial prejudice in acts of discrimination. The needs of immigrants are not in essence different from those of the native population, among whom also there are poverty, unemployment, derelict housing, educational backwardness, invalidity and deprivation. But all these troubles are magnified in a group which enters the society laterally from outside instead of growing up vertically from within, a group which is culturally alien, linguistically handicapped and often in addition visibly distinguished by colour. In principle, social policy makes no distinction between immigrant and native: their rights and claims are the same. In practice, they present different problems which in the case of immigrants call for special skills and special understanding on the part of the people who handle them, whether they be housing officers, teachers, policemen, child care officers, social workers, or nurses. But to regard immigrants, and more particularly coloured immigrants, as a special category to be accorded positive discrimination would almost certainly increase their detachment from, and impede their integration with, the rest of the community, which is exactly the opposite of what is desired. There cannot, for instance, be a separate housing policy for immigrants, although immigrants may figure prominently among those who are the object of a special policy for 'twilight areas'. When particular attention is paid to the needs and interests of immigrants, this is not a privilege, but a means of ensuring that the opportunities and assistance provided them are in substance equal to those enjoyed by others. This principle is recognized today, particularly in projects for priority areas of mixed population. But progress is slow, precisely because it involves changes in the complex of community relations to which there is still considerable resistance, both conscious and subconscious.

When we say that the aim of a policy is to maximize welfare, or anything else, we mean that it is trying to do the best it can for all concerned with limited and inadequate resources. Its most fundamental task, in such circumstances, is to establish a system of priorities, on the basis of which it can balance competing claims and harmonize growth rates within the area in which the policy operates. This calls for an appraisal of the relative importance and urgency of the needs to be satisfied which must be made or endorsed by outsiders (Parliament, government, local authorities and their agents), all in their various ways and according to their various lights drawing inspiration and guidance from the values current in their society. As so often happens in politics, it is an impossible task which must nevertheless be carried out.

These battles over priorities are not only a matter internal to the area of social policy. They are fought also at a higher level over the claims of the social services as a whole to a share of the national budget, as well as the claims of their various branches to resources, human and material, which are equally in demand for other purposes. It is not enough to prove that there is a shortage of houses or nurses; it must be established that the need for the additional quota is more urgent than that for the schools and the teachers for which the education authorities are clamouring. But since the government does not direct labour nor generally allocate materials the fight for resources is reduced for the most part to competition for funds.

On the budgetary aspect there is the obvious point that a large social service budget implies high taxes and insurance contributions, which may have a depressing effect on the economy and impede economic growth. Rather more subtle is the question whether this is true of money passing through the channels of income redistribution. For this process does not increase spending power but only reallocates it, and it makes no new demands on national resources. But there is more in it than that. One possible result of the transfer of income from the richer to the poorer is that saving is reduced; the recipients are given the money because they need it to spend, and presumably they spend it. On the other hand commercial insurance, as is well known, is one of the major sources of saving in modern societies, and some national insurance schemes perform a similar function, though usually less intensively. It depends to what extent they work on the 'pay-as-you-go' system and to what extent by funding their receipts. Most Western European insurance funds, as we saw, invest considerable sums in low-rent housing and welfare institutions, and in many economically backward countries social security funds contribute substantially to the financing of economic development.

Secondly, the effect of income transfers will depend on the point in the economy at which the income is collected. In most cases the bulk of it is today collected by a graduated pay-roll tax, a part of which is usually borne by the employees. Whether the whole of this, or less than the whole, becomes an item in the cost of production depends on how far and how soon the deductions from earnings are made up in the course of the negotiated wage increases which are a permanent feature of modern industrial economies; and this is not an easy matter to determine. One may conclude that it will prove difficult to introduce a new scheme of this kind, or to raise the level of an existing one, except when the economy is prosperous and progressive enough to absorb the consequent increase in the labour costs of production. But once it has successfully absorbed it, as it has always managed to do in the past, the continued operation of the scheme need present no special problem.

When all this has been said it remains true that costs set limits to the expansion of social policy, and this is often a cause of anxiety to governments. Their anxieties are unnecessarily increased by the natural tendency of the public to think in terms of absolute figures instead of ratios. This underlay the alarms of the 1950s. But the calculation of ratios is tricky, and international comparisons are trickier still. Estimates made by Professors Peacock and Wiseman showed expenditure on social services (including two large items not included in this survey, education and food subsidies) rising as a percentage of GNP from 2·6 in 1900 to 11·3 in 1938 and 17·8 in 1961.[11] This shows that the escalation associated with the Welfare State, when compared with the first phase of expansion up to the first World War, was not as spectacular as is often imagined. More relevant to our subject are the figures showing the change in the proportion of public expenditure devoted to the social services covered in this book, i.e. social security, health, personal social services and housing, since the establishment of the Welfare State. These are: 28·8 per cent in 1951, 31·7 per cent in 1961 and 36·0 per cent in 1972. This shows that in twenty-one years the *share* of public expenditure devoted to these services rose by 25 per cent or one quarter. The greediest sector was social security, whose share rose by 60 per cent, for most of which payments in respect of old age, death and illness were responsible, and which represents redistribution of income, not of resources. These figures reveal a considerable shift in budgetary allocations, but it falls far short of what happened in education which (at 12·9 per cent of the total in 1972) had increased its *share* by 90 per cent since 1951.[12]

Most European countries were undergoing a similar experience, and there is some evidence to suggest that, in recent years, the increase in the cost of the social services was causing anxiety.

In France four *Ordonnances* were issued in August 1967 to introduce measures rendered necessary by the deficit in the finances of the social security administration. They included the increase of the *ticket modérateur* from 20 per cent to 30 per cent already mentioned, a levy on motor insurance policies, a pruning of family allowances, and changes in financial procedures leading towards the abolition of the income ceiling for the contributions of the insured, which could bring in some useful additional income. Germany carried out extensive fiscal reforms in 1967 because, it was said, of an anticipated excess of expenditure which might endanger economic stability. These reforms extended far beyond the area of social policy but included the imposition of a 2 per cent contribution on pensioners and the removal of the income limit above which salaried employees were not included in national insurance. In the same year Japan was obliged by the rapid growth of medical expenditure to increase the proportion of the costs paid by the patients.[13]

In Britain the increase in the charge for medicines under the NHS was a small item, justified by the fall in the value of money, but the introduction of proportional charges for dental treatment involved a significant change of principle which reflected some financial troubles. The relation between the basic retirement pension for a couple and the average take-home pay of an industrial wage-earner was being well maintained at around 40 per cent, having risen to that level from the 34 per cent at which it had started in 1948, but this put an increasing strain on income which led eventually, in the 1970s, to the acceptance by both parties of the expedient of imposing graduated contributions to finance flat-rate benefits. But the principal way in which the limitations of cost disclosed themselves was in the flood of complaints that too little was being spent, especially on health care and the personal social services, and the embarrassing demands for higher pay by some of those working in the services, notably the hospital nurses. But it is not possible to assess long-term trends by what happens at a time when the government is fighting the menace of inflation. Inevitably the rate of progress is checked. What one must look out for, in estimating the long-term effects of rising expenditure, is some sign, not merely of postponement of desired advances, but of a change of direction involving a sacrifice of principle. At present there does not seem to be any evidence of this.

Another potent cause of anxiety about social security expenditure was the prospect of an ageing population and a greatly increased demand for pensions. This was based partly on forecasts which proved wrong and partly on inadequate analysis of the problem; in part, however, it was well-founded. The magnitude of the burden placed on producers by the need to support non-producers is measured by the ratio between the two groups and this is determined partly by demographic and partly by social factors. There has been a tendency to underestimate the importance of the latter and to focus attention too much upon the old non-producers—the retired—and too little on the children. Beveridge based his plans on the assumption that 21 per cent of the population would be of pensionable age (men over sixty-five, women over sixty) in 1971. The population projections calculated by the Registrar General in the early 1960s put the peak figure, due in about 1980, at 16·4 per cent to be followed by a fall to as low as 13·5 per cent in 2001. The earlier forecast was falsified by the rising birth rate, which increased the proportion of the population in the youngest age groups. But in the mid-1960s this rise stopped and the rate began to fall, making it necessary to raise the peak figure (still in about 1980) to 17·4 and the level in the first decade of the new century to between 16·0 and 16·4—compared with the 16·3 actually recorded in 1971. But even if the percentage is about the same in 2011 as in 1971, there will nevertheless be about a million more people of pensionable age in the population.[14] If one is wondering how society is going to carry this burden, it is more realistic to compare those of working age with the combined forces of the pensionable and the children below school-leaving age. This gives us what is called the 'dependency ratio'. But it still omits the social factor. Age groups are not a satisfactory measure for our purpose, since they do not correspond to the workers and the dependants. Many young people over the age of fifteen are not working (especially students and mothers with young children), and quite a lot of those over pensionable age continue to work. The number of women in paid employment has been increasing steadily in the last twenty years or so, and this was largely responsible for the rise in the percentage of the population over the age of fifteen who were in employment, full or part-time, between 1951 and 1971 from 59·6 per cent to 61·2 per cent, in spite of the growing number of old people.[15] Looking at the situation in the mid-1960s Dr Benjamin concluded that 'a comparatively modest growth in national productivity would permit of a substantial increase in the standard of living of the active population in spite of the growth in the numbers and claims of old people'.[16]

Note the words 'and claims', which imply that the circumstances of the old could not only be maintained, but be bettered. Today it is clear that the incomes of some old people are still minimal, or even sub-minimal. Is this because productivity has not risen, or because our system of income redistribution is faulty, or because our wage differentials make personal saving during working life impossible, or what?

This is a typical example of a problem of policy co-ordination, involving the regulations about pensions and the practices of the labour market. It raises the general question of planning. Attention has been drawn more than once in this book to the haphazard way in which social policy has developed in some areas. We have also seen that in recent years major reorganization has been undertaken in several fields, notably health care, the welfare services and local government as a whole. These have continued the work of integration which was already noted as a prominent feature of the social policy scene when the first edition of this book was published in 1965. But it cannot be assumed that what has been done has solved all the problems to everybody's satisfaction. There are already signs of a recognition that what can be achieved by purely structural and administrative change is very limited and easily exaggerated, and that it often has unwelcome side-effects which had not been foreseen. Secondly, if services are to be co-ordinated, it must be clear on what principles the administrative division of labour is to be based. It can be, and has been, based on categories of persons or on categories of needs. The attack of the Webbs on the Poor Law was aimed at substituting the latter for the former. The poor, they said, were not a true social category, since poverty might include problems of health, housing, education, delinquency and unemployment. But this policy, as we pointed out, had the unfortunate side-effect of disintegrating the family as a unit of attention and making it the target for a number of unco-ordinated services. It encouraged what the Seebohm Committee called the 'symptom-centred' approach to social problems.

The solution to this dilemma of the categories, however, is not easy to find. Policy with regard to the homeless provides a recent example. Responsibility for them had been divided on the basis of the cause of homelessness and of the need it created, whether due to an emergency like a fire or flood, or to some disturbance in domestic circumstances which created a welfare problem, or to delay in carrying out the general housing programme. The Seebohm Committee recommended that order should be brought out of a chaotic situation by treating the homeless (whatever the cause of their plight) as a single category of persons for whom one authority, that for housing, should take full responsibility. The change was made, but it has not met with universal or unequivocal approval. In its general recommendations for a single social service department and a staff of 'generic' or all-purpose professional social workers, it could be said to favour the elimination as far as possible of all categories, whether of persons or of needs, leaving them as it were to emerge and define themselves in the course of treatment, when it is found that a symptom-centred approach is needed in a particular case. It is too early to judge how successful this policy will prove to be.

A third possible base for an integrated social policy is the local area or community. The educational priority areas and the National Community Development Project described in the previous chapter are examples of positive discrimination used in this way, but they are not the only ones. Writing in 1974 David Donnison remarked that 'during the last six years Britain has had a boom in priority area policies', including the 'six cities project' of the Department of the Environment. It was indeed high time, he wrote, that 'we bridged the gap between "spatial" and "social" thinking—between geography and town planning on one side, and social policy and administration on the other'. But he doubted whether 'a few hurriedly carpentered programmes' would suffice to achieve this. It was time for a reappraisal of the whole subject of deprived areas.[17]

The bridging of gaps, or co-ordination of policies, can take place at various levels. The purpose of priority area projects is to bring it about at ground level. At the opposite extreme we have seen moves in recent years to bridge gaps at the top, for instance by establishing a Department of the Environment to cover all aspects of housing, town and country planning, conservation and pollution, and a Department in which Health and Social Security can be united, and by seeking ways to fuse social security finance with personal taxation. This kind of structural change should make it easier to take political decisions which are consistent with one another. In between these two levels lies the area of planning proper, if by this we mean, not the taking of the political decisions, but the objective study and analysis of situations and measures in order to provide a basis on which the decisions can be taken and guidance as to the means by which they can be put into effect. Planning of this kind must go into considerable technical detail and get down to the roots of the matter; this, as we saw, is being advocated, and to an increasing extent practised, in the field of medicine.

It is also making progress in social security, which offers considerable scope for the use of quantitative methods. Two international conferences on social security planning were held in 1970 and 1972 under the auspices of the International Social Security Association.[18] At these were discussed both the general issues involved and also technical matters like forecasting, the use of social indicators to estimate the magnitude of social problems and to measure change, the value of computer-based models to calculate the nature and distribution of the effects of a proposed change in a social security system, and so forth. The discussions were lively and to the point, but when it came to reviewing what had actually been achieved in overall social planning, let alone in co-ordinated social and economic planning, the results were rather meagre. It was reported that France had included social security in her fifth plan (1966–70), but only with a view to reducing expenditure; in the sixth plan (1971–5) she intended to examine the objectives of social policy and its shortcomings, and propose appropriate action. West Germany had adopted a comprehensive social budget in 1969, and in 1972 laid down the percentages of national income to be devoted to various social purposes. Belgium produced an overall plan of social security expenditure for 1971–5, but ran into difficulties because of the lack of unanimity on the principles of social policy. Italy had similar problems about making definite choices between fundamental alternatives. The official British reply to a questionnaire contained the information that in this country policy developments and changes 'arise from the interplay of political programmes, administrative planning, pressure groups and public opinion' (Report No. 2, p. 39). A French spokesman (and member of the sponsoring body) made a significant comment about a situation from which, he thought, social policy still has some difficulty in extricating itself. He said: 'The evolution of social expenditure is still planned as a burden, certainly inevitable but all the same troublesome, in a national accounting system entirely conceived in terms of market values, and not as a desirable result, positive and conducing to the increase of available wealth.'[19]

Postscript

The expected autumn election was held on 10 October 1974, and gave the new Labour government an overall majority of three. This meant that their programme could go forward, but that the passage of complex or controversial legislation might be a laborious process. The White Paper on pensions (Cmnd. 5713) issued by Labour in September reactivated the Crossman Plan, with modifications including better terms for wives, widows and widowers (a new category). In one respect the gap between it and the Joseph Plan appeared to be narrowed. The revised Labour scheme contains what is virtually a basic guaranteed minimum pension for all insured persons, whether 'contracted out' or not, which looks very much like the State Basic Pension of the Joseph Plan, except that it is built into the earnings-related structure instead of being financially and administratively separate from it. Since both plans allow for company 'occupational' schemes to take over responsibility for retirement pensions above the basic level, the crucial question is what conditions such schemes must fulfil in order to be judged acceptable for this purpose. Conservatives think Labour's conditions are too exacting; on the other hand the Labour attitude towards partnership with occupational insurance is markedly warmer than it was in Crossman's day. There is room here for negotiation, especially with the companies. But there is no place in the Labour programme for the supporting device of tax credits which the Conservatives, in their election manifesto, called 'the centre-piece of our social policy'.

On housing there is a measure of consensus on two points. The policy of encouraging Housing Associations, as expressed in an Act passed by the previous Parliament (1974 c.44), has general approval; and all parties favour measures to keep mortgage rates at a tolerable level, especially for first-time buyers of houses, though the Conservatives would do more here than Labour proposes. In the matter of rents there are two controversial issues. The Opposition is sharply critical of the Act already passed (1974 c.51) giving security of tenure to occupants of furnished dwellings, on the grounds that it will drive this kind of accommodation off the market, and it has been alleged that this is already happening. Secondly, the Conservative Housing Finance Act applied the 'fair rent' system to council houses and ordered rents to be stepped up towards the expected higher level. Labour has frozen rents till April 1975 and will repeal that section of the Act, thus restoring to councils the power to fix their own rents, provided that they are 'reasonable'. This, say the critics, will make the level of rents uncomfortably dependent on the state of the local Housing Revenue Account. How much difference the shift from 'fair' to 'reasonable' will make in the long run depends on the generosity of government subsidies and the amount that can be added from the rates, which is likely to be small. It is assumed that, when rents are unfrozen, they will rise, and Labour proposes to regularize the use of means-tested rebates by retaining the system in the Conservative Act and providing a 'rent rebates subsidy' to cover 75 per cent of the cost. But the most far-reaching measure proposed may well prove to be that imposing on local authorities a *duty* to bring into public ownership land scheduled for development for ten years ahead. This is a long-term measure, however, which a future government could easily suspend or amend.

The election campaign revealed a unanimous will to extend family allowances to the first child and to create a comprehensive pension for the disabled. Expectations have been disappointed on both points. Family allowances will be increased, but the first child is left out. A non-contributory pension is to be given to those of working age whose disablement prevented them from ever working (and contributing), and an invalid care allowance to those devoting themselves to the care of a disabled relative. This falls so far short of what the various organizations were demanding that they have united to form a new Disability Alliance to strengthen their campaign for further measures. Clearly what was said above (pp. 188–9) on the subject was over-optimistic.

We may probably attribute this failure to fulfil declared aims to the stresses of the economic situation. All branches of social policy are oppressed by rising costs and wages. The personal social services are suffering from an acute shortage of staff, and the state of affairs in the National Health Service is still more serious, though statements that it is 'grinding to a halt' are, as yet, exaggerated. It has suffered from industrial action by its employees, including refusal by some to serve private patients in NHS hospitals. This issue rose to confrontation proportions when the government reaffirmed its intention to 'phase out' the hospital pay-beds in which consultants can treat their private patients, adding to an already critical situation.

References

Chapter 1 *The legacy of the Victorian era*

1. Leonard Woolf, *Sowing*, Hogarth Press, 1960, pp. 151 and 160.
2. e.g., J. A. R. Marriott, *Modern England 1885–1932*, Methuen, 1934, p. 155.
3. G. M. Trevelyan, *History of England*, Longmans, 1926, p. 50.
4. R. C. K. Ensor, *England 1870–1914*. Clarendon Press, 1936, p. 109.
5. Royal Commission on Labour, 1894, vol. xxxv, p. 36.
6. Cited by Sir Ivor Jennings in H. J. Laski (Ed.), *A Century of Municipal Progress*, Allen and Unwin, 1935, p. 57.
7. Children's Employment Commissioners, 1864, quoted in B. L. Hutchins and A. Harrison, *A History of Factory Legislation*, London School of Economics, 1911, p. 224.
8. Harold E. Raynes, *Social Security in Britain*, Pitman, 1957, p. 175.
9. A. Bevan, *In Place of Fear*, Heinemann, 1952, pp. 73–4.
10. David Roberts, *Victorian Origins of the British Welfare State*, Yale University Press, New Haven, 1960, p. 315.

Chapter 2 *Problems and policies at the turn of the century*

1. Edward R. Pease, *The History of the Fabian Society*, 2nd ed., Fabian Society, 1925, p. 13.
2. Godfrey Elton, *England Arise!*, Jonathan Cape, 1931, pp. 123–30.
3. John R. Commons, *History of Labour in the United States*, vol. iii, Macmillan Co., New York, 1935, pp. 128 and 219.
4. R. C. K. Ensor, *England 1870–1914*, Clarendon Press, 1936, p. 111.
5. Richard Hofstadter, *The Age of Reform*, Jonathan Cape, 1955, p. 166.
6. Charles Booth, *Life and Labour of the People*, vol. i, Williams and Norgate, 1889; R. Seebohm Rowntree, *Poverty, a Study of Town Life*, Macmillan, 1901.
7. L. G. Chiozza Money, *Riches and Povery*, Methuen, 1905, p. 5.
8. D. Lloyd George, *Slings and Arrows* (Ed. Philip Guedalla), Cassell, 1929, p. 6.
9. Parliamentary Papers, 1904, vol. xxxii, p. 92.
10. Royal Commission on the Housing of the Working Classes, First Report, 1885, p. 4. (Cd. 4402).
11. J. M. Mackintosh, *Trends of Opinion about the Public Health, 1901–1951*, Oxford University Press, 1953, pp. 42–3.
12. A. V. Dicey, *Lectures on the Relation between Law and Public Opinion in England during the Nineteenth Century*, 2nd ed., Macmillan, 1914, p. 64.
13. R. L. Hill, *Toryism and the People*, Constable, 1929, pp. 5–6.
14. Dicey, op. cit. p. 256.

15. S. MacCoby, *The English Radical Tradition, 1763–1914*, Nicholas Kaye, 1952, pp. 201–2.

16. *Fabian Essays* (Jubilee Edition, 1948), pp. 194–7.

17. *The Nineteenth Century*, 1899, pp. 10 and 23–7.

18. 'Lord Rosebery's Escape from Houndsditch' in *The Nineteenth Century*, 1901, p. 366.

19. W. S. Churchill, *Liberalism and the Social Problem (Speeches 1906–1909)*, Hodder and Stoughton, 1909, pp. 71–8.

20. *Fabian Essays*, p. xxii.

21. ibid., p. 137.

22. Helen Bosanquet, *The Strength of the People*, Macmillan, 1903, p. 208.

23. William Stanley Jevons, *The State in Relation to Labour (The English Citizen)*, Macmillan, 1882, pp. 9 and 12.

24. E. Halévy, *History of the English People in the Nineteenth Century* (trans. E. I. Watkin and D. A. Barker), 2nd ed., vol. v, Ernest Benn, 1951, p. 231.

Chapter 3   *The problem of poverty*

1. Emily Greene Balch, *Public Assistance of the Poor in France*, American Economic Association, Baltimore, 1893.

2. George P. Nelson (Ed.), *Freedom and Welfare—Social Patterns in the Northern Countries of Europe*, Arbejds- og Socialministeriet, Copenhagen, 1953, p. 457.

3. Jean S. Heywood, *Children in Care*, Routledge and Kegan Paul, 1959, pp. 71–2.

4. *Provision for Old Age by Government Action in Certain European Countries*, P. P. 1899, vol. xcii; *Memorandum on New Zealand and Germany*, 1908, vol. lxxxviii.

5. K. de Schweinitz, *England's Road to Social Security*, Oxford University Press, 1943, p. 180.

6. S. and B. Webb, *English Poor Law Policy*, Longmans, 1910, pp. 214–15.

7. W. H. Beveridge, *Unemployment—A Problem of Industry*, Longmans, 1912, pp. 154–6.

8. Grace Abbott, *From Relief to Social Security*, University of Chicago Press, Chicago, 1941, p. 17.

9. W. J. Braithwaite, *Lloyd George's Ambulance Wagon*, Methuen, 1957, p. 136.

10. S. and B. Webb, *English Poor Law History*, part ii, Longmans, 1929, pp. 529–31.

11. Majority Report of the Royal Commission on the Poor Laws and Relief of Distress, 1909, vol. xxxvii, p. 294, para. 220.

12. ibid., p. 421, para. 604.

13. ibid., p. 529, para. 10.

14. Minority Report, pp. 284–5.

15. Beatrice Webb, *My Apprenticeship*, Longmans, 1926, p. 195.

16. Minority Report, p. 405.

17. ibid., pp. 670–3.

18. Majority Report, p. 597, para. 4.

19. S. and B. Webb, *English Poor Law Policy*, Longmans, 1910, p. 302.

20. W. S. Churchill, *Liberalism and the Social Problem (Speeches 1906–1909)*, Hodder and Stoughton, 1909, p. 87.

Chapter 4   *The coming of social insurance*

1. L. K. Frankel and M. M. Dawson, *Workingmen's Insurance in Europe*, New York Charities Publication Committee (Russell Sage Foundation), 1910, p. 395.
2. H. du Parcq, *David Lloyd George*, vol. iv, Caxton, 1912–13, pp. 643 and 778.
3. Majority Report, p. 528, para. 2.
4. Beveridge Report (*Social Insurance and Allied Services*), p. 12, para. 24.
5. A. Birnie, *Economic History of Europe*, Methuen, 1957, pp. 223–4; *Provision for Old Age by Government Action in Certain European Countries*, P.P. 1899, vol. xcii.
6. Dermot Morrah, *A History of Industrial Life Assurance*, Allen and Unwin, 1955, pp. 29–35.
7. Gertrude Williams, *The State and the Standard of Living*, P. S. King and Son, 1936, pp. 67–8.
8. *Provision for Old Age* [. . .], pp. 14–19.
9. Minority Report, p. 274.
10. W. H. Dawson, *Social Insurance in Germany*, T. Fisher Unwin, 1912, pp. 14 and 19.
11. *Memorandum on Old Age Pensions*, P.P. 1908, vol. lxxxviii, p. 393.
12. J. M. Mackintosh, *Trends of Opinion about the Public Health*, Oxford University Press, 1953, p. 33.
13. W. J. Braithwaite, *Lloyd George's Ambulance Wagon*, Methuen, 1957, p. 71.
14. The *Lancet*, 1895, p. 476.
15. I. G. Gibbon, *Medical Benefit: A study of the Experience of Germany and Denmark*, P. S. King and Son, 1912, pp. 27 and 236–9.
16. Dawson, op. cit., p. 85.
17. Majority Report, p. 630; W. S. Churchill, *Liberalism and the Social Problem* (*Speeches 1906–1909*), Hodder and Stoughton, 1909, p. 254.
18. S. and B. Webb, *English Poor Law History*, part ii, Longmans, 1929, p. 663.
19. W. H. Beveridge, *Unemployment—A Problem of Industry*, Longmans, 1912, p. 322.
20. Frank Tillyard, *Unemployment Insurance in Great Britain*, Thames Bank, 1949, pp. 3–4.
21. Churchill, op. cit., pp. 309 and 315–16.
22. W. S. Churchill, *The Second World War*, vol. iv, Cassell, 1951, Appendix F, p. 862.
23. E. M. Burns, *The American Social Security System*, Houghton Mifflin Co., Boston, 1951, p. 36.
24. Braithwaite, op. cit., p. 121.

Chapter 5   *The inter-war years*

1. C. W. Pipkin, *Social Politics and Modern Democracies*, vol. ii, Macmillan Co., New York, 1931, p. 196.
2. ibid., pp. 202–5.
3. Paul Douglas, *Social Security in the United States*, McGraw-Hill, New York, 1936, p. 11.

4. Arnold Wilson and G. S. Mackay, *Old Age Pensions*, Oxford University Press, 1941, p. 203.

5. ibid., pp. 88–9.

6. Beveridge Report, Appendix F, p. 287.

7. R. C. Davison, *British Unemployment Policy since 1930*, Longmans, Green, 1938, pp. 111 and 128.

8. W. H. Beveridge, *Unemployment—A Problem of Industry*, Longmans, 1930, pp. 288–9.

9. Douglas, op. cit., pp. 12 and 130; *The Social Welfare Forum*, Columbia University Press, Columbia, 1962, p. 9.

10. D. V. Glass, *Population Policies and Movements*, Clarendon Press, 1940, ch. 3.

11. Norman Wilson, *Municipal Health Services*, 1938, pp. 87–99.

12. André Rouast et Paul Durand, *Sécurité sociale*, Dalloz, Paris, 1960, pp. 473–505; Henrich Braun, *Industrialisation and Social Policy in Germany*, Carl Heymanns Verlag, Köln, Berlin, 1956, p. 90.

13. George P. Nelson (Ed.), *Freedom and Welfare—Social Patterns in the Northern Countries of Europe*, Arbejds- og Socialministeriet, Copenhagen, 1953, pp. 446–60.

14. Hilary M. Leyendecker, *Problems and Policy in Public Assistance*, Harper and Bros, New York, 1955, pp. 52–5 and 82–5.

15. Edith Abbott, *Public Assistance*, vol. i, University of Chicago Press, Chicago, 1940, p. 125.

16. Marian Bowley, *Housing and the State 1919–1944*, Allen and Unwin, 1945, p. 3.

17. G. Slater, *Poverty and the State*, Constable, 1930, pp. 243–8.

18. Bowley, op. cit., *passim*; John Greve, *The Housing Problem*, Fabian Society, 1961, p. 11.

19. Pipkin, op. cit., vol. ii, pp. 156–7.

20. Alva Myrdal, *Nation and Family*, Harper and Bros, New York, 1945, p. 242.

21. ILO, *Housing Policy in Europe*, 1930, *passim*.

22. Davison, op. cit., ch. 5.

23. A. C. F. Bourdillon (Ed.), *Voluntary Social Services*, Methuen, 1945, p. 164.

24. ibid., p. 57.

25. ibid., p. 26.

Chapter 6   *The war and the Welfare State*

1. R. M. Titmuss, *Problems of Social Policy*, in *History of the Second World War*, UK Civil Series, 1950, p. 507.

2. ibid, p. 504

3. A. G. B. Fisher, *Economic Progress and Social Security*, Macmillan, 1945, p. 23.

4. Beveridge Report, para. 459.

5. ibid., para 8.

6. ibid., para 14.

7. ibid., para 31.

8. *Social Insurance*, part i, 1944, para. 1 (Cmd. 6550.)

9. H. D. Henderson, *The Inter-war Years and other papers* (Ed. Henry Clay), Clarendon Press, 1955, pp. 192–207.

10. Bulletin of the International Social Security Association, 1959, vol. xii, no. 8–9.

11. Hansard (Lords), 1953, vol. 182, cols. 675–6.

12. Arnold Wilson and G. S. Mackay, *Old Age Pensions*, Oxford University Press, 1941, p. 193.

13. W. H. Beveridge, *Insurance for All and Everything*, *Daily News*, 1924, pp. 6–7.

14. J. L. Cohen, *Social Insurance Unified*, P. S. King and Son, 1924, p. 23.

15. Beveridge Report, para 288.

16. ibid., Appendix F, para. 6.

17. ibid., para. 294.

18. ibid., para. 369.

19. *Social Insurance*, part i, paras., 12–13.

20. Hansard (Lords), 1953, vol. 182, col. 677.

21. Beveridge Report, para. 302.

22. Hansard (Lords), 1945–6, vol. 143, col. 78.

23. Henry Brackenbury, *Patient and Doctor*, Hodder and Stoughton, 1935, pp. 149–50.

24. Joan S. Clarke, in W. A. Robson (Ed.), *Social Security*, Fabian Society, 1945, pp. 92 and 121–3.

25. Consultative Council on Medical and Allied Services, First Interim Report, 1920, vol. xvii, para. 3.

26. Royal Commission on National Health Insurance, 1926, vol. xiv, p. 138.

27. ibid., p. 152.

28. Harry Eckstein, *The English Health Service*, Harvard University Press, Massachusetts, 1959, p. 142.

29. A. Massey (Ed.), *Modern Trends in Public Health*, Butterworth, 1949, p. 130.

30. Aneurin Bevan, *In Place of Fear*, Heinemann, 1952, p. 73.

31. Vincent Brome, *Aneurin Bevan*, Longmans, Green, 1953, p. 198.

Chapter 7   *Re-assessment of the Welfare State*

1. *The Times*, 25 February 1952, p. 7.

2. Iain Macleod and J. Enoch Powell, *The Social Services—Needs and Means*, Conservative Political Centre, 1952, p. 5.

3. R. M. Titmuss, 'Crisis in the Social Services', *The Listener*, 14 February, 1952.

4. *The Times*, 26 February 1952, p. 5.

5. *Crossbow*, Autumn 1960, p. 25.

6. Alan Peacock, *The Welfare Society*, Liberal Publication Department on behalf of the Unservile State Group, 1961, p. 11.

7. Geoffrey Howe, 'Reform of the Social Services' in *Principles and Practice*, Bow Group, 1961, p. 61.

8. ILO, *The Cost of Social Security 1949–1957*, p. 205.

9. *The Times*, 24 May 1961, p. 17.

Chapter 8   *Social security*

1. EEC, *Exposé sur la situation sociale dans la Communauté*, 1958, p. 71.

2. *International Labour Review*, vol. lvii, p. 566; J. E. Russell (Ed.), *National*

Policies for Education, Health and Social Services, Russell and Russell, New York, 1961, pp. 275–6.

3. EEC, *Etudes-Série Politique Sociale: Sécurité Sociale*, 1962, pp. 14–23.

4. Paul Fisher, 'Developments and Trends in Social Security, 1967–69', *International Social Security Review*, vol. xxiv, no. 1, 1971, p. 24.

5. EEC, *Sécurité Sociale*, p. 8.

6. OASIS, August 1960, p. 8.

7. Conservative Political Centre, *The Future of the Welfare State*, 1958, p. 18.

8. Social Trends No. 4, 1973, Tables 49 and 50.

9. White Paper on Provision for Old Age, 1958, Cmnd. 538.

10. *Occupational Pension Schemes*, Third Survey by the Government Actuary, 1968, pp. 7–13.

11. Richard Crossman, *The Politics of Pensions*, Liverpool University Press, 1972, p. 21.

12. Sir John Walley, *Social Security—Another British Failure?*, Knight, 1972, pp. 146–7 and 170–1.

13. Barbara N. Rodgers, John Greve and John S. Morgan, *Comparative Social Administration*, Allen and Unwin, 1968, pp. 34–5 and 289–90; EEC Social Policy Series No. 17, 1966, *Supplementary Social Security Schemes*.

14. Barbara N. Rodgers *et al., op. cit.*, p. 110; T. H. Kewley, *Social Security in Australia*, Methuen, 1965, p. 214.

15. 'Women and Social Security—Study of the Situation in Five Countries', *International Social Security Review*, vol. xxvi, nos. 1–2, 1973, pp. 73–106.

16. *National Superannuation and Social Insurance*, 1969, Cmnd. 3883, Appendix 1, para. 27.

17. 'Women and Social Security [. . .]', pp. 104–5 and 93.

18. Report of the Committee on Abuse of Social Security Benefits, 1973, Cmnd. 5228.

19. François Lafitte, 'The History of Family Help', *New Society*, 26 July 1973.

20. *Journal of Social Policy*, vol. i, part 4, October 1972, p. 347.

Chapter 9 *Health care*

1. *International Social Security Review*, vol. xxii, no. 3, 1969, pp. 327–9.

2. Odin W. Anderson, *The Uneasy Equilibrium: Private and Public Financing of Health Services in the United States 1875–1965*, College and University Press, New Haven, Connecticut, 1968, p. 137.

3. Thomas McKeown, *Medicine in Modern Society*, Allen and Unwin, 1965, p. 13.

4. M. M. Hauser (Ed.), *The Economics of Medical Care*, Allen and Unwin, 1972, p. 19.

5. Ruldolf Klein, 'An Anatomy of the NHS', *New Society*, 28 June 1973.

6. *Private Practice in NHS Hospitals*, 1972, Cmnd. 5270, p. 5.

7. *The Cost of the National Health Service*, 1955–6, Cmd. 9663, p. 9.

8. *A Review of the Medical Services of Great Britain*, Report of the Medical Services Review Committee of the BMA, 1962.

9. *Management Arrangements for the Reorganised NHS*, HMSO, 1972 (The Grey Book), p. 12.

10. *National Health Service Reorganisation: England*, HMSO, 1972, para. 134.

11. *National Health Service Reorganisation: Consultative Document*, 1971, para. 20.

12. *NHS Reorganisation: England*, para. 66.

13. Royal Commission on Medical Education, 1968, Cmnd. 3569, paras. 133–7.

14. *Doctors in an Integrated Health Service*, HMSO, Edinburgh, 1971, para. 107.

15. *Working Party on Collaboration between the NHS and Local Government*, HMSO, 1972 and 1973.

16. 'Community Care: Fact or Fiction' in H. Freeman and J. Farndale (Eds.), *Trends in the Mental Health Services*, Pergamon Press, 1963.

17. Kathleen Jones, *Mental Health and Social Policy 1845–1959*, Routledge and Kegan Paul, 1960, pp. 109–10.

18. *Better Services for the Mentally Handicapped*, 1971, Cmnd. 4863.

19. *The Field of Work of the Family Doctor*, HMSO, 1963, para. 206.3.

20. J. Enoch Powell, *A New Look at Medicine and Politics*, Pitman, 1966, p. 33.

21. *The Organisation of Group Practice*, HMSO, 1971, p. 89.

22. *On the State of the Public Health in 1971*, HMSO, 1971, p. 151.

23. Joint Report of the Royal College of Physicians and the Royal College of General Practitioners, *The General Practitioner in the Hospital*, 1972, p. 3.

24. WHO, *First Report on the World Health Situation*, 1959, p. 33.

25. *The Future Structure of the National Health Service*, HMSO, 1970, p. 1.

26. I. Douglas-Wilson and Gordon McLachlan (Eds.), *Health Service Prospects*, 1973, cited in *New Society*, 18 October 1973, p. 160.

27. Milton I. Roemer, *The Organisation of Medical Care under Social Security*, Report to the ILO, 1969, p. 31.

28. *International Social Security Review*, vol. xxiv, no. 4, 1971, pp. 562–4.

29. *Bulletin of the International Social Security Association*, 1966, no. 9/10, p. 348.

30. *International Social Security Review*, vol. xxv, no. 1/2, 1972, pp. 84–6.

31. Roemer, loc. cit.

32. *Private Practice in NHS Hospitals*, 1972, Cmnd. 5270.

33. British Medical Association Report on Health Service Financing, 1970.

Chapter 10   *The welfare services*

1. S. K. Ruck, *London Government and the Welfare Services*, Routledge and Kegan Paul, 1963, p. 9.

2. Edith Abbott, *Public Assistance*, vol. i, University of Chicago Press, Chicago, 1940, p. 60.

3. Charity Organisation Society, *How to Help Cases in Distress*, 1945, p. 18.

4. Barbara Rodgers and Julia Dixon, *Portrait of Social Work*, Oxford University Press, 1960, p. 31.

5. Report of the Assistance Board for 1944, 1945, p. 8.

6. Health Services and Public Health Act 1968, ch. 46, para. 45 (1).

7. Noel Timms, 'Foster Parents and the Child Care Service', Case Conference VII, 6 November 1960, p. 147.

8. Report of the Care of Children Committee, 1946, paras. 62 and 32. (Cmd. 6722.)

9. Hubback Committee on *The Neglected Child and his Family*, 1948.

10. Report of the Departmental Committee on the Adoption of Children, 1972, Cmnd. 5107, p. 133.

11. Peter Townsend, *The Last Refuge*, Routledge and Kegan Paul, 1962, p. 133.

12. ibid., pp. 511 and 143.

13. Ethel Shanas *et al.*, *Old People in Three Industrial Societies*, Routledge and Kegan Paul, 1968, especially ch. 2, 7 and 9.

14. J. H. Sheldon, *The Social Medicine of Old Age*, Oxford University Press for the Nuffield Foundation, 1948, p. 197.

15. Margaret N. Hill, *An Approach to Old Age and its Problems*, Oliver and Boyd, 1961, p. 86.

16. *The Purpose and Content of the Youth Service*, Second Report of the Youth Advisory Service, 1945, paras. 2 and 7.

17. C. L. Mowat, *The Charity Organization Society 1869–1913, its ideas and work*, Methuen, 1961, pp. 70–1 and 112.

18. Barbara Wootton, *Social Science and Social Pathology*, Allen and Unwin, 1959, pp. 284–97.

19. E. M. Goldberg *et al.*, *Helping the Aged*, Allen and Unwin, 1970, p. 197.

20. Association of Social Workers, *New Thinking about Welfare, values and priorities*, 1969, p. 81.

21. Adrian Sinfield, *Which Way to Social Work?*, Fabian Tract No. 393, 1969, p. 10.

22. Report of the Committee on Local Authority and Allied Personal Social Services, 1968, Cmnd. 3703.

23. *Social Work and the Community: Proposals for Reorganising Local Authority Services in Scotland*, 1966, Cmnd. 3605.

24. D. V. Donnison, *The Neglected Child and the Social Services*, Manchester University Press, 1954, pp. 72–3.

25. Eileen Younghusband (Ed.), *Social Work with Families*, Allen and Unwin, 1965, p. 28.

26. *Community Work and Social Change—A report on training*, Calouste Gulbenkian Foundation, 1968.

27. Maurice G. Speed in Kathleen Jones (Ed.), *The Year Book of Social Policy in Britain 1971*, Routledge and Kegan Paul, 1972, pp. 65 and 67.

28. George Meredith in Kathleen Jones (Ed.), op. cit., p. 46.

Chapter 11 *Housing*

1. *Fair Deal for Housing*, 1971, Cmnd. 4728, para. 5.

2. *Housing*, 1963, Cmnd. 2050, p. 2.

3. *Old Houses into New Homes*, 1968, Cmnd. 3602, para. 6.

4. Quoted in David Donnison, *The Government of Housing*, Penguin, 1967, p. 164.

5. *New Society*, 28 February 1974.

6. Donnison, op. cit., pp. 103–4 and 94–5.

7. Paul F. Wendt, *Housing Policy: the Search for Solutions*, University of California Press, Berkeley and Los Angeles, 1962, pp. 67–8.

8. EEC, *Exposé sur la situation sociale dans la Communauté*, 1959, p. 259; 1961, pp. 214–6.

9. *Exposé* [. . .], 1958, p. 99.

10. Lord Beveridge, *Voluntary Action*, Allen and Unwin, 1948, p. 106.

11. Social Trends, 1972, Table 113.

12. Mark Abrams, *The Condition of the British People*, Fabian Society, 1946, p. 84; Ministry of Labour Family Expenditure Surveys; Paul F. Wendt, op. cit., p. 75.

13. C. A. R. Crosland, *Towards a Labour Housing Policy*, Fabian Tract No. 410, 1971.
14. *Skilling* v. *Arcari's Executrix, Scots Law Times*, 8 February 1974.
15. *New Society*, 28 June 1973.
16. *Local Authority and Allied Personal Social Services*, 1968, Cmnd. 3703, 390–5.
17. *Council Housing Purposes, Procedures and Priorities*, HMSO, 1969, p. 3.
18. David Donnison, 'A Housing Service', *New Society*, 11 November 1973.

Chapter 12 *Poverty*

1. *Research on Poverty*, Social Science Research Council Review of Current Research, 1968, p. 5.
2. R. J. Lampan, 'Ends and Means in the War against Poverty' in Leo Fishman (Ed.), *Poverty amid Affluence*, Yale University Press, Connecticut, 1966, p. 212.
3. Robert Holman, 'The American Poverty Programme 1969–71', *Journal of Social Policy*, vol. iii, part 1, January 1974, p. 32.
4. A. H. Halsey, 'The Dilemma of Educational Priority Areas', *Encounter*, May 1969, pp. 93–6.
5. Eric Midwinter, 'The Strategy of the EPA Movement', *Year Book of Social Policy in 1972*, 1973.
6. The National Community Development Project: Inter-Project Report, 1973, p. 26, para. 4.11.
7. Family Service Units, 25th Annual Report, 1974.
8. G. C. Fiegehen and P. S. Sansley, 'The Tax Credit Proposals', *National Institute Economic Review*, May 1973.
9. *Administration of the Wage Stop*, Report of the Supplementary Benefits Commission to the Minister of Social Security, 1967, para. 36.
10. Report of the Select Committee on Tax Credits, vol. iii, 1972, pp. 24–6.
11. Audrey Hunt, Judith Fox and Margaret Morgan, *Families and their Needs, with particular reference to one-parent families*, vol. 1, HMSO, 1973, pp. 31, 36, 81.
12. R. M. Titmuss, *The Social Division of Welfare*, Eleanor Rathbone Memorial Lecture No. 6, 1956.
13. David Barker, 'Negative Income Tax', in David Bull (Ed.), *Family Poverty—Programme for the Seventies*, Duckworth, 1971, ch. 5.
14. *Proposals for a Tax Credit System*, 1972, Cmnd. 5116.
15. J. E. Meade, *Poverty in the Welfare State*, Oxford Economic Papers, vol. xxiv, no. 3, 1972, p. 305.
16. Richard Crossman, *The Policy of Pensions*, Liverpool University Press, 1972, p. 18.
17. R. M. Titmuss, *Commitment to Welfare*, Allen and Unwin, 1968, p. 122.
18. Barbara N. Rodgers, John Greve and John S. Morgan, *Comparative Social Administration*, Allen and Unwin, 1968, p. 237.

Chapter 13 *Problems and Prospects of the 1970s*

1. Brian Abel-Smith, 'Whose Welfare State?', in Norman Mackenzie (Ed.), *Conviction*, MacGibbon and Kee, 1958, p. 57.

2. Richard Titmuss, 'Equity, Adequacy and Innovation in Social Security', *International Social Security Review*, vol. xxiii, no. 2, 1970, pp. 259–67.

3. Margaret Wynn, *Fatherless Families*, Michael Joseph, 1964, p. 45.

4. Herman Miller, in Howard S. Becker (Ed.), *Social Problems: A Modern Approach*, Wiley, 1966, p. 472.

5. Robert Pinker, *Social Theory and Social Policy*, Heinemann Educational, 1971, p. 141.

6. W. H. Beveridge, *Voluntary Action*, Allen and Unwin, 1948, p. 31.

7. R. M. Titmuss, *Problems of Social Policy*, in *History of the Second World War*, UK Civil Series, 1950, pp. 261–2.

8. *New Society*, 12 July 1973.

9. *New Society*, 2 May 1974.

10. Bill Jordan, *Paupers: the making of the new claiming class*, Routledge and Kegan Paul, 1973.

11. A. T. Peacock and J. Wiseman, *The Growth of Public Expenditure in the UK*, Oxford University Press, 1961, p. 86; A. T. Peacock and D. J. Robertson (Eds.), *Public Expenditure—Appraisal and Control*, Oliver and Boyd, 1963, pp. 114 and 119.

12. Social Trends No. 4, 1973, p. 187, Table 168.

13. *Social Security Abstracts of the International Social Security Association, 1968*, vol. iv, nos. 6, 7, 18, 31 and 35.

14. Census of Population Reports, Population Projections, 1974.

15. Social Trends No. 4, 1973, p. 85, Table 17.

16. B. Benjamin, 'Demographic and Actuarial Aspects of Ageing', *Journal of the Institute of Actuaries*, September 1964, pp. 218–9.

17. David Donnison, 'Policies for Priority Areas', *Journal of Social Policy*, vol. lii, no. 2, 1974, pp. 127–35.

18. International Social Security Association, Studies and Research Reports, No. 2, 'The Planning of Social Security', 1971, and No. 4, 'Current Issues in Social Security Planning', 1973.

19. Clément Michel, in ISA Report No. 4, above, p. 48.

Select bibliography

Historical background

BRUCE, MAURICE, *The coming of the Welfare State*, 4th ed., Batsford, 1968.
Fabian Essays, Jubilee edition, Fabian Society, 1945.
FRASER, DEREK, *The Evolution of the British Welfare State*, Macmillan, 1973.
MARTIN, E. L. (Ed.), *Comparative Developments in Social Welfare*, Allen and Unwin, 1972.
WEBB, SIDNEY and BEATRICE, *English Poor Law History*, part ii, vol. ii, Longmans, 1929.

General

BROWN, MURIEL, *Introduction to Social Administration in Britain*, 2nd rev. ed., Hutchinson, 1971.
COOPER, MICHAEL H. (Ed.), *Social policy: a survey of recent developments*, Blackwood, Oxford, 1973.
FAMILY WELFARE ASSOCIATION, *Guide to the Social Services*, 63rd ed., MacDonald and Evans, 1974.
HALL, MARY PENELOPE, *The Social Services of Modern England*, 6th ed., Routledge, 1965.
PINKER, ROBERT A., *Social Theory and Social Policy*, Heinemann, 1971.
ROBSON, W. A., 'The Welfare State' in *Hobhouse Memorial Lectures 1951–60*, Athlone Press, 1962.
SLACK, KATHLEEN, *Social Administration and the Citizen*, Michael Joseph, 1966.
TITMUSS, RICHARD M., *Essays on the Welfare State*, Allen and Unwin, 1958.
—— *Commitment to Welfare*, Allen and Unwin, 1968.
TOWNSEND, PETER (Ed.), *Social Services for All*, Fabian Society, 1968.
WARHAM, JOYCE, *Social Policy in Context*, Batsford, 1970.

Economic and financial

CULYER, A. J., *Economics of Social Policy*, Martin Robertson, 1973.
HAUSER, M. M., *The Economics of Medical Care*, Allen and Unwin, 1970.
HOUGHTON, D., *Paying for the Social Services*, Institute of Economic Affairs, 1967.
PEACOCK, A. T. (Ed.), *Income Redistribution and Social Policy*, Cape, 1954.
Proposals for a Tax-Credit System, Cmnd. 5116, HMSO, 1972.
RICHARDSON, J. HENRY, *Economic and Financial Aspects of Social Security*, Allen and Unwin, 1960.

Social insurance

BEVERIDGE, W. H. (Lord), *Insurance for All and Everything, Daily News,* 1924.

GEORGE, VICTOR, *Social Security: Beveridge and After,* Routledge, 1968.

MARSH, DAVID C., *National Insurance and Assistance in Great Britain,* Pitman, 1950.

National Superannuation and Social Insurance, Cmnd. 3883, HMSO, 1969.

ROBSON, W. A. (Ed.), *Social Security,* 2nd ed., Allen and Unwin, 1945.

Strategy for Pensions, Cmnd. 4755, HMSO, 1971.

Social Insurance and Allied Services, (Beveridge Report), 1942.

WALLEY, SIR JOHN, *Social Security: Another British Failure?,* Charles Knight, 1972.

WILSON, SIR ARNOLD and MACKAY, G. S., *Old Age Pensions,* OUP, 1951.

Poverty

ABEL-SMITH, BRIAN and TOWNSEND, PETER, *The Poor and the Poorest,* Occasional Papers on Social Administration no. 17, Bell, 1965.

ATKINSON, A. B., *Poverty in Britain and the Reform of Social Security,* CUP, 1967.

BULL, DAVID (Ed.), *Family Poverty: Programme for the Seventies,* Duckworth, 1971.

MARRIS, PETER and REIN, MARTIN, *Dilemmas of Social Reform: Poverty and Community Action in the United States,* Routledge, 1967.

STEVENS, CINDY, *Public Assistance in France,* Occasional Papers on Social Administration no. 50, Bell, 1973.

STEVENSON, OLIVE, *Claimant or Client? A Social Worker's View of the Supplementary Benefits Commission,* Allen and Unwin, 1973.

YOUNG, MICHAEL (Ed.), *Poverty Report 1974,* Temple Smith, 1974.

Health

BROWN, R. G. S., *The Changing National Health Service,* Routledge, 1973.

FARNDALE, W. A. J. (Ed.), *Trends in the National Health Service,* Pergamon Press, Oxford, 1964.

FORSYTH, GORDON, *Doctors and State Medicine,* Pitman, 1966.

Future Structure of the National Health Service, HMSO, 1970.

JONES, KATHLEEN, *A History of the Mental Health Services,* Routledge, 1972.

LINDSEY, ALMONT, *Socialized Medicine in England and Wales,* University of California Press and OUP, 1962.

MACKINTOSH, J. M., *Trends of Opinion about the Public Health 1901–1951,* OUP, 1953.

MCLACHLAN, GORDON (Ed.), *Challenges for Change: Essays on the Next Decade in the National Health Service,* OUP, 1971.

MENCHER, S., *Private Practice in Britain,* Occasional Papers on Social Administration no. 24, Bell, 1967.

National Health Service Reorganisation, Cmnd. 5055, HMSO, 1972.

POWELL, J. ENOCH, *A New Look at Medicine and Politics,* Pitman, 1966.

Social welfare and social work

1. General

JEFFERYS, MARGOT, *An Anatomy of Social Welfare Services*, Michael Joseph, 1965.

Report of the Committee on Local Authority and Allied Personal Social Services (Seebohm Report), Cmnd. 3703, HMSO, 1968.

RODGERS, BARBARA and STEVENSON, JUNE, *A New Portrait of Social Work*, Heinemann, 1973.

RUCK, S. K., *London Government and the Welfare Services*, Routledge, 1963.

2. Voluntary action

AVES, GERALDINE, M., *The Voluntary Worker in the Social Services*, National Council of Social Service report, 1969.

BEVERIDGE, LORD, *Voluntary Action: A Report on Methods of Social Advance*, Allen and Unwin, 1948.

MOWAT, C. L., *The Charity Organisation Society 1869–1913*, Methuen, 1961.

WOODROOFE, KATHLEEN, *From Charity to Social Work in England and the United States*, Routledge, 1962.

3. Social casework

FOREN, ROBERT and BAILEY, ROYSTON, *Authority in Social Casework*, Pergamon Press, Oxford, 1968.

GOLDBERG, MATILDA E. *et al.*, *Helping the Aged*, Allen and Unwin, 1970.

MAYER, J. E. and TIMMS, N., *The Client Speaks: working-class impressions of casework*, Routledge, 1970.

TIMMS, NOEL, *Social Casework, Principles and Practice*, Routledge, 1964.

YOUNGHUSBAND, DAME EILEEN, *New Developments in Casework*, Allen and Unwin, 1966.

4. The old and disabled

BAYLEY, MICHAEL, *Mental Handicap and Community Care*, Routledge 1973.

HUNT, P. (Ed.), *Stigma: The Experience of Disability*, G. Chapman, 1966.

SHANAS, ETHEL *et al.*, *Old People in Three Industrial Societies*, Routledge, 1968.

TOWNSEND, PETER, *The Last Refuge*, Routledge, 1962.

5. Family and children

DONNISON, D. V., *The Neglected Child and the Social Services*, Manchester University Press, 1954.

MARRIS, PETER, *Widows and their Families*, Routledge, 1958.

PUGH, ELIZABETH, *Social Work in Child Care*, Routledge, 1968.

WYNN, MARGARET, *Fatherless Families*, Michael Joseph, 1972.

6. Race relations

CHEETHAM, JULIET, *Social Work with Immigrants*, Routledge, 1972.

ROSE, E. J. B. (Ed.), *Colour and Citizenship: A Report on British Race Relations Part IV*, OUP, 1969.

Housing

BOWLEY, MARIAN, *Housing and the State 1919–1944*, Allen and Unwin, 1945.

CULLINGWORTH, J. B., *Housing and Local Government in England and Wales*, Allen and Unwin, 1966.

DONNISON, D. V., *The Government of Housing*, Penguin, 1967.

GREVE, JOHN, *Voluntary Housing in Scandinavia*, Centre for Urban and Regional Studies, Birmingham University, 1971.

HOWES, ERIC G., *Housing in Britain, France and Western Germany*, PEP Planning, vol. 31, 1965.

NEVITT, ADELA A., *Housing, Taxation and Subsidies: a study of housing in the United Kingdom*, Nelson, 1966.

WATSON, C. J., *Social Housing Policy in Belgium*, Centre for Urban and Regional Studies, Birmingham University, 1971.

Periodical Publications

Among the many periodicals carrying articles on social policy the following are likely to be the most useful:

British Journal of Social Work
International Social Security Review
Journal of Social Policy
New Society (weekly)
Social and Economic Administration

And the following annual publications:

Social Trends 1970– , published by the Central Statistical Office.
Year Book of Social Policy in Britain, 1972– , edited by Kathleen Jones, Routledge.

Index